Salena Godden FRSL is an award-winning author, poet, memoirist and broadcaster of Jamaican-mixed heritage based in London. Her debut novel *Mrs Death Misses Death* won the Indie Book Award for Fiction and the People's Book Prize, and was shortlisted for the British Book Awards and the Gordon Burn Prize. Her work has also been shortlisted for the 4thWrite short story prize, the Ted Hughes Award, Jerwood Compton Foundation, the Saboteur Awards and The Bridport Prize. Salena Godden is one of the UK's foremost poets, often topping the bill at national and international literary events and festivals. She is widely anthologised and broadcast on BBC radio, TV and film. Her poem 'Pessimism Is for Lightweights' is on permanent display at the People's History Museum, Manchester. She is a Fellow of the Royal Society of Literature, an Honorary Fellow of West Dean, Sussex, and a patron of Hastings Book Festival.

@salenagodden | salenagodden.co.uk | @salena.godden

'[Salena's] writing is urgent and detailed, colourful and clamorous. Like all love stories, her memoir is intense, intimate'

The Times

'Godden writes about a past that is at once deeply personal yet also belongs to the everyman figure; her descriptions of childhood are simultaneously timeless and yet rooted in a particular period of British history'

The Literateur

'A lyrical and witty memoir painting a portrait of the artist as a young girl . . . *Springfield Road*'s prose wavers effortlessly throughout, from tender poignancy to raw, gritty realism and this book serves to remind us that how in the last forty years, in many

iet

'In this timely and exquisite meditation on breath and its best rhyme, we see a stunning performance poet crowding all the energy, wisdom, passion and laughs of her live work into the solid ingot of this astounding novel, as profound as Cohen, as playful as Brautigan. Salena Goddess, more like'

ALAN MOORE

'It's light, it's dark, it's twisted and it's brilliant. As we all encounter life, so too we should all encounter Mrs Death. Poetry, prose, life and death. Salena Godden brings them together with ease'

BENJAMIN ZEPHANIAH

'Godden reinvents the form while staying true to an emotional honesty that's as forthright as it is courageous. Some of the most powerful writing I've read in years. Here is necessary, beautiful work. Thank God for Godden'

COURTTIA NEWLAND

'Timeless, brave and beautiful'

JOHN HIGGS

'What a writer. What a novel. The inventiveness of this use of story and form to delve in and out of loss, grief but ultimately hope and friendship had me hooked until the last page'

TRAVIS ALABANZA

'A modern-day *Pilgrim's Progress* leavened with caustic wit . . . an elegant, occasionally uproarious, *danse macabre*'

Guardian

'A thought-provoking novel that travels across time and place to question the value of life, the experiences of womanhood, and grief in all its forms'

Observer

'Lyrical, abstract and utterly original'

iPaper

'Godden's writing bypasses tired adages, zooming in on specifics that become loaded and devastating . . . *Mrs Death Misses Death* is both a balm to a bad year and a reassuring accompaniment to a new one'

Irish Times

'Celebratory and life-affirming, aglow with love, fortitude and compassion'

Mail On Sunday

'Lyrical, powerful and definitely one you need to read'

Stylist

'Unlike any other book I've ever read . . . I will be shouting from my window to anyone who can hear me; *Mrs Death Misses Death* is a masterpiece of modern literature'

The F-Word

'Godden strikes the perfect balance between humour and effective insights into grief, trauma, living, and dying . . . an irresistible novel which speaks equally to the act of living as it does to the inevitability of dying'

RTÉ

Also by Salena Godden

With Love, Grief and Fury
Canongate, 2024

Pessimism Is for Lightweights
— 30 Pieces of Courage and Resistance
Rough Trade Books, 2023

Mrs Death Misses Death
Canongate, 2021

Pessimism Is for Lightweights
— 13 Pieces of Courage and Resistance
Rough Trade Books, 2018

LIVEwire
Nymphs and Thugs, 2016

Springfield Road
Unbound, 2014

Fishing in the Aftermath: Poems 1994–2014
Burning Eye Books, 2014

Under the Pier
Nasty Little Press, 2011

springfield road
a poet's childhood revisited

Salena Godden

CANONGATE

This Canongate edition published in Great Britain, the USA and Canada in 2024
by Canongate Books Ltd, 14 High Street, Edinburgh EH1 1TE

Distributed in the USA by Publishers Group West
and in Canada by Publishers Group Canada

canongate.co.uk

First published in Great Britain in 2014 by Unbound

I

British Library Cataloguing-in-Publication Data
A catalogue record for this book is available on
request from the British Library

ISBN 978 1 80530 024 3

Typeset in Centaur MT by Palimpsest Book Production Ltd,
Falkirk, Stirlingshire

Printed and bound by CPI Group (UK) Ltd, Croydon CR0 4YY

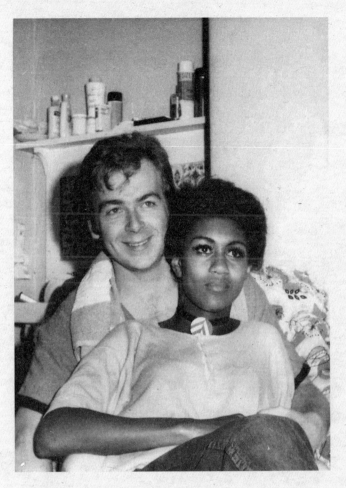

Mum and Dad, Springfield Road, Hastings, 1968

For my mother

The continuity of this love remains,
and shall remain unbroken.
There is nothing encountered big enough
to fracture or reduce, what's bigger than time
and shall outlive time's use.

Do not be afraid then, worry nor even
miss me overmuch. Between us, over us,
longer than us both, this love.
Circumstance, separating miles
or chance, but aspects of the one
insoluble thing, this love.

Excerpt taken from 'Birthday Ode A Month Late'
written by my father, Paul Godden, to his mother,
22 October 1964

Contents

SUMMER

Introduction / Spain 2010	3
When We Were Three	11
The Right Excellent Nanny of the Maroons	18
The Man of the House	31
My Mother's Words	38
Love-Drunk	43
Paint It Black	50
Paint It White	53
Tales from My Mother's Kitchen	58
Our Real Dad	67
A Letter from Paul to Edith	74
Tea and Crumpets	75
Grandpa George	82
The Heart of Springfield Road	89
The Wendy House	99
Kiss Chase	102
Mrs Tiggy-Winkle	111
Princess Leslie	115
Spaghetti Legs and Curly Top	122
Once in a Lifetime	125

AUTUMN

The Other Woman / London 2009	139
Bonfire Treacle	146
Doughnut and Lolly	155
Black Ice	159

Tiny Tears   166
Stepbrother   171

                        WINTER

Wish Upon a Star   181
Christmas   188
The End   192
The Silence   196
Fishing   201
Golliwog!   206
The Day the Joke Glass Broke   210
Swings and Slides   216
Coffee and Sherbet   220
Game, Set and Match   226
The Nightmare   229
69 Pink Pass / Bristol 2007   234

                        SPRING

Mickey   245
Six Times Six   249
The Red Suitcase   253
The Big Lesson   257
Runaway   260
One Knife, One Fork, One Cup, One Plate   266
Patriarch   269
Voodoo   276
And We Don't Wear No Shoes   283
Facebook 2008   291
Eulogy   295
Kingston, Jamaica / January 2011   299
Afterword / London 2024   316

SUMMER

In Nanny's garden, Danesholme

Introduction

La Casa de las Almendras
Andalucía, Spain
August 2010

My Dears,

These are the memories of my life as a child. This is the story of the world before I was here, the universe I was born into, that I came to love before I had to grow up, find rent and suffer hangovers. This is the story of how I became this overgrown adult with scars and wonky teeth.

I am alone in the mountains behind Málaga, at the highest point of Andalucía. The truth is, I feel as though I am peeling myself off the ceiling, coming down from the gigs and festivals, and I'm swapping the microphone for a pen.

I came here with the sole intention of writing some new work. But something happened here yesterday, and I'm now compelled to open the pages of this memoir and share this story — and this new version I write for you — especially for you, who have waited so patiently to read it. This is the memoir of our old house, our family home in Hastings. How I remember those first mornings of the school holidays, stretching under musty blankets and sheets, in that house, in that bedroom, on Springfield Road. Awaking to the sounds of Grandpa's mantelpiece clock chiming downstairs, the distant church bells and seagulls. This is the story of that home and those who lived here, namely my absent father, Paul Godden, who left such a trail of debris in his wake that as I read and write this memoir I feel like his personal road-sweeper, picking through the litter and leaves, letters and photos, for nuggets of truth and revelation.

It's important you should know this is not written from the perspective of a time-travelling superhero – quite the opposite – this is just how I can best remember my child self, how we have all changed, and yet not at all.

Now all I require you to do is read this and click your fingers and say, *Hey! I remember, we did that too!* I want you to say you remember not how things could have been, but how they really were. You might say, I remember being closer to the ground, to the cracks in the pavement; I remember liking being upside down; I remember being afraid of the dark; I remember being lost in daydreams; I remember discovering life is unfair; I remember riding my bike with my feet off the pedals and I remember freewheeling down hills with the wind in my hair; I remember losing my front teeth; I remember being forced to eat my greens; I remember how summers were longer and how oranges were bigger; I remember struggling to comprehend sex and death, heaven and hell, war and God and perhaps, you'll say, I remember I missed my dad too.

In my life I have found it much easier to get up on stage in front of people and talk openly, humorously, about cervical smears and one-night stands, rather than reveal the story of my interior world, my childhood and especially my father. But, as someone once told me, you cannot climb a well from the middle. You must fall right to the bottom. Once you are there, in the cold, alone and ankle-deep in slime, you'll look up and you'll get a real sense of the dark and the work involved to climb towards the light and the truth.

If this book were an animal, it would be a stray kitten that has been passed around between us, fed and stroked. This story has grown into a strong and handsome alley cat, an animal that will likely bite and scratch you if you hold it for too long.

I have often wondered if this book is cursed; sometimes I have believed it is haunted, for it has surely haunted me. This writing is my *Red Shoes* and when I hear its tune I dance, even though I know I am dangerously close to leaping off the edge. And as I fall, time and time again, I catch myself rethinking and rewriting this book. We see what we want to see, and sometimes we are shown the threads that connect us all. I believe that if you are focused on a certain person or a particular time and place, if you listen keenly, the world will reveal clues, like bridges and doorways, that guide you onto the right trail and encourage you to keep going against all odds. No matter what I do, all roads lead me back to *Springfield Road*.

It's August 2010. I left London and came to Spain for a month, alone and quite impulsively. The solitude and silence were startling at first. As I write this, I am overlooking almond and olive trees under big starry skies. The moon is full, white and hot. I've been working on new poetry, reading a stack of books and talking to myself out loud. On the drive from the airport and up the mountain I saw a sign with the word *Cardobe*. I couldn't figure out what memory it was tickling, then yesterday as I drank coffee and smoked, serendipity came knocking. *Cardobe*. I threw the word into my computer's search engine and it led to the folder of the first-ever draft of this book from 2006. My gaze fell upon a discarded letter from my dad to his mother, Edith, a letter we found in the basement of Springfield Road, that had been edited out of the manuscript, considered inconsequential, backstory, because it was written before my father met my mother. But I now notice the postmark of this letter: my dad posted it from here, this very spot, in the mountains behind Málaga, Andalucía, 1965.

Did we forget that my father, as a young jazz poet and bachelor, ran away to Europe in 1965? Is this fate? Is this significant? Am I being led by nostalgia? Am I grabbing at straws?

I phone home and speak to my mother. She believes that yet again my dad is watching over me, guiding me back on his trail, this trail.

'I have taken to myself a Spanish 'Cardobe' hat. It is a wide-brimmed black hat they use to dance flamenco in . . .' he writes, and yet again my present is illuminated by a light from the past, just like a lighthouse. In 1965 he described *the silent white houses, the twisting streets and the glittering sea* – the very view I can see now, as I write this in 2010. So what choice do I have but to continue pushing on with this story and for it to be told my way for you? Here I am quite literally walking in his footsteps, down narrow Andalucían streets. I sit at bars he must have drunk in more than forty years ago.

Like many of his letters it is written in a steady hand, in green ink, looped and slanted words like music notation on thin paper. The envelope is marked with the red and blue striped edges of airmail. I am guessing 'Easter 1962' is the title of a poem but so far there are no clues who 'K' might be.

Casa del Poeta Pedregalejo, Malaga Somewhere around 8th Dec.

Dearest Mum,

Thank you for your regular, encouraging and ultimately lovely letters. K hasn't written still. Don't understand but maybe I am a little slow. Listen I shall telephone you Christmas Day at 4pm afternoon if you can pay for the call. It costs 10/ - a minute. Is that OK? I shall probably just cry for three minutes but there you are. I feel so terribly lonely at the moment, I'm vastly terrified to come straight home. What would that prove? That I was just as weak as everybody else, wanting security and peace. I want peace but of a different kind. You understand, so why do I talk so much. The Rector wrote and said he sent 'Easter 1962' to a publisher, just for an opinion. Might be very interesting. We must wait and see. There is a full moon tonight and it glitters silver on the sea and lights the white and silent houses and the twisting streets. On Saturday we went up into the mountains behind Malaga. Was very exciting, you looked down on the whole coast or so it seemed.

The trumpet is [unreadable] very well. All afternoon I have been practising carols. Incongruous in that I was sitting on the porch in a bathing costume at 65 in the shade, sweltering from the hot sun playing 'In the bleak mid winter'! It's early days though. We are thinking of going into Malaga at Christmas to perform and see if we can get any money.

You know my usual outfit, jeans, Pa's jacket, jumper, it has taken an addition. I have taken to myself a Spanish 'Cardobe' hat. It is a wide-brimmed black hat they use to dance flamenco in. Anyway exhibitionist as oft- I am well known throughout the (dives) town as 'Cardobe Poeta'. Cardoba is the place where they dance most flamenco. Flamenco is just the [unreadable] dance. In the little bar in Pedregalejo on Sunday nights they have a sort of beano. The bar is no bigger than my bedroom at home. Last Sunday night two little girls aged 10 or 11 were dancing. It was quite beautiful but awfully disturbing for both before the age of puberty had all the bumps and grinds necessary. I have become vaguely acquainted with a Spanish girl but all that happens is an exchange of language

7

lessons. I wonder why K hasn't written. Anyway I am writing quite a lot, some not too bad. I miss you, shall hope 4pm Christmas day. OK? Lots of love. F in F.G.B.W.Y., Love Paul

*   *   *

And I now have no choice but to open the kitchen door to this gnarly tomcat of a book. I will give it some food, some light, water and warmth knowing this is bound to hurt a bit. There are going to be things we all thought we had forgotten and also things we wish to forget. Things that will remind you of yourself. I came here to begin a new story, but maybe all my stories begin with this one story, this love story, this ghost story. As I type that, the tinny radio fizzes with Bob Marley singing 'Buffalo Soldier'. His lyrics remind me to remember history, where I come from and who I think I am.

All I know is that I have been nurturing these stories for you for thirty-eight years. I never married and I do not have any children. Home is a run-down fishing town by the sea called Hastings, East Sussex. And home is London. I didn't go to a posh school or even university. I moved to London at the age of nineteen and began my big city life by working two jobs, backstage at the Drury Lane Theatre at night and as an A&R assistant at Acid Jazz Records by day. As a young poet in the 1990s I lived predominantly on Marmite on toast and instant ramen noodles. I was constantly hungry; I feasted on books, nourishing my writing in the warmth of Swiss Cottage and St Pancras libraries. At night I read my poetry in the backrooms of pubs and bars for free wine and laughs; or I spat lyrics over beats in clubs and raves hiding under the punk-poet moniker, Salena Saliva. I always called myself Jamish: Jamaican, Irish, Scottish, English. I have very few regrets, I have nothing to lose and I have no savings.

They say that it is always poets who die in wars, and I never got over a sense of being in the trenches. I have a bizarre and outdated sense of fair play and team spirit. I have been my own worst enemy. My heart is wide open, I have fallen in love too quickly, too often and too easily. I believe we are running out of time, I don't believe we have any time to waste. I give myself a hard time and I am impatient. I am impulsive. I throw in all I have in a game of poker, but I reckon that is the only way to truly win. And these are some of the phrases I use to define who the heck I think I am.

I spent the latter half of the last decade dwelling in the flesh and blood of this story, our history. It ought to make a person a special kind of weird to live in the past for so long. I feel a special kind of strange every time I sit here reading through these pages. But the past is here in the present and on the tip of my tongue. I now know I was always heading to this very ledge here today, on a mountaintop. I contemplate the space I inhabit between the past and the future, between the deep night sky and the rocky drop below. And as I do so, I remember home and Springfield Road.

How I would peer from that attic window and imagine my father looking out of that very same window when he was a boy. Outside, Hastings would be fresh with spring, the buds and pale blossoms hanging on the apple and pear trees. That attic room was my father's bedroom when he was a boy and when I was there, I suppose I was always looking for him, the materials of his existence. I remember the lavender mothballed paper-lined drawers of the furniture in that particular room. I remember once finding a king-size marble, how I held it up to the light, squinting with one eye into the swirling blue and green glass. It was well scuffed and a sure winner. I told myself it was once my father's marble. I gave it a squeeze as I tucked it safely into the pocket of my pink pedal-pusher jeans, convinced it would be lucky some day. In the distance I could make out the steel-blue line of sea on the horizon and overhead I heard the constant cry of seagulls on the slanted slate roof. I imagined what it might be like to call the house on Springfield Road my home and what it would be like to live in the holiday forever.

Salena Godden
Spain, 2010

PS: This book has been separated into four pieces and named after the four seasons rather than the years. More for the emotional images that come with each season than the actual date or time. While writing this I found there was a time of innocence and with it came sunshine and there was a time of grief and with it came the darkness. For me, whatever year it was, it was always spring-like and summery at Springfield Road, and when I was there it always seemed to be alight and hopeful. Autumn and winter in my recollection were times of cold hardship and difficulties and so these sections reflect this. You will notice the summer section is longest, because the school holidays seemed endless in childhood.

When We Were Three

The day we left my father, I remember orange lights. I was wrapped in the familiarity of my soft blanket, and the luminous streetlights were wrapped in their own black blanket of night. Lying on the back seat, I watched them pass the car window, how they sped towards me and then slowed down. We were on a long journey. We were in motion, moving forwards, fast, and we would never go back.

Stars dangled; I saw the lights dancing on see-through strings. I called out for my mother. She turned to pat me and made a *shush* noise. *There, there,* she said, *shush.* Her face, though smiling, was strange, contorted with shadows and ghosts of amber lights. I struggled to sit up to see the world the right way round, to see where we were, and she said,

'Lie still, be a good girl, we're nearly there now, love.'

My eyes fixed on a yellowish light moving towards me from the other side of the road; it was a lighter orange than the others. It stuttered like a falling star, disappearing into the distance. I tried to stay awake to watch this particular light as long as I could. My eyelids grew heavier until it was pin-sized and lost, the hypnotic lights blurred and the monotony of the car engine lulled me back to sleep.

* * *

I was in a jungle one hot afternoon. At least, I believed I was in a jungle, and there, deep down in the tall grasses, nothing kept still for a minute. It was crawling in there, fizzing with life. Millions of tiny bugs buzzed and jumped, flew and hopped about me. I could not see over the top of the long grass, with its spikes and thorns. My nose tingled with the smell of earth and grass. There were fluffy spores in the air, dandelion clocks. A white butterfly settled on a cowslip and I moved to touch it; I can recall my chubby hand reaching out as it flew away, up into the endless blue above me. Down in the tall grass it was cool, shadowy. I looked up into the cloudless sky and listened. There were no human voices, nothing familiar, just the rustling of insect monsters and a humming of six-legged traffic. Suddenly for me it was all over, it was the end of the world, I was lost and I was crying. I dropped my empty jam jar and sobbed. It was hay-yellow in every direction and my ears burned with the itch of grass life as something jumped on my arm. I cried out, then stopped to listen, then cried out louder. Suddenly he appeared like a giant saviour, the sun his halo,

'Ah, come, Salena, don't cry, look.'

My big brother Gus, my hero.

'Don't cry, look, I caught two grasshoppers!'

His jam jar was filled with grass and spindly legs. He was proud, but I didn't know what a grasshopper was. He started half-singing the song from *Pinocchio. My name is Jiminy Cricket . . .*

Then he lay down and rolled off down the hill. My big brother Gus, four years older than me, and hurtling ahead. With outstretched fingers we rolled fast down the slope, tumbled down the bank laughing. Until the grass was suddenly soft, short and green and I now knew where we were. We were at the front door of our new home.

* * *

Then this is one beginning, we could begin this story here: I was coming up to my third birthday in the spring of 1975 and this was our fresh start. We were three, my brother, my mother and me. Our dad went away to play in the resident jazz band on a ship called the *QE2*. My mother had moved us to a house on an ugly concrete council estate called Danesholme, near Corby, Northamptonshire. Northamptonshire is in the Midlands, the green and flat middle of England's waist.

In this new house, we lived around the corner from my mother's parents, Nanny and Grandad, and my Uncle Gerry. My brother had gone ahead of us with Nanny and was staying with her for us when we arrived. He was so relieved to see us again that he cried at first. He missed us horribly. I could tell by the way he clung to Mum.

The houses in Danesholme were grey boxes, built in squares facing each other, with a hump of grass and bush in the middle of each, identical to the last. It was a Legoland of concrete play bricks. It was very different from the pastel fishermen's cottages of Ramsgate and the seaside where we had lived in a marshmallow-pink house with my father before.

We didn't have much furniture, and certainly not enough to fill an entire house. When I ran across the uneven wooden floorboards the rooms echoed, resounded hollow. I can picture my mother with her headscarf on, smiling, the portable radio playing. She was always busy, my mum. She'd smoke her ciggy and she'd whistle and sing along to the radio. She'd wink down at me, then take a swig of tea from a paint-smeared pint glass and gasp, *Ah, that's better.*

She threw the doors and windows open while she painted the house. I remember the kitchen was bright green and she painted a hippy daisy chain along the wall. This is a borrowed memory,

13

I don't remember the daisy chain – she does. I do however remember this industrious period. Most of all I remember she painted my bedroom in tones of violet and lavender. My mother taught me the words for colours, the names of rare and subtle hues. I loved these pretty words my mother used. The words for my new bedroom were indigo, lilac and purple, and when she put me to bed for my afternoon nap those particular colours were lit in shafts of sunshine; ultraviolet swam behind the backs of my eyes and etched into my memory forever.

*　*　*

I made a friend; her name was Mary and she lived across the square from us. She was Irish, with black hair and vivid violet-blue eyes. I recall we played together every day, pushing our prams, wearing our mothers' beads and high heels. We collected and squashed berries with sticks. While we played, we listened out for the ice cream van, the tinny trickle of the 'Teddy Bears' Picnic'. Although we were not to talk to strangers, the ice cream man was a pink and jolly man. I remember he took us by the wrists and ankles and gave us swings and aeroplanes. He gave us penny sweets and drum-stick lollies for nothing.

One day Mary and I wandered further away from our square than we had before. We were hiding and spying on my brother and his friends. We followed them through the tunnel that led under the motorway and towards the woods on the edge of the estate. We weren't allowed to go there. It was dark and cool beneath the underpass, with the steady roar of traffic above us, and we made a racket, roaring and shouting as we ran through the dark and the urine stench towards the sunlight.

We believed that there were real grizzly bears in Danesholme woods, so we didn't follow my brother any further at first. We stayed safe in the sunshine, peering at the edge where the trees started, before the long forest shadows began. We ran back excited and scared, jumping and squealing at the sound of anything rustling in the bushes. *It's the bears*, we repeated to each other, clutching each other's hot hands, dipping into the cool gloom of forest and then dashing back into the sunshine.

Our bare arms goosepimpled as we dared to enter the woods, stepping into the shadows, dapples of sunlight trickling through the canopy of forest above us. Gus and some boys were looking up into a tree.

'Shushh! I've found some chicks . . . be very quiet or you'll scare them,' Gus said, as he very carefully gathered the tiny creatures in his jumper. He set off and we followed him, the chicks cheeping as we were chirping and begging to hold one.

Once at home, we looked at the three chicks on the kitchen table, fragile, purple and papery, their eyes hardly open. Their beaks were wide, letting out tiny croaks and cries.

I asked, 'Where's the mummy gone, Gus?'

'Don't know, they've been abandoned.'

'But why?'

'Don't know, maybe the mother was scared off or something . . .'

Our mother said softly, 'Poor things!'

'The mother bird would smell us humans on them now, wouldn't she, if she came back, wouldn't she, Mum? Mum?'

Mum didn't say anything.

Gus continued urgently, 'Mum, we can't take them back to the woods. They'll perish out there in the wild.'

'Mummy, would the mummy-bird smell human bean on them now?'

'Human bean? It's human being!' Gus laughed at me.

'Yes, I am afraid she would, and she'd abandon them.'

'Yeah,' Gus butted in, 'so we best keep them, hey? Mum, can we, hey?'

We pleaded at a high pitch until Mum smiled and said we could keep them if we looked after them properly.

Gus said, 'They'll be eaten by cats or foxes if we don't take them in, hey, Mum?'

'And the bears will eat them all up, won't they, Gus?'

'Yes, Salena, if you say so.'

We made the chicks a cosy nest in the airing cupboard where Mum said it was warmest. Mum remembers we let them free and they cheeped and hopped along the top landing of the house. We gave them tiny pieces of bread dipped in warm milk and broken-up cereal.

Then, one chilly morning before Gus left for school, we went to feed them their breakfast but found the corridor silent. When we opened the airing cupboard door they were all dead. Maybe they were scared to death in the dark airing cupboard. My brother and I had shaken hands, choosing which chick was to be whose. We had imagined a future with our chicks for pets. One day, they were to be our own tame birds. We could have trained them to follow us to school, to sit and wait on the school fence and then follow us home again. Now, wiping our eyes, absorbed in our young grief, my brother and I made the necessary arrangements. We filled a shoebox with toilet paper and tissue, and used an old cotton handkerchief to cover the chicks up and keep them snug. We dug a hole with spoons and buried them in the public front garden, right by our front door. Mum led with a sombre funeral speech, helped us say our prayers, and said, *Ashes to ashes and dust to dust*. Mum told us the chicks went to God in bird heaven. I squinted up into the cold morning sky to see bird heaven. I imagined it was behind the clouds and just before the stars. We made a lollipop-stick cross to mark the final resting place, but a few days later they were dug up by cats.

The Right Excellent
Nanny of the Maroons

Every morning in Danesholme, my mother dropped me off at my grandmother's on her way to her new job working in the local Co-op supermarket. She sat me in my grandmother's living room, put the radio on very low for me and told me to be good. I knew that I had to be very quiet; Nanny worked nights as a nurse in a hospital and I had to wait for her to wake up to see to me. I'd play alone, taking in the spicy smells, the tall leaves of the rubber plants and the exotic red ginger flowers. I remember the collection of wooden ducks on the stairway, the maps of Jamaica on bamboo trays, and a blue and yellow budgie in a cage. I'd lift the night-cover on the cage to see if the budgie was sleeping. I chattered to the little bird, hearing the rustle of its feathers, and I'd poke my fingers into the cage to feed him seeds as he nipped me with his beak. Whenever his cage door was opened, he'd fly around the living room and perch on the curtain rail.

Waiting for Nanny to get up, I'd listen to the radio while spinning around in a circle for hours. This was my favourite game – to try to stand for as long as I could no matter how dizzy I became. I loved the melodies of 'Lazing On A Sunny Afternoon' and 'Raindrops Keep Falling On My Head'. I sang, spinning on the spot, until the fuzzy shagpile carpet came up to meet me, orange waves of brown circles and red patterns rising. I stood there fixed, trying not to fall over, with the room spinning about. Once I had fallen and the room stopped racing before my eyes, I struggled up to do it again and again. I never grew tired of the rush of blood to my head and making myself dizzy, either by spinning or hanging upside down off the back of the sofa. I loved this sensation: enjoying being dizzy and upside down has followed me into adulthood.

Eventually I'd hear my grandmother in the bathroom upstairs. I'd creep up to the L-shaped landing halfway up the stairs to watch her. I crouched and spied on her, ducking down out of sight when she looked over, though she knew I was there – it was all part of the game. Watching my grandmother dressing fascinated me: the preparation and piecing together of this magnificent tiger-eyed woman. Just out of the bath, she was engulfed in clouds of powder, a soft dusting of sweet scents of lavender, lily-of-the-valley or roses. Chalky white talc against her soft brown skin.

I studied my grandmother and her underwear. My nanny's bra was just like my mother's, but so much bigger and stiffer to hold her wondrous bosoms in pointed peaks. Each breast was protected, separated and mountainous. Even though I had seen this a hundred times, I was mystified by my nanny's pillowy bosoms. She'd put on another contraption, a girdle, with a million hooks and buttons, until it seemed she was bound in with underwire and lace. The process was unfathomable to me; the undergarments were master-pieces of engineering. I felt it was important for me to watch, because, one day, I hoped I might develop such a chest and I'd need to know how to ease myself into such interesting articles.

I moved up a step and held my breath, watching as Nanny sat and gathered the nylon material of her stockings expertly in her hands. I liked the way she pointed her toe into the silken material. Then she stood and pulled her full petticoat over her head. She'd call my name and tell me to come and I'd obediently go and sit on her bed and watch as she finished dressing. She'd put on her beige skirt and button her blouse and cardigan. Finally, she sat at her dressing table and brushed her hair through, the brush making a rasping noise through her tight knotted curls. Then with her lips clenched around pins, I watched as she gripped her wig into place. She wore a reddish-auburn wig, with shiny fat curls. As she creamed and powered her face, I'd see her look at herself in the mirror, and I'd see the reflection of me looking at her looking back at me. In that moment, I adored my grandmother, mesmerised and in awe of her quiet power, wisdom and beauty.

✳   ✳   ✳

Nanny, my maternal grandmother, was the fifth of ten children born to Rudolph Robinson and his wife Theresa in the hills of Clarendon – there were thirteen babies in the Robinson brood, but only ten survived to adulthood. Clarendon is on Colonel's Ridge on Bull Head Mountain, a couple of hours' drive from Kingston; to get there you drive high into rainforest, following a shady, green and winding road. My grandmother was the daughter of a tailor and farmer. Her father, my great-grandfather, Papa, was also a lay preacher and elder at the Mount Carmel Church, which Nanny told me meant, among other tasks, he had to give the sermon if the priest was away.

'But everyone did a little bit of everything,' Nanny said, 'everybody helped each other as best they could, not like now, there was no, not my job, not your job, we all just got stuck in as best we could.'

Nanny told me that although it was beautiful on Colonel's Ridge, life was very hard. Every morning before they walked many miles in the heat down the potholed track to school, Nanny and her siblings bathed in the river and did their chores, milking goats and fetching the water from the river on a donkey. The Robinson children loved school, though, and were very eager to go. The way she spoke it was as if school and church were social events.

My grandmother had the most beautiful gold eyes, like a tiger's eyes. Her eyes were magic. As a child I was convinced my great-great-grandmother Marma was also somehow magic – to the English ear it sounds like Mar-ma although I never saw it written. There was always a black and white photograph of her on both my mother's and Nanny's bedside tables. This one picture of Marma is so striking and unforgettable. She looks so content in her rocking chair on the porch. She wears a bandana, long lace petticoats and smokes a clay pipe. Nanny told me that she smoked that pipe all the time. She said that Marma spoke of the Hebrew Moors, that she was a descendent of the Moors who lived in Spain and assisted the Spanish in their navigation of the new world. How on reaching Jamaica our ancestors joined the Maroons and fought the British with what is now known as guerrilla warfare.

Now, as a child I believed that my grandmother's eyes had turned that pale amber and saffron-gold from one of Marma's spells to cure her from going blind, and as is often the case, these stories had some grains of truth in them. Our ancestors were Maroons, today recognised as an indigenous people by the United Nations. Using guerrilla warfare, the Maroons would camouflage themselves with leaves and ambush their enemies at night. They were said to be able to slit a man's throat before he'd seen or even heard them coming. They were fierce and proud and rumoured to be unafraid of death, and I've read that the Maroon mantra was:

to never bow head or knee, to hear only their own voice, to stand in the shadow of none and to be masters of their own destiny.

The British called them the 'relentless rebels' as they made cross-country travel treacherous in Jamaica and fought hard for the liberation of enslaved people and freedom. Many plantations simply surrendered or were abandoned. An initial offer of land and freedom was shunned by the Maroons, resulting in warfare. Eventually, in 1739, peace treaties were signed and bribes accepted in return for land, freedom and independence.

Nanny told me that Marma was something like a herbalist or a healer, and that she was present in the community as a midwife and doula. Nanny said that even though Marma couldn't read or write, she instinctively learned the properties of all the herbs and plants through a lifetime of watching. She had an intuitive natural talent for alternative medicine. Now, all grandparents have stories they tell the grandchildren over and over. And my grandmother always told me stories about Marma and the day Nanny went blind.

'Back home, if anyone went into labour, Marma was there; when people were sick she'd be there for them too. Then when I got malaria I got so sick, I went blind and I couldn't go to school, I'd just sit on the porch all day and hear the other kids playing. I felt very lonely and left out. Marma, she go fill a metal bathtub with water, roots and herbs. Then she leave them in the water to soak and let them get sun-drenched. She boil up herbs and make me drink it down, boy oh boy, it was bitter. I would have to sit in that tub as Marma pressed the sun-drenched leaves on me, applying pressure, over and over again. I got better, eventually, but my eyes were like this, light colour, from that day on. You know, when Marma died she told me, I'm going to follow you, uh huh, that's what she said. I am going to follow you. And she did, oh yes, she keeps an eye on me.'

As Nanny told me these things, with her face so deadly serious, I would look past her shoulder and above her head for the ghost of Marma.

Nanny taught me to believe there are greater forces in the world than us and I trusted her every word. As a child I always believed this; I took it for granted that the dead were somehow watching me – not just God, or the tooth fairy and Father Christmas, but my elders and ancestors too. This was a confusing contradiction for how could people be both in heaven and also down here watching us? Bedtime was quite crowded, what with all the dead people, ghosts and spirits standing at the end of the bed and watching over me. I feared the dark and all the dead that lived there.

Nanny had a quiet influence and she captivated me as a small child. She was kind but firm. She could be quite strict, and so I was sure to be particularly well-behaved for her. I would do anything she said whenever she finished the command with *for Nanny*. And she used it to full effect: clean your teeth for Nanny, tidy your toys for Nanny, finish your greens for Nanny. Nanny made steamed greens and she got her fish fresh from the fish-van man who drove around the Danesholme estate and rang a bell so you'd know he was there. I'd pull a kitchen chair to the sink and stand on the seat to watch her gutting the bloody veins, all that filmy, grey mucus and muck out from inside the fishes. I'd watch with great morbid fascination as she dismembered a mackerel with practice and precision, opening the gills with her thumbs under cold running water and scraping off the scales. The skin seemed slippery but she held it sure and fast in her firm grip. She chopped through fishy tissue and fibre. Then she cut the heads off with a sawing motion.

I hated fish, loathed it. I disliked the smell and the taste, but was mostly afraid the bones would get trapped in my throat and choke me. I always complained, but Nanny was convinced the properties of fish made children brainier somehow. She made me stay at the table until I finished my lunch. Sometimes I was there almost all afternoon, it felt like an eternity, staring at my plate of cold fish and soggy greens, my legs swinging, agitated, my bottom getting numb. Screwing up my nose, I would chew it with my very front teeth to keep the bones away from my throat as Nanny said, 'Don't play with your food.'

I pretended to eat: chewing fresh air and swallowing imaginary bites while I watched Nanny have her lunch, the way she ate all of it, sucking the skin and the bones. I studied her as she spat bone into her hand delicately and left it carefully by the side of the plate. She was like an owl regurgitating pellets. I would look up in astonishment at the way my grandmother ate, the way she consumed apples whole, even the core. My nanny, she sucked the marrow out of chicken bones.

At school I used to boast that my nanny had a choice between either Grandad or Harry Belafonte. I shamelessly used to wish my grandmother had married Belafonte instead. The truth was that Harry was a schoolfriend of hers. She told me that nobody back then had any idea what Harry would achieve. Harry Belafonte was to become one of the first great Jamaican singers to cross over into mainstream America and Europe. He was a trailblazing civil-rights and human rights activist. When I quizzed my grandmother about Belafonte she would just shake her head and laugh, her golden eyes twinkling. She was clearly very fond and proud of him and all he did with his life.

At the age of ten, Nanny left Colonel's Ridge and went to live in Port Antonio with her eldest sister, Viola, to study millinery and dressmaking. While she was there she liked to ride bicycles, go to

24

church and practise with the choir, and go to the cinema to see films with Tyrone Power and Errol Flynn. Errol Flynn lived in Port Antonio at the time; Nanny and her friends would often talk to him and ask him when another film was coming out.

'He was very friendly, like one of the locals. Errol Flynn was a very nice man.'

Nanny's house smelled spicy with a combination of Nanny's rice and peas, oxtail, goat or chicken stew and Grandad's home-brewed beer in various stages of fermentation. It was noisy too, with the barking of my grandfather and his gravelled laughter.

My mother's brother, Uncle Gerry, was usually hovering in the background or upstairs in his bedroom playing the albums of Bob Dylan, Jimi Hendrix or The Beatles, still in his late teens but never to leave home. He was always very much in his own world, keeping himself to himself, appearing only for tea. Thin and tall, he religiously wore skintight black T-shirts and dark skinny jeans. He'd leave the room as soon as he could after family meals, head upstairs and close his bedroom door. To me he seemed to spend hours lying on his bed, staring past the garish floral yellow wallpaper, lost in space, deep in poetic dreams. Or he'd play his unplugged electric guitar, his long black fingers holding a plectrum, strumming the chords of his muted rock solo.

Downstairs, my grandfather was a noisy man; a big personality, you felt his presence before you heard him. He was rarely calm, always agitated or agitating, loudly whistling or singing. When he spoke his voice was a booming tenor and he had a dirty, rum-toasted laugh. When my grandfather was home from work, I can recall the unnerving vibration; it was a jostling place, with the news on the television blaring at top volume, my grandfather shouting at the screen that the politicians were all crooks and thieves and sucking his teeth. It seemed this was a place where kids were to be seen and not heard, where children were not to get underfoot. I can remember peering through the baby-gate fixed across the kitchen door to keep us out of the way. My grandfather drinking brown liquor, whisky or rum, the ice jangling in his tumbler. I remember how he rattled his pocket change. How he chewed on his own tongue as though he were Humphrey Bogart. You did well to be quick off the mark, to make sure to keep out of his way and to try to stay on the good side of him. We all worked hard for his approval but rarely got it.

My grandfather was an only child, born in the early 1920s; he was brought up by his grandmother from the age of four. I have always been led to believe that he had a particularly tough childhood, but he never spoke about it in any detail. I know he originally studied agriculture and during the Second World War he signed up to the RAF. Occasionally Grandad would take the bamboo tray with the map of Jamaica on it off the wall and point out the geography of home, the names of the places where the family were born and where they all grew up. He came from the Buff Bay area. Nanny and Grandad met when she was seventeen and he was nineteen on holiday in Balaclava. Then Grandad went to live in the States for a year studying agriculture. By the time he came back they were recruiting volunteers for the war.

Nanny told me, 'It seemed to be the thing to do, everybody was signing up and getting paired off. There was this big rush to get married and, well we loved each other, so we went to Kingston and got married on the third of May 1944.'

During these rare softer moments with my grandfather, I thought of Jamaica as a faraway place on a shiny, varnished bamboo tray, with the different parishes of Jamaica depicted alongside images of hummingbirds, flowery birds of paradise, palm trees and coconuts.

In 1951 Nanny followed him to England with my seven-year-old mother. Grandad was stationed in Dover. Soon after she arrived in the UK, Nanny came down with malaria again. And here is Nanny's other story, the other one to tell us grandkids.

One night her fever was so bad they got their heavy greatcoats and laid them on her to try to make her sweat it out, Grandad's coat and four others, piled high. And that night Marma appeared to Grandad and told him to give Nanny nothing but pure Jamaican coffee and pure rum she had just brought from home.

'Pure coffee . . . the real stuff, and the 100% proof pure white rum we used to have back home, uh hum . . . and it was so strong, it knocked me out and I was sweating under those heavy greatcoats. Your grandfather, he says, 'you are not to be sick, "you keep it in", and I did but I was so out of it. I never touch that rum again without it making me want to be sick.'

The next morning Nanny was up and out of bed, getting my mother ready for school. When the doctor came to check in on her and told her she should be back in bed she said, *Oh, I am all right now, thank you.*

And she was.

*   *   *

Every day Nanny and I would take a morning walk to the shopping precinct where my mother worked in the Co-op supermarket to get the day's newspapers. There she would be in her turquoise-green gingham supermarket uniform with her pricing gun. The cool refrigerators made the hair on my arms stand on end.

27

'How much am I today, Mum?'

Clin-ker-ching went the gun.

'38p! I am 38p!'

I wore the 38p price tag with joy. The other ladies who worked there with Mum made a fuss, standing around and patting my head and telling me I was going to be a right heartbreaker when I grew up. It didn't sound very nice, the breaking of hearts, but they cooed at me and made a fuss about my curly hair and the colour of my eyes.

'Green? Or are they blue? Ohhhh! She's going to be a heartbreaker that one all right, aren't you love, eh? Right little heartbreaker!'

'They are blue, green and grey. It changes with her mood,' my mother told them proudly and squeezed me around the back of the neck. My mum always told people that like it was a fact. She said that if I had been crying, they appeared more green, when I was happy, my eyes were blue and when I was angry, they turned a stormy grey. I grew up believing my own eyes would betray me, that they were as easy to read as the weather, as the sky and the sea.

'Little heartbreaker.'

The ladies grinned down at me, making me squirm. I looked over at the yoghurts. If it was a good day, Mum would let me choose one to take home; if it was a supreme day, I could pick a miniature pot of my favourite blackcurrant cheesecake.

With our dad away at sea, my brother at school and my mother working in the supermarket, I revelled in those plump and idle days with my grandmother. I watched TV, *Sesame Street*, *The Monkees* and movies with the young, handsome Elvis. I lay on the carpet glued to the television screen and watched him kiss the ladies. In those pre-school days I remember making mud pies, having carpet tea-parties and picnics for my dolls. I remember I liked to bury all the cutlery in the public garden as though it was treasure, and had my mother in fits trying to find it and dig it up again at dinner time. I recall I had a play nurse's uniform to dress up in to mimic my grandmother. While my brother played on his bike and seemed to get away with dull domestic tasks scot-free, Nanny ensured I was programmed to be self-sufficient and capable. This is the Jamaican way – girls in the kitchens and boys free to play in the sunshine. My grandmother stood over me and carefully taught me to sew on buttons; how to iron Grandad's handkerchiefs; she told me to be helpful around the house. I learned how stand on a chair to make my own tea for breakfast and to wash the dishes. I was a very independent child. I asked *why* to everything. My mantra was *I can do it* and that has not changed.

'I can do it'

The Man of the House

When Gus began to go to primary school every day, I would try to follow him to his bus stop. I remember he kissed me goodbye by the underpass, before the bears' woods, and he'd tell me to 'Be a good girl, you look after Mummy, now go back home, I'll be back later, OK?' Gus was the man of the house now. Mother and Nanny often told him so, and he took this title very seriously. Gus could run fast and jump off high walls. He could ride his bike, gather speed and then skid, he could do wheelies like Evel Knievel. He was rarely ever out of his Spider-Man pyjamas and I wanted to be just like him.

While Gus was at school, I sometimes played with my dolls with Mary and waited for his school bus to bring him home at teatime. I was happy and content, but soon it was time for me to start to go to a pre-school nursery every morning. It was in a pointed building, shaped like a witch's hat, situated opposite my mum's Co-op supermarket. I liked it there; they gave us biscuits and orange squash. We painted and sang and they read us stories. There were lots of other children to play with and so I was happy to go.

* * *

My brother was always a lovely-looking boy. With shiny black curls and striking eyes, dark as coffee beans, and very long curly eyelashes. He has a Y-shaped scar between his eyebrows because he once ran into a metal pole in the launderette before I was born. The scar accentuates the crease when he frowns and knots his brow. He was always browner and redder in skin tone than me. As an infant I was blondish, pale yellow and chubby, where Gus was beautiful and dark and lean with a slighter bone structure. Often, to our absolute horror, people would think he was the tall and slender girl and I was his robust and rotund, pale and pot-bellied little brother.

I remember when we took our baths together he'd squeeze the sailor-shaped bottle of Matey bubble bath and scoop white handfuls of bubbles onto our faces to make Santa Claus beards and say, *ho-ho-ho*. And when we cleaned our teeth side by side we used to aim to spit at each other's hands accidentally on purpose.

I copied everything my brother did, and being a curious little girl, I tried to straddle the toilet seat to wee standing up like my big brother. This was something I attempted more than once and every time I made a mess everywhere. Once, I remember Gus busting into the downstairs toilet and catching me mid-experiment, I was facing the cistern and toilet bowl and trying to take aim as he burst in and into laughter, yelling, 'Mum! Come and look what she's doing this time! Quick, Mum . . .'

It seems my brother was always laughing at me. And it's worth mentioning that his laugh is an unusual, fast machine-gun laugh that rat-a-tat-tatted from the back of his throat and resonated in his chest and belly: ha-ha-ha-ha. There are two things that always follow this laugh; his tutting, *what's she doing this time?* or, if it looked as though I'd hurt myself, *you all right, sis?* To this very day these are still the two phrases I most often hear Gus say to me.

*   *   *

I have pale memories of two visitors during those early times in Danesholme and the beginning of life without our father. Grandpa George came on the train all the way from Hastings. He had known us when we were babies; Gus being older remembered him more than I did. Grandpa George smelled like sandalwood, mothballs and dusty books. I sat on his knee at the kitchen table and I could tell that although he was very kind he was not used to affection or children climbing on him. He sat stiffly and gave me funny little pats on the head. His white hair was combed to the side, and he wore a three-piece suit and a tilted green beret. He sat with my mother at the kitchen table and they had cakes and tea from the teapot. He spoke courteously as he drank his tea. My mum told us to go out to play and they talked in hushed adult tones.

We were also visited by an Uncle Peter from Germany, who was fostered and brought up with my father on Springfield Road. Not a real uncle and not my dad's real brother – but kind of. He spoiled us with sweets and gifts and gave me a Slinky. What I recall most, though, is that during these two particular visits, Gus and I knew the adults were talking about our dad. I remember we asked after him intentionally, because there were strange pauses when we came back into the room, and my mother shot us looks and gave contradictory replies in front of the guests. Gus and I picked up on the awkwardness that came with the answers, like, *he's away at sea* or, *he'll soon come*, followed by the standard – *wait and see*.

During those early days, I'd catch my mum sighing into the washing up, looking out of the window into the distance, lost in worries. I

33

saw her weepy after phone calls and muttering over the post. She dreaded letters. She'd say, *what is it this time?* Then she'd take a deep breath and roll her eyes heavenwards as she opened the mail.

I know now that my mother must have found it difficult to ask her parents for help. I also now know that it was a struggle being a single parent in the early 1970s and working at the supermarket to keep us together. I have a distinct memory of her cleaning up a spillage on the kitchen floor – she has stopped wiping, she sits on the floor with her hands covering her face. I bend down to look at her, I am trying to peel her fingers away. She shakes and makes no real noise. I begin to cry, hating seeing my mum weep like that,

'Stop now, don't you start crying, love, you don't understand, you're too young.'

I did understand, at least I understood enough to know my mother's heart was broken; to know there were bigger things than puddles of spilt juice on her mind. Wishing I were older, wanting to take care of her, I remember trying to wrap my arm around her neck. She found a tissue and blew her nose. She stared at the floor and at the mess. Then, standing up, she smiled, the corners of her mouth forced upwards, her dark eyes still sad with black streams of mascara running down her cheeks.

My mother's moods were always hard to predict. I remember after our baths how we would happily scamper about naked, and how we loved that freedom. Mum laughed and chased us to bed, threatening and singing: *Bite your bum, bite your bum, here I come to bite your bum.*

But at other bathtimes she'd cry out, 'How am I supposed to cope without your dad if you kids are going to play up? I thought I told you to get into your pyjamas, you'll catch your death running around naked and barefoot!'

And with that she'd burst into furious tears.

I soon understood there was a pressure and a strain my mother was under. I knew she was often tired, but I also often couldn't tell whether she was serious. She could play-act that she was angry to tease me and I would be overly sensitive and believe her. But I knew there was a boiling point, that there were times when it wasn't an act but a reaction triggered by something deeper and darker. It wasn't that she was quick to anger or bad-tempered, I believe that she got exhausted wearing that optimistic mask. My mother was a fine actress. Mostly she appeared in a calm and serene mode or she was sunny and positive. She always put her chin up and her best foot forward. However, it all depended on the colour of the day, how much energy there was, how tight money was. The messy toys or muddy shoes were never the real issue.

Once the drama was over there was a long and awful silence. The tension was palpable. The only sound was the crash of crockery as she washed up or the scratch of the brush as she attacked a stain with vigour, on her hands and knees, working up a sweat. It wasn't until I was much older that I found out this was perfectly normal, that universally when mothers are angry they do fierce housework. My mother vacuumed up a storm and slammed the kitchen cupboard doors. She swore under her breath as she crossed the street in her slippers and hurled the rubbish into the back of the dustbin man's truck *her bloody self.* She wouldn't speak to us for what seemed hours, as she cleaned and battled and cursed inanimate domestic objects, like the jammed ironing board or a wonky cupboard door. We knew she meant business when she had her apron and pink rubber gloves on.

We'd beg her to speak to us; we'd write notes or draw pictures and promise to be ever so good, to never ever be naughty again, beside ourselves for want of her affection and forgiveness. She would finally call us to come to her. Gus and I would be quiet as she spoke to us firmly and asked us if we had learnt our lesson. These speeches were delivered in a slow, stern voice used specifically to make us listen. Often she said something wrong or backwards and we would all crack up laughing, because Mum was funny that way. She got muddled and used the wrong words; she would tell us: *I'm gonna put my foot down with a firm hand.*

Then we'd all say sorry, my eyes welling up with relief that she was speaking to us again, and we'd all be laughing and crying at the same time. At times like these her frown dissolved and the sunshine mask returned, her forgiving smile just like sunlight through a cloud as she hugged us and told us she loved us very much. Then we'd put the dishes away together, the three of us, industriously, picking up what was broken, clearing away what was spilt and putting the kettle on. She'd promise something nice for tea, like our favourite chewing-gum cake – malt loaf, a doughy fruitcake which was delicious toasted and heavenly with melted butter.

As I grew older I learned to read the changes of tone signalling one of my mother's thunders. When I was older still I even became an accomplice in them. We mirrored each other and eventually we learned to laugh at our reflections. I came to understand that as much as there are sunny yellow days there are blue days, grey days and black days, days when it's all too much, depressive days when the wintry rain is as sad as tears. There were also days to see red, days when Mum smashed empty milk bottles against the wall at the side of the house on purpose, her eyes glittering with satisfaction. (Many years later, after a teenage disagreement, I remember my mother saying *don't take it out on me* and taking me around the side of the house on Springfield Road to smash empty milk bottles against the wall. She was right – the explosion of glass was hugely gratifying and momentarily relieved my angst and frustrations.)

During my childhood, on more than one occasion, I caught my

mother alone in her bedroom crying. She'd ask me if I thought she was a bad mother. I never had any idea what prompted her to ask me that. I'd throw my arms around her and kiss her wet cheek and tell her again, 'You are the best Mum in the world and I love you forever and ever.'

This was the time when my mother was my universe. My infant images of her and of those days are like this: she sits curled on the sofa, eating something salty and tangy like tinned sardines on toast, utterly absorbed in a Dick Francis novel. She has washed all of our clothes and hung the damp laundry on the radiators to dry. The house is hot; it smells of clean washing, humid and soapy, some stew or curry is simmering and bubbling in a pressure cooker on the stove and the windows are steamed up with condensation. Later that day, she sits at the kitchen table holding a pen, smoking, pensive and staring into space. The cigarette smoke rises and curls, and she is silhouetted by dusky light at the window. There are envelopes in separate piles in front of her, official-looking letters from the bank and her solicitor, leaflets about single-parent child support. She's trying to make sense of it all. She is dyslexic and she bites her lip and writes very carefully, arduously, with loopy handwriting on a lilac writing pad. She always uses the lined guide so her writing will cross the page in a straight line. Remembering her like this, I sense my mother's solitude. This was our early life living without our dad, when there was a big hole and we were standing on the edge, waiting. We could not turn around or go back, we were in transition and biding our time.

My Mother's Words

Excerpts from my mother's diary written in 1974:

*I am seven years old. I come from a warm place, a settled home on the planta-
tion in Jamaica, to a cold and indifferent father. The war is over but I do not
know of any lack of chocolate, fruit, sugar or know the terror of bombs. I am
full of trust, a free child, natures child. I could have died twice though, at birth
and at the age of four when I had pneumonia. I believe everything happens for
a reason, I am full of love and trust.*

*I arrive in Dover 1951, winter. 'Who is King George, Mummy?' I ask, 'and
why is the flag at half mast?' 'Quiet child, can't you see I am talking to your
mother?' That is the first thing he said to me. I drop back one pace and follow
behind and see my mother change. I sense I am alone from now on and looking
back I never knew how right I was.*

*It's England and it's so cold and I have only a cotton dress and jumper, white
socks and red shoes, I hate to wear shoes. The tall block of flats we live in are
cold. It's not a friendly place. Crying is out of the question, I unpack. Oh, to
be in my feather bed where the hot rain beats on the tin roof and lulls you to
a sweet slumber.*

38

My mother falls very sick and I am not allowed to go to her. He says 'go downstairs with the nice lady, go do as you are told.' 'Yes sir,' I say and turn on my heels. I want my mother so much, I fell silent, I didn't speak until I saw my mother again.

I have nightmares. The bedroom is cold and still unfamiliar. My mother comes to comfort me and my father storms in and says 'what the hell's going on in here?' 'There's somebody at the window!' I say and so my father switches off the bedroom light and we wait until we see it was my malt bottles making shadows on the walls. I have to drink malt to build me up because I am too skinny, my father says. I ask if I can sleep in the bed with my parents and my father tells me, 'no, you are a big girl now' and 'your mother is too soft with you.' I find solace in remembering Jamaica, the noon-day sun and walking with my grandfather. I remember how I went to stay at my loving aunties sometimes and swim in a sea the colour of malacite with white, white sand. I remember the sugar mill, the smell of the bubbling golden sugar, mangoes fresh off the tree, swimming and splashing in the cool river and walking through the coffee groves. In the evenings there is story-telling and my great-grandmama, Marma, feeds us fruit and smokes a clay pipe and wears a red bandana. One morning I slept in past the cock crow and they found me asleep in Marma's bed. When she died, my afternoon naps were taken on her grave of white marble under the mango tree.

Sleep was always a great healer.

My father taught me to polish his RAF buttons and badges and his boots and shoes and if they were not to his satisfaction or liking I was beaten and if mum got in the way she got it too. I remember him waking me from bed to beat me because I had forgotten to brush my teeth.

We moved to London, where I join the International Ballet School, but then we moved on to Hong Kong. We sailed on the Georgie, a lovely ship. In Hong Kong, Mum and Dad are out most nights and I go to ballet classes. My school is twenty miles away. To get there I travel first by RAF lorry with a crowd of others to the Hong Kong Ferry, then across the harbour and by bus to Lion Hill. We are in Hong Kong for three and a half years. I learnt from the Chinese and I enjoyed their way of life. I absorb it all, I go everywhere, see everything, nothing is hidden and nothing my father could do can harm me. I learn tolerance.

By the age of thirteen I break the school sports records and jump my own height, 5'1. I saw Richard Third and I dance in nightclubs and start to learn to play the drums and to sing to please people. I had spoken to Robert Wagner and Kitch Kendal whilst still going to school.

Then, one day my teacher notices blood on the back of my shirt and how I flinch if anyone tries to put an arm around me or touch my back. For the first time I am encouraged to talk and my dad has to see the headmaster. I see school as an escape and I perk up and take more interest in my studies and my father lays off for a while.

Leaving Hong Kong was like a bit of me dying. I loved that place and still do. My babysitter Lee with her one gold tooth and chopsticks. The rooftops with everybody doing tai chi every morning. I learnt something about inner calm there, inner strength.

I am fourteen when we go to live in Deal, where my father has been posted, mum having not found much work as a nurse in London. We live in a grand house with Susan's aunt and uncle. Susan and I hang out in our Smoky Joe's, sloppy jumpers with a belt, we have frothy coffee and walk down the road with our thumbs in our jeans singing, we go for fish and chips. That was our big splash, walking home eating fish and chips.

We move to Bournemouth. They stop calling out my name every Monday in assembly for my weekend achievements wherever I had been running and winning, in Southampton, Portsmouth and everywhere else. Dave, John and the gang all called me their shapely javelin or iron drawers.

Dave is the first to kiss me. I am fiftteen and he is seventeen. He has a motor-bike and is off to college at the end of that term. He comes to meet me from school one day and all the other girls run into the school cloak room at Boscombe, all talking at the same time and saying there is a fabulous boy on a motor bike asking for me. I take my own sweet time and when I see him I wave nonchalantly. All the other girls are two paces behind me talking in loud voices but I stay cool and quiet. He takes my books and puts them in his side saddles of the bike and we ride off, waving.

We go down the beach and walk and then he takes me in his arms and for the first time in my life I am really kissed. My knees give way and we flop on to the sand dunes. I wish he'd stop and talk about the track and the following weekend inter-school sport of England meet in Southampton, but he has other things on his mind. He is kissing my ear and I start laughing and say, it tickles. We laugh and roll about in the sand, chasing and dodging, and he rugby tackles me and my school shirt comes untucked from my school skirt and he kisses my belly and for a brief moment he puts his hand on my thigh and then I sit upright and we sit side by side. I don't want to spoil the moment but I say, we had better be going home. My voice is no more than a whisper as I brush the sand off his cheek. He takes my hand and kisses my palm, he gets up and helps me to my feet. He jokes about the sand getting everywhere then we ride home. He parks and takes both my hands in his and says, 'you are still a virgin aren't you? I won't bite you.' I stand there smiling and say, 'I am, does it matter?' I take my books and my hands are trembling. 'No,' he smiles, and he kisses me on the cheek, starts his bike and rides off.

Then when we got to Southampton I didn't notice Dave until the event had started. I could see love in his eyes and it is enough for me to drive me to come second in the All England Championship.

One day I come home tired from my usual daily five-mile run and notice my mother has been crying. She says goodnight and goes to work her night shift at the Boscombe hospital. My father has been drinking. I smell whiskey on him. I run into the bathroom and lock it and then he comes looking for me and he bangs on the toilet door it seems for hours. He keeps saying, 'you are no good at anything, you will never be any good at anything.' I pray for God to help me. My father stops banging on the bathroom door and passes out. I drink port, thinking it would keep me awake all night until mum got home . . .

Love-Drunk

Quite suddenly, my mother changed: she was a sing-song of summer joy and she seemed to laugh more. She played Gilbert O'Sullivan records and sang along triumphantly to the songs 'Matrimony' and 'Nothing Rhymed'. She took my hands in hers and danced with me. I followed her and got under her feet as she got ready to go out. I watched as she ironed her hair in the kitchen. I'd see the flat irons heating up on the stove top, glowing blue and searing orange on the gas cooker rings. I recall there was a turquoise tub of straightening lotion and how she'd prop a mirror against a pot and I can recall that smell, the lotion and the sizzle of steamed hair.

'Promise me you will never straighten your hair.'

'I promise.'

'You promise! I wish I hadn't started . . .'

I watched her as she morphed from this soft, curly-haired mother to a beautiful and elegant lady, with her black hair all sleek and glossy.

'Does it hurt?'

'No, darling.'

She grinned down at me from her reflection in the mirror, patting at her silky and straightened hair. My mother sprayed my wrists with

Chanel N°5. I sniffed them and watched as she put the finishing touches to her make-up, gazing at the way she used those delicate brushstrokes to apply mascara with her mouth half open and her eyes wide. Her pretty perfume hung in the air around us. Being only so tall, I admired the shine of her stockinged legs and turn of her tiny ankles in her strappy high heels, the shimmer of her silvery evening dress. Then she tucked me up in bed, leant over me, engulfing me in her loveliness, and told me to be good. *Sleep tight and don't let the bed bugs bite*, she always said, then when she was most mesmerising and intoxicating, she kissed me so I could have some of her lipstick on my own lips. I'd feel the sticky gloss on my mouth and rub my lips together, and as I fell asleep I sniffed my wrists.

The next thing I remember was my mother's bedroom becoming out of bounds. I recall my bare feet padding across the floorboards to find myself at her now closed bedroom door, hearing voices and hesitating to go in. My early morning time snuggling in her bed seemed interrupted. I was nosy and curious hearing someone else in there but when she heard me she called out, 'Go put your slippers on, there's a good girl or you'll catch cold, we'll be down in a minute.'

We'll be down. There was now a *we*, not just Mum. In the stillness of the sleeping house, I can easily picture my child self in the dark kitchen making tea, climbing on a chair to reach the cupboard with the intention of getting two cups down, instead of just Mum's. I can see my pleasure in making a tray of breakfast, clumsy toast and jam, proud as a house cat with a dead bird. I had been taught to knock, so with my hands full I said *knock knock* out loud, balancing my offering, my bid to be allowed to join the laughing people behind the closed bedroom door.

That whole first year with Mum's new boyfriend was a rush of impressions, a sped-up montage of falling in love. For me, it was a rollercoaster of sensations. This new person took us out in his car for trips to the countryside, to see castles and stately homes. At one, perhaps it was Hampton Court, I remember a beautiful rose garden with water fountains and a maze of tall, trimmed hedges where we lost them both, this man and my mother, in a game of hide and seek. I remember the anxiety of being lost in a maze. That my mother had got herself lost with her new friend, of being left out, but worse than the sense of abandonment was the nagging feeling that although it was a game, she did so intentionally. It was all fun and games: we had water fights, pillow fights, snowball fights. He gave us aeroplanes, swinging us by our arms and legs, spinning us through the air. He gave us killer dead legs and Chinese burns and pinned us in wrestling holds. He had one trick where he bent my finger in on itself, towards my palm, pushing the fingernail up into itself. It hurt. He laughed. He squeezed my knee hard just above the kneecap and he wouldn't let go until I repeated, *surrender, surrender.*

One lazy summery day we went on a picnic. There were millions of fluffy dandelion seeds in the air and we took a rowing boat down a slow river, water splashing the seat. I leaned over the edge of the boat, staring into the algae-green water looking for fish. It was a dreamy summer's day and I was witness to a blossoming love affair going on above my head in the realm of the adults. I recall my mother smiling and laughing, looking so gorgeous in a pretty pink gingham sundress, a stalk of straw between her teeth as we walked through fields, climbed into a tractor and sat on hay bales.

Have you ever had a close friend besotted with a new lover, and do you remember how annoying it can be? Although we want to be happy for the friend and we are excited to meet the new addition, sometimes we all secretly wish things hadn't changed. You suffer tiny stabbing pains of possessiveness and jealousy. You try

45

extra hard with him, because you need to be liked by the new boyfriend so he won't freeze you out or turn her against you. More to the point, there is a love-drunk glaze that comes over your friend as she falls under the spell of the new man – and so it all seemed with my mother. Often with new couples there is a power struggle, a balance to find. Someone is the lover and someone is the loved, someone does the running and someone does the chasing, someone is the giver and someone is the taker. And so before we knew it this new boyfriend was the boss. He was at our house all the time and swiftly things changed. Now when we asked for anything Mum began to surrender to him. This man became the law, policing the washing of hands and the tidying of toys. Soon he installed more regimented routines, bedtimes and teatimes. He already had two children from a previous marriage, who lived with his ex-wife, so apparently he knew how to bring up children. He was about ten years older than my mother and she thought he knew best.

But the truth is you cannot make a first impression twice.

I was three years old, overexcited and overtired – or maybe I was having a tantrum – when he looked down at me and said, 'Do you want a real spanking? You carry on like that I'll give you a spanking!'

I laughed nervously and answered yes, believing he wouldn't really do it, thinking he was playing and that this was a new game. But this man lifted me up in a flash by my arms, he swung me around, put me over his knee, pulled down my knickers and slapped my bare bottom hard with the flat of his hand. With the shock of this I urinated all over him and his lap and he quickly threw me off. Towering above me, Gus, Mum and her new boyfriend looked down, the expressions on their faces a mixture of anger and amusement. Gus sniggered as this man made a huge fuss about the wet on his jeans. Blood rushed, flushed red under his skin and his top lip curled as pointed to the wet stain on his trousers. I never forgot the look of disgust on his angry pink face or the precision with which he grabbed me and pulled my pants down. I never forgot that when he swung me by the arms and slapped me, it didn't feel like a game, it felt like he really meant it.

∗   ∗   ∗

Soon after this my mother disappeared and we had to stay with Nanny and Grandad for what felt like ages. Nanny ran a tight ship and Grandad frightened me. Gus was always in Gerry's room playing records and locking me out, keeping boy secrets and teasing me. We all had to be on our best behaviour and I remember just crying a lot and missing my mum.

When everyone was still asleep in the early morning, I climbed out of my cot and crawled to the corner of the room to a box where Mum put some of her precious belongings for safekeeping, including a blue jewellery case. I especially liked to play with my mother's magic seahorse necklace: a seahorse skeleton with silver eye sockets set in a diamond shape of clear Perspex; if you looked at it very closely, the skeleton was surrounded by microscopic rainbow-coloured air bubbles. It hung down to my feet from a black velvet ribbon when I put it around my neck. Just as the seahorse was frozen and suspended, I was waiting for my mother to come back to me.

When my mother did return she was glowing and grinning and she was married. She might have asked our permission to marry, but I don't remember that chat or any warning, but I know I probably would have gone along with it. Whatever Mum wanted, I wanted too, and I simply liked things to be organised. In my child mind it would be normal, we would be two grown-ups and two children, we were a four, two girls and two boys, and now we'd all live together happily in our house in Danesholme. However, my big brother Gus was no longer *the man of the house.* More to the point, Gus knew that this meant our real father was not coming back. My brother was loyal to our real dad. He remembered our father clearly; he also must have understood that from now on if our dad ever returned, it would be only as a visitor, not as our parent. During this period my brother started getting into trouble. Aged seven or so, he was expelled from his first school for breaking a boy's nose with a dustbin lid. In his defence Gus told us the boy was a bully who had been picking on the smaller children. For the rest of our lives as children together, this became a pattern with my brother: always getting into scrapes for protecting himself and others, he was always being singled out and scapegoated for standing up to racists and bullying. I remember my mother taking us with her to talk to his headmaster about Gus's behaviour. His school was an austere red-brick building that smelled like hospitals, bleach and rubber-soled plimsolls, the empty corridors echoed with the determined click of my mother's heels as she frogmarched the doomed Gus out of the school with an angry *Wait until I get you home!*

* * *

It was to be our first Christmas together as a family and we went out shopping. Fizzy with excitement I skipped ahead down Kettering High Street. I looked back to see Mum and her new husband arm in arm and I cried out, 'Come on, Mummy! Come on, Daddy!'

We were outside Woolworth's, with the flashing fairy lights and pretty tinsel and paper stars and snow in the window, Christmas carols being merrily played, when I was told quite clearly, 'Don't ever call me dad or daddy. I am not your daddy.'

'This is Patrick. Salena, you are to just call him Patrick.'

I recall that memory as clearly as if it happened this very morning, as succinctly and sharp as that first spank. I know in that moment, as a little girl, that I saw the trick, and realised this cold man was to be my stepfather and that he would never replace my real dad.

Paint It Black

On Saturday mornings, Patrick and Mum started to drop us kids off at a local community centre, where we would spend most of the day with other children doing creative activities and sports. It was a Saturday school where children took extra classes and did activities. I remember there was a balloon game at the end of each session, and at home time, all of us joined in, scrabbling to bop the balloons up into the air so they never touched the floor.

One of my favourite songs was 'Paint It Black' by the Rolling Stones. I thought the lyrics were: *I see a window and I want to paint it black.* I first heard that record when my Uncle Gerry played it to us and I imagined painting window panes so no one could see in or out. I found that idea and the song itself exciting; it made me feel rebellious as I sang: *I see a window and I want to paint it black.* I sang it at the top of my lungs. I'd gallop, punching the air, leaping higher on the chorus of *black, black, black,* to the recollection of the rhythm of the drums, which sounded to me like racing horses' hooves.

At the Saturday school they separated us into groups by age. My brother was at the other end of the hall with the big boys. I was alone with my painting, wearing a back-to-front old man's shirt with the long sleeves rolled up to protect my clothes underneath.

I was humming to myself, *I see a window and I want to paint it black*, painting with a rainbow of colours, a picture of a pink house, red apples growing on green trees and the yellow sun in a blue sky.

'Blackie!' spat the mouth of a plump seven-year-old child with a red face and crooked plaits. The child with her chubby fingers stood close enough for me to smell the cheese and onion crisps on her breath.

'Blackie!' she said again.

She frothed the word up, over and over, in a singsong of spit: 'Blackie, Blackie, Blackie!'

I looked over her shoulder across the hall for my brother but I couldn't see him. My heart pounded and my eyes misted over so I couldn't see to pick the colours. I knew this was a bad word. I took my brush and slathered it in gloops of black paint. Concentrating on the paper in front of me, keeping my chin tucked in and my head down, I drew the brush across the painting. I looked through hot watery eyes at my house now swimming in ugly mud, the butterflies I had been trying to conjure now a swirl of brown sludge and mess.

'Blackie . . .'

I smelled again the acridity of cheese and onion.

'Blackie, Blackie, Blackie . . .'

It was over as soon as it started. I stood with all the fury of a nearly four-year-old who believed she was in the right and I threw myself at the girl, who was twice my size. It was so fast and so sudden, it was easy. She fell to the ground, and I sat on her chest, pinning her down with my knees, while I painted her scrunched-up face black. Paint splashed and flicked off my brush, a half-chewed mush of crisps between her teeth mingling with black globs of paint.

I was picked up by my arms and ripped off her and my paintbrush was snatched away. I looked up at the adults who had suddenly appeared as they fussed over the seven-year-old, as she howled, *it went in my mouth!*

They washed her face and mouth out while she bawled. I was scolded and told to fold the soggy paper that had once been my glorious, colourful painting and throw it in the bin. That was the part that made me cry.

Gus thought it was hilarious. He shook his head and put his hand over his mouth to hide his laughter, saying, *ha ha, that's my sister, look what she's doing now.* Then he helped me get cleaned up and as usual he told me to say, *sticks and stones may break my bones but names will never hurt me.* No matter how many times he said that, it was not true – those names *did* hurt and they made me feel dirty. Kids in the streets often yelled 'golliwog' or 'Blackie' at us when we were out playing. *Golliwog, Golliwog, get back on your marmalade jar* was a nasty sing-song taunt we heard most often. This popular playground racial slur came from a long-running advertising campaign that depicted a golliwog sitting on the Robertson's marmalade jar. The golliwog symbol was finally removed in 2001.

And as suddenly as it all flared up it was forgotten. It was nearly home time and then we all played the balloon game, keep the balloons up, keep the balloon in the air, whatever you do don't let the balloon touch the ground. Gus and I never went there again, to that strange Saturday school, because shortly after that we left Danesholme and moved to a new bungalow in Desborough.

Paint It White

Our new house was a two-bedroom, semi-detached bungalow in a village called Desborough, also in Northamptonshire, in the green belly of England. My newlywed mother had to give up her job in the supermarket and this meant she stayed at home to look after me. I recall enjoying having my mother to myself for this brief time before I started full-time education. I also remember the new house was startling white, spotless and modern. Even the television was a white space-age cube.

In the two-bedroomed white bungalow I now had to share a room with my brother. We slept in bunk beds in new sleeping bags; we thought it was what camping must be like, and being the smallest and lightest I got to sleep in the top bunk.

The decoration of this house was minimal; it was painted in muted and neutral tones, slate grey and white. There was no hippy daisy chain painted on the kitchen walls here. There was an oval framed picture of Mum and Patrick's wedding day above the mantelpiece. I wished we'd been invited to the wedding; it seemed that my mum had looked so pretty, her dress all lace about her throat. Gus and I sniggered that our stepfather looked like the Hulk with an afro.

In the new house there were many precious things we weren't allowed to touch, tennis trophies and crystal wine glasses to be kept for best. Looking back I think it was a bizarre foreshadowing, that this man had married my mother with her two fun-loving, rough-and-tumble children and then proceeded to carpet the whole place in a scream of tell-tale white. And that white carpet was our worst enemy: it not only betrayed tiny drips but also showed up indented footprints, giving away any scuffle or play. And we soon discovered that Patrick was fastidious enough to know if we had been in the living room by whether the nap on the carpet was brushed wrong or lay differently. Before long, we were forbidden from being in the living room at all – except for special occasions or when we had visitors.

My stepfather installed cowboy saloon doors in the archway to the dining room. When Patrick was out, the swinging saloon doors were excellent for playing at cowboys and gangsters; we'd fling ourselves through them, falling dead onto the sofa, pretending to shoot each other. There were wicker baskets for our laundry, which were nearly as tall as me and big enough to climb in and hide. I played my recorder and writhed, slithering up through the lid like a hypnotised snake. I recall my childhood in that white bungalow was governed by two sets of rules – the way we were when Patrick was in versus when Patrick was out.

My stepfather was a curly-haired Irishman. He was very vain about his hair; he fluffed it up in the mornings with an afro comb so it might double in volume. He had sharp features and pale skin that burned lobster red in the sun. He smelled of Germolene all the time, which was a pink antiseptic cream he applied after shaving. He had pale, ice-blue eyes. If you squinted, he looked a little like

Paul Michael Glaser, the curly-haired one in the hit TV show *Starsky and Hutch*. With Patrick at the head of the house, there were now new petty laws and strict regimes. They started as small rules and got more and more controlling. For a start, Gus and I were not permitted to watch television. We sneakily watched TV when they went out, so then we were not permitted in the house alone. If they went out, we had to go out too and we could come back inside only when they returned. We would roam the streets waiting for them to return. We were taught to feel that we were in the way, too noisy and messy. If my mother was too soft towards us, she was told not to spoil us. I assume looking back this was where I first learned to go without, to take the back foot, to shelve my needs and make an apology to keep the peace, even if I didn't mean it. And it's taken decades to unlearn all of this.

Soon Patrick decided that my brother and I were to eat in the kitchen, standing up at the counter. He said we were messy and we ate like pigs. He said he was sick of the mess we made in the dining room after meal times. At tea time they closed the partition of frosted glass, slid the door shut between the dining room and the kitchen, between them and us. It was not so bad eating standing up. My brother and I still fought for the one cherry in the tin of fruit cocktail and swapped food we liked and disliked. We learned to wolf our food down fast to get meal times over and done with so we could go back out on our bikes to find our friends to play in the street.

My stepfather liked processed, English, bland food: shepherd's pie, sausage and mash, bacon sandwiches, roast dinners. Nothing too *fussy* or *foreign*. However, this didn't stop Mum constantly trying to add exotic flavours and Jamaican flair and spices to her cooking. She made curries and took pride in using the herbs, fruit and vegetables she had grown herself in the back garden. But I recall food being a huge issue. Amongst other things, my stepfather was bizarrely territorial about cheese. He ate cheddar cheese and pickle sandwiches on Saturdays watching sport on television while smoking Rothmans cigarettes. He'd eat cheese in chunks. He'd often take the cheese out of the fridge and scrutinise it, weigh it with the palm of his hand and say accusingly, 'Who's been at my cheese? You been eating my cheese? That's my cheese that is . . .'

It was difficult to look innocent when you really were – the idea of being wrongly accused and found guilty of cheese-theft was so terrible. Believe me: I never ever ate my stepfather's cheese. It was always me who stole the cream off the top of the milk without shaking the bottle, but I promise I never touched the cheese.

* * *

Soon after moving to Desborough those brief luxurious days of being at home alone with my mother ended. On my first full day at infant school I remember being alarmed by the number of children who were crying and afraid to go inside the school. Some mothers had to come into the building and struggle to pull coats off rigid, stubborn arms. Children clung to their mothers' legs like koala bears, hiding their faces in their mothers' laps.

But not me. I waved goodbye from the playground, leaving my mother at the gate with other parents, all teary and choked up. I watched a tiny girl with long plaits start bawling and how she was given a lolly. I wanted one too; it didn't seem at all fair that the cry-babies got rewarded with sweets. All around me there seemed to be blubbering hysteria, a snuffling of sucked thumbs, snot bubbles wiped across cheeks. The teacher seemed kind and soft-spoken and I could see there was plenty to do: there were coloured bricks, pictures on the walls of numbers and letters and a wooden playhouse. During that first day one child worked himself up into such a fit he had a nosebleed and had to be taken to a special quiet room. There was a smell of disinfectant in the corridor.

Mum always said I tried to run before I could walk, and those first days at school I was keen, eager and impatient. I had watched *Sesame Street* daily at my grandmother's. Both my mother and Nanny had read and sang to me and fed me books. Like a parrot, I repeated my numbers and letters, so as a result, I could write my own name and count and knew most of my alphabet before I started school. I confidently shouted out answers in class, and when the teacher sang us a song, I was the only child who could click my fingers as required. I picked up the sing-along precociously fast and sat in class bolt upright, able to click the fingers on both hands, a feat that even the teacher couldn't manage. After a day or two of this overzealous, admittedly annoying behaviour, the teachers took me into a special quiet room and gave me a little test with picture cards. I was hoping for a lolly. The next day I was put up a class and placed with the second years. The children were so much bigger than me, I stopped shouting out the answers and I listened and took my first brave steps on that brilliant journey of learning to read and write all on my own.

Tales from My Mother's Kitchen

Sometimes on Sunday afternoons, my mother and I would cook the roast together, and we often made apple crumble. For the crumble part, I was the boss – I rubbed the butter and sugar and flour together between my thumbs and fingers and ate sweet, buttery nuggets. The greasy, crunchy crystals dissolved on my tongue. At times like these, the kitchen was a cacophony of bubbling pots infused with the sweet smell of apples stewing with cloves, nutmeg and cinnamon.

My mother checked the apples by poking them with a knife, leaning over so the pots steamed up the lenses of her round owlish spectacles.

She nodded and then said, 'Oh, that's strange, look at that! Look at my arms . . .'

'What?'

I looked up from my crumbly, brown-sugared world as she held out her arm for me to examine.

'Goosebumps! Look!'

Her arms were goose-pimpled, but I didn't understand what this signified.

'I could swear I just felt a cat wrap around my ankles, it tickled, how funny, just then . . . Oh, there it is again.'

We looked at her feet but there was no cat there. I looked up at her face again and then back at her feet. Her face was lively with mischief and her dark eyes glittered.

'I think it's the ghost of our old cat Presley! I just felt its tail wrap around my legs. Come on, boy, come on, Pres, outside . . .'

I watched as my mum opened the kitchen door and motioned as if to a cat. She waited with the door wide open, smiling at the cold air as she ushered clean nothingness out with her hand and softly whispered, 'Outside now, there's a good boy, there you go . . .'

I shivered and watched my mother as she shooed air, saying, 'Outside, Pres, there you are, good boy . . .'

Then, as if that was the most normal behaviour in the world, she closed the door and returned to the cooker, lifted the lid and stirred the apples. There was a very long pause, during which she knew I was looking up at her, waiting for her to laugh or tell me she was joking. Her eyes shone as though lost in memory, and then finally she smiled and started a story.

'You see, your dad and me, we used to have this cat called Pres. We named him after Elvis Presley. Pres was a lovely tortoiseshell tomcat who followed me everywhere around the house. He'd even be there at the bottom of the street waiting for us when we got in late from a gig.'

She paused and lightly bit her bottom lip. Even though she told me these stories over and over again, I always couldn't help smiling. I liked to hear them as much as she liked to relive the time when we were babies and when my real father and my mother were young and hopeful. No matter how brief it was, I loved to hear tales about my father being a good dad and a loving husband, and to imagine the two of them happy and in love together.

'The thing is,' she continued, 'I didn't know I was pregnant with you at first. I was still dancing, go-go dancing until four, sometimes five in the morning, and there would be Pres, sitting on the steps of our pink cottage. It was in Shaftsbury Street in Ramsgate, where all the fishermen's houses are all painted different pretty colours, ours was the pink one. We'd take your brother with us . . . he would have been only two or three then. He'd sleep backstage in the dressing room . . . he'd be fine, such a good little boy.'

My mother sighed, remembering happier times. She always sighed like that when she talked about my father. Over the years, Mum told me that they both thought it was for the best, that as far as break-ups go, it was quite an amicable split. They were skint and totally broke when Dad was offered a job on the QE2. It was steady work and well paid, and she encouraged him to take it. When he left she hoped for a new life, something more stable, away from the touring, the rock-and-roll and the financial uncertainty. As the years passed we hardly heard from our father, and Mum would say it was because he was still away at sea or that it would upset us too much to see him. Gus and I, however, always suspected it was because Patrick wouldn't like to meet the real love of my mother's life.

Piece by piece, I created a mental scrapbook story of who the other half of me was. By borrowing memories from these kitchen stories I imagined our life before he left. I vaguely remember the house in Ramsgate and shadows of railings against sunny pink walls. As I rubbed buttery sugar to make the crumble fine, with that sweet smell of stewing apples, I wanted to remember it all, remember my father's presence, remember the cat called Pres, the ghost that curled around my mother's feet that afternoon.

I have seen a photograph of Pres, lying on his back in a pool of sunshine with his paws in the air, wanting his belly scratched.

In the family album it sits beside one of the only photographs of my father and me together. It is a black and white photo, but I have coloured it in. We are sitting in the sun on the doorstep, I am in between the legs of my father, and there are the shadows of the railings against the pink, sunny walls behind us. Half of my dad's head is cut out of the picture because the photographer, probably Mum, hasn't stepped far back enough, but my father is smiling. He has long hair to his shoulders. He has leather sandals on his feet, his ankles are skinny, and he wears a long-sleeved T-shirt covered in a pattern of bathtime rubber ducks – he looks like a hippy. A cigarette dangles from his lips and he grins down the lens, never knowing the top of his head and his eyes are out of the frame. There he is then, one bright morning, he sits on the door-step in the sunshine with me sitting the next step down and I am his toothless daughter, grinning, sitting between his feet and holding onto his legs.

*   *   *

My father flirted with my mother when they were driving from Margate to London for a gig, performing with the Skatalites. My mother was riding in the Bedford van with the equipment in the back and Dad was shotgun in the other car, a dark green Humber, with the trumpet player and the other dancer. He dared her to and so my mum passed the bottle of wine across the busy motorway to my father, the trombone player wearing the cravat and the shades. And that night my mother was the leggy dancer in sparkling tights while my father looked up from below, playing in the band, admiring her. That's my dad, down in the pits, looking up at the legs. In her words, he threw her a rose and she caught it and has kept it forever.

As happy newlyweds in the late 1960s, my mother and my father lived in Leeds but often stayed in the house on Springfield Road, my father's family home, with his parents, George and Edith. Mum fell pregnant and had my brother almost immediately. Gus was a beautiful eight-pound-ten baby with a full head of jet-black hair. At the indignation of being slapped on the bottom Gus screamed relentlessly until he was locked onto my mother's breast. He was a very loving and easy-going baby and, being the first born, he was pampered and spoilt rotten by everyone, namely Grandma Edith and her home cooking. The family house in Hastings was often a pit stop between gigs and a place for my parents to gather themselves on rainy days.

* * *

With the late afternoon sun streaming through the small square of gold, with the windowsills cluttered with plants and the leaves casting shadows on the kitchen's turquoise wallpaper, my mother regaled me with these tales of the past. I remember the kitchen wallpaper so well; it had a pattern of sea-blue and green heart-shaped flowers with violet centres. I remember the wallpaper so vividly partly because of the hours I spent watching my mother cook, and also because we covered all my school books in it to keep them nice. Sitting up on the side with my legs swinging against the cupboard below, I felt I could ask my mother almost any question. As she peeled, chopped or stirred, I coloured in the outlines she drew of our life before.

I was conceived during the lazy dog days of the summer of 1971, at a holiday camp on the Isle of Man. Dad was playing in the jazz band and Mum was go-go dancing. They lived in a caravan with three-year-old Gus. 'It was the end of the summer season and we were at the Douglas holiday camp, your dad was playing with Ray Ellington—'

I interrupt, 'There was a magic bridge, right?'

Mum rolls her eyes, then nods, indulging me. 'Yes, there was a fairy bridge. When you cross it to go from Douglas into Castletown, you have to say 'hello fairies' three times and make a wish or you will be cursed by the witches who were burnt at the stake at an old mill nearby.'

As a child, I loved this story, imagining this place of wizardry and fairy magic during that warm September just nine months before my birth. I imagined a ducking stool by a humpback bridge over a fast green river, the spirits whispering through its rickety wooden frame, surrounded on each side by wildflowers that littered the grass and nearby woodland. I could see the river, winding towards a crooked windmill on the distant horizon, where ghosts of drowned girls haunted the cold shadows of the rocky river bed. I imagined the mischievous laughter of fairies skipping across the glimmering, sunlit surface of the shallows. Then I pictured my mother laughing, being chased by my father across the bridge, hiding beneath it as he caught up and kissed her. He might have said something daft and sloppy like, *if we weren't already married, I'd ask you to marry me.* That was when I was a twinkle in my dad's eye and that was when my parents were in love, kissing under the dog star.

'Really? I was made under that magic bridge?'

'Well, no! Not exactly there, under the actual bridge, but later on, when we knew I was pregnant, we did wish for a little girl there.'

*   *   *

As a child, I stared at the sun. I tried to capture a memory of what it was like to be inside my mother's womb, to then be born, the first sensations of first light and life. I believed that if you look through your eyelids directly at the sunlight, maybe that is something of what you saw, you saw the veined inside of red skin. When I was a very little girl, I dreamt I was inside my mother's belly. For many years, I was convinced it was my first and earliest memory, as it was as vivid and real as one.

I was once growing inside my mother. I could think and feel, but I was wordless. I was inside a dark place with a glimmer of red, a dim glow in the dark like a ruby in the bottom of a pint of Guinness. I gave that warm glowing colour, that essence of ruby, a made-up name: *rubiessence.* I could hear music, the way you hear sound from below the surface of the bathwater. There was a muffled rhythm, something like a drum, my mother's heart beating, blood in my ears, pulsing. Most prevalent and unforgettable though, was the sense of total peace I felt, and an acceptance that this was all there was, all there ever could be, and whenever I remembered this place, this *rubiessence,* be it a dream or a memory of a dream, I could conjure how I had once felt there: safety, peace, comfort and pure contentment.

Tipping my face towards the sun, and through my closed eyelids, I compared this memory-dream of my birth to scenes in films of people drowning, the serenity on the face of the drowning person once he or she stops fighting for air. It seemed peaceful, beautiful, the most graceful of deaths, to sink down below the surface forever, like floating off into space. I imagined that being born was like drowning but backwards, as violent as not being able to breathe any more. From the essence of ruby, the dark red cave and heat of the womb to the bright, white glare of a hospital. Noise and first light would feel like a sharp, cold slap and I believed that was

64

why babies screamed so much when they were new born; the outside world would be just too bright and too cold and too loud.

Maybe this is what all mothers tell their daughters, but my mother always told me that they wanted a little girl and that I was made on purpose. She told me I was a love child. I was born in June, midsummers, and I arrived early, impatient as ever. When my mother went into labour, my father was performing in Canterbury in a jazz concert. In one version of the story she told me, when my father heard my mother was in labour, he literally leapt, grabbing onto the velvet curtains, and joyously swung across the stage. Either way she told it – and the story does alter – my father was wild and excited at the news. A bandmate drove him to the hospital to be at my mother's side and, as my mother put it, we both popped our heads out at the same time. He appeared as I arrived. I weighed eight pounds six, but when I was born I was silent and refused to scream or cry. Apparently, I started breathing on my own and then immediately put my own thumb in my mouth. Mum always said, *it was as if you had been here before, you just stared at us and sucked your thumb as though you knew us.* The doctor told my mother, *you've got an independent one there,* while my father kept telling Mum how clever she was. Dad was pickled, half-drunk, merrily singing in the hospital corridors to anyone who'd listen: *come and look, I've got a beautiful baby girl!*

Mum insists that I was also a mother's dream, an easy-going baby. She says we were a happy young family for a while, that my parents believed that somehow things would work themselves out. However, a dancer and a session musician do not make much money, particularly off-season and between gigs. So my mother picked potatoes at a local farm for fifty pence a day. In those days, we lived hand to mouth. Mum could make a chicken last seven days: a roast chicken on Sunday would be a stew come Tuesday, then by adding some spice and love it became a chicken curry, and after boiling the bones for broth, it was reduced to a soup by the end of the week.

I have pale but warm, talc-powder memories of our pink fisherman's cottage in Ramsgate. With a smoky jazz soundtrack in the background of Dicky Wells, Gene Krupa, Coleman Hawkins and Lester Young, this era was a rose-tinted time. My brother Gus remembers it more keenly. He remembers our dad taking him behind the bar in a pub and teaching him to pour a pint, and he remembers going go-kart racing. My brother remembered my father more clearly and during our shared childhood his absence was suffered most acutely, and also privately, by Gus.

PAUL GODDEN (trombone)

Paul is our trombonist, although he is another newcomer to the show this is no new venture for Paul as he started playing trombone at the age of 12. After University he played a night club in Vienna. Has played with the well-known " Sounds Incorporated " and in 1967 recorded on the Sergeant Pepper L.P. Summer seasons in Blackpool and engagements on the Q.E.2 go to make up Paul's wide experience. He is married and has one child. He met his wife in the business, she is a dancer and they live in Hastings.

Programme from Granville Theatre, Ramsgate, 1970

Our Real Dad

When you travel to a new city, you can imagine what it must be like, even if you have never been there. You can conjure up London, New York or Paris by their names alone, picturing your destination while on your way there. This journey is in reverse – my father is the stop I missed, he is the station I dreamt of when I was sleeping.

We all have a store of scenarios of how it might have been. I have imagined him being a loving father. I have pictured him throwing me into the air and catching me, then sniffing me the way I have seen all parents do, putting their faces close into the centre of a bare-bellied baby and blowing raspberries. I am sure my father did this to me: threw me high in the air, made me fly and blew onto my belly. When he changed my nappy, I imagine I caught my own foot and sucked my toes. My skin was once as soft as all babies', and just like all our fathers must have – your father, our father, my father – he held me and I felt safe in his arms. With his mouth pressed against the crown of my head he inhaled as he soothed and patted my back. He saw himself in me, I'm sure, in my features. I was his echo and he must have said what all fathers have always said, that looking into my face was like looking in the mirror.

I can picture the familiar shape of my father in the early morning. Then I can imagine my chubby infant self, dribbling, standing up in a cot in a messy bedroom. There's a gas fire, the bars are glowing orange, and I smell toast. I have torn off my nappy and thrown it out of the cot. I know I used to do this, I know I am naked and laughing, funny Daddy, I clap, although when I clap I let go of the side of the cot and fall. I am only just learning to stand, so I must be seven or eight months old. I haul myself back up by the cot bars and he says something like, *that's my girl.* He would, wouldn't he? I think he'd say something like, *that's my good girl.*

It is dawn, early in the morning and he is melancholy, probably hungover. It's the grey morning after a gig and he didn't get paid or he subbed all the fee already. The money is always spent before he sees it. He has post-gig blues, is unshaven, and his mouth tastes of stale fags and booze. He looks down at me and wonders how on earth he is going to cope. He licks the cigarette paper and puts the rolled-up fag in his mouth, sighs, shakes his head. He lights a match and inhales smoke.

I can now recognise sounds and shapes, objects and people. Shoe. Dog. Milk. Mummy. Daddy. I must know that word and try to use it. This is one time when I get to say 'Daddy' to my real dad. If I am eight months old, then it is winter and he is in mourning. Cancel the summer sunshine I had previously imagined, making an arc of light across the smoky, shabby room. If I am eight months old, let's say, then it is cold and about to snow outside on the cobbled street in Ramsgate, on the pink house, on the row of pretty fishermen's cottages in February 1973.

Or maybe we are not in Ramsgate but in Hastings, visiting Grandpa George on Springfield Road. They are in grief. Now I do know how that feels. I know what the view looks like from that window, I have touched the old wallpaper in the room we would

68

have slept in. I know the red brick and slate rooftops of the houses opposite and the grey sea on the distant horizon. Snow is falling diagonally and disappearing as it touches the wet ground.

That moment then, he loves me, doesn't he? Dare I write that? Yes, I dare and I know it. If there is one thing I know, it is that in this snapshot, this imagined scene, he loves me. He scoops me into his arms and takes me to the window to show me the snow. Let's say he did, for now it makes no difference. I am in his arms and I can see the snow outside, feathers falling from above. I can also see our reflection in the glass, my dad holding me in his arms, us together, father and daughter. The hairs on his arms and the warmth of his chest against my soft, naked baby form. I nuzzle into his neck, his unshaven bristles and sideburns. We are framed by the windowpane and faintly etched into the glass. The snowflakes are tapping the windows, erratic as shoals of fast white fish in light and water, changing directions in swirling gusts of salty wind.

Dad. Your cheek is pressed against me, you sniff my hair and kiss my head. 'Daddy,' you say slowly. You put my hand on your mouth and I feel the sound, the resonance of the word vibrating through my fingers. 'Dad.' You are holding me and moving from foot to foot, slowly rocking us as we look out at the grey-mauve of first light, and the sky is the colour of pale wisteria, swollen, mottled and lilac.

This is what we all owe ourselves: the shape of a memory of a moment of love and intimacy. A flash of how it might have been, how they told you it was. Once upon a time, when you were too small to remember, there was tenderness and you were cherished. Imagine your own father. Your real dad brushed your hair away from your forehead with gentle fingertips, he gave you the sweetest light kisses and watched over you when you were in your cot. That is all always yours, forever. This life, it is a long journey and this is the station you passed when you were sleeping but will always dream about.

✳   ✳   ✳

My father was born in Kent on 24 April 1941. According to my mother, he was a clever and gifted boy with a propensity towards chubbiness. Mum said he was nicknamed Porky at school and this made him self-conscious about his pot belly. He was very smart, and he shot through school and was awarded a scholarship to grammar school. He lived on Springfield Road from the age of about ten.

As a young man my father went travelling around Europe. He visited Spain and Italy, he studied music in Vienna and then came back to England to study at the new music college in Leeds. During this time he met my mother, Lorna. He played sessions for the BBC then he graduated to session work for the London Philharmonic. He also played sessions for Miles Davis and on The Beatles' *Sgt. Pepper's Lonely Hearts Club* album.

The summer when I was born, my father was playing with the great jazz singer Salena Jones — my namesake. I was honoured to have the opportunity to interview Salena Jones once for the BBC; she was so warm and generous and so beautiful. She told me she took the spelling 'Salena' from her heroes and friends the great jazz legends Sarah Vaughn and Lena Horne, Sarah-Lena, Sa-Lena. Since learning this, I always felt there is so much powerful black beauty, black history and jazz ancestry in that chosen name and that particular spelling of Salena.

My parents toured with the likes of television gameshow host Larry Grayson and legendary ska band the Skatalites, until my father took that job playing in the jazz band on the *QE2*. By the late 1970s, he was resident at the London Palladium and then . . .

I combined my mother's accounts of my father with the odd snippets I gleaned from Grandpa George and the anecdotes that came out during rare visits from his old jazz pals in my teens.

I heard that my father was a brilliant musician, that he could play almost anything you put in front of him – the piano, the trumpet, the clarinet, the trombone. He was a drinker and a great laugh down the pub. My mother tells me that as a young man the local police in Hastings knew him by sight and often found him after closing time, singing in the street and along Hastings seafront, and would bring him home to Springfield Road. He hated to wear a suit; when he did it looked like it had been thrown at him and just missed. He was a writer of poetry, a lover of jazz, a wearer of cravats and neckerchiefs. He was a bohemian and a libertine. The life and soul of the party, he had time for a drink with everyone and Mum told me this was his downfall. He gave it all away, he left nothing for himself. He gave himself such a hard time that the people who loved him had to work hard too. He never went straight home, he never did anything the easy way. He seemed to me to be sexually ambiguous, I have always suspected he was bisexual, and that he was struggling with that. Either way, attitudes to sexuality and mental health were so different in those days. It is a fact: he gave himself a hard time and he'd drink until drunk after every gig.

As I grew up, when I played the fool or read my stories or poetry aloud, my mother's face would light up and she'd tell me I was being like my father. That was how I was rewarded and how I grew up to know this much and this little. My mother tells me that we would have had great debates, we'd have had each other running in circles of wordplay. I revelled in the notion that my father was a poet and a showman, that he was infectiously funny, mischievous, and above all that we would have made each other laugh. I reckon that I could have drank him under the table and enjoyed trying to beat him at blackjack too. But all I could ever do was digest these statements, his poems, letters and fragments

71

of stories and deduce truths from the materials of my own DNA. Nature or nurture – could I really be a copy of a man I never truly knew? Often I didn't want to believe my mother's portraits of my father, based as they were on her memories of being in love with the smell of the man and his laughter, and the details always changed with her mood and the weather of her own remembering. Her ex-husband Paul Godden was not the same as the dad-man-hero I invented. The father I knew was in my bones and blood, I felt I knew him in the reflection behind my eyes in the mirror.

My creation of him was all my own.

When your father is absent you collect all they have said and all they have told you, you look at photographs and letters, and you stir these ingredients together and bake your own dad. It doesn't matter now if he had faults and flaws. When you haven't known your father, he can be anyone you like and anything you choose to believe. So I made my father out of jigsaw pieces of other extraordinary men. I believed he was gentle and quirky like the American author and poet Richard Brautigan. I imagined he could be a merry rogue, maybe like Oliver Reed in *The Three Musketeers*. He had the look and flair, I thought, of a young and distinctly English Dirk Bogarde. Something of the poetic heart and wanderlust of author Laurie Lee. He was rock-and-roll with the hedonistic jazz persona of a haplessly destructive and depressive Chet Baker. My version of my father was anything but ordinary.

When I was at Springfield Road I was closest to his life as a boy and young man. The fact that he had lived there, and was a teenager in that very house, was all I had. I knew he was confirmed and that he sang in the choir at Christchurch, and I knew that he read and wrote music and poetry. I imagined he probably composed those songs and poems while walking on Hastings' pebbled beaches, and later as a teenager I often walked along the same beaches and sat under Hastings Pier writing poems and tried to recreate or emulate this.

It is necessary to mention that my father was adopted and that he searched all his life for his birth parents. So more than anything, my father and I shared a perpetual sensation of seeking, the unbearable state of looking. His children inherited that longing, the sense of waiting to be found, to be rescued.

It's not that we are not loving, living in the present with our loved ones, but when you have an absent parent or parents, there is an itch and yearning to have more. It's as though we are looking over your shoulder when we say hello. We are gazing across the water at the receding horizon, with a glimmering hope to find lost blood, to catch a familiar eye across a strange and crowded world.

A Letter from Paul to Edith

Hello My Dear Old Mum

How are you this bright windy day? Thanks very much for the bread my mum and for Cressendo which has just arrived. I am glad to hear you had a nice birthday, I thought of you all day. I have written a begging letter to Nell, I asked for 30 quid to pay the rent. That way she might send ten but if she comes around moaning don't blame me it was your idea. Tonights the night I find out about the job. So by the time you get this . . . we'll know. The food parcels haven't arrived yet but I expect they'll take a little while. Thanks for them in advance. Dyson my trombone teacher is a gas. He's teaching me things I never knew on the horn and he's got such a beaut tone. He's a gentleman like Mr Chapman. Truly family man with nice hands and a little moustache. He thinks I should grow one (a tache not a family) to strengthen my lip, so don't be surprised if? What do you think of the enclosed, my first (BBC) contract. One whole guinea, hang on to it we'll frame it one day. Well I must go and do some more practice. Lorna says she'll marry me which would be nice but I will say it for you 'What on?' It's nice to know she goes along with the idea. Sorry this letter is late I have been so busy. Take care of yourself, love your unworthy son, Paul x

Tea and Crumpets

It was a long drive from Desborough to Hastings to visit Grandpa George for the holidays. It took all day, the entire family rising as the sky was just light and lavender. We were like an army about to go on manoeuvres. We crawled along motorways behind queues of cars pulling caravans heading for holidays on the coast. The radio announced that it was *going to be a scorcher*, making us fast-forward to images of Hastings, the promenade, Knickerbocker Glories and splashing in the green and salty sea. My brother and I were squashed among luggage and the picnic bag. There was a stink from the grey hard-boiled eggs in our packed lunches. Gus had had a growth spurt and was suddenly very tall, bony and spindly. He sat with his legs wide apart and constantly complained of cramps. *I need more leg room!* I wore shorts, and the leatherette seating always stuck to my bare legs, leaving a red mark of the linear grooved pattern on the backs of my skinny thighs.

On long car journeys I had a preoccupation with needing the bathroom or with car sickness, and thinking of either made it worse. Trying to concentrate on not thinking of it made those journeys unbearable for me. Being told that it was impossible to stop and being warned to *go now because we are not stopping* instilled a terrific dread that stopping, that pulling over, was a very bad thing to ask for. Now as an adult I must admit I get overexcited at petrol stations and truck stops on road trips with friends. I look forward to the pit stops and choosing snacks and treats most of all.

For the first half hour or so, my brother and I read out the road signs and bet on who would be first to see the sea, which was still a good seven hours' drive away. We played games: I-Spy, Battleships and Top Trumps. He cheated, I cheated, we bickered. The air outside was hot through the open windows but it was suffocating, stifling with them closed. There was no such thing as air conditioning – not in Patrick's queasy margarine-yellow Mazda, a clapped-out rust-bucket that rattled down the motorway.

Heat oozed off the tarmac, shimmering like water in the distance, and I'd say to myself: *it looks like an oasis.* With the windows wide open, the car filled with country smells and the ripe stench of cow dung. The nose tickled with the smell of petrol as the car was filled in the garage.

Gus drew an invisible line with his finger down the centre of the back seat, marking his territory. We squabbled about which was my side and which his, hoarding prisoners of war, claiming toys and comics. We passed fleas, playing IT, which escalated to dead legs and silent, swift, thigh-stinging punches. Gus gave me a Chinese burn and I tried to bite his hand as he twisted my wrist. He said, *she started it,* I said, *he started it,* and then as we bickered we were told to 'Give it a bloody rest for Christ's sake or you can both bloody get out and bloody walk!'

The car was quiet after that. I escaped into my top three favourite indulgent daydreams of discovering I was adopted, being an Olympic gymnast or being a pop star, while staring at the country-side and listening to the radio DJ say, 'Annnnd it's gonna be a scorcher and you know, folks, you could fry an egg on your car bonnet, today we're reaching highs of ninety-two in the south . . . and now I'd say it's about time for some summer loving, here's John Travolta and Olivia Newton-John . . .'

When we were all in the car Patrick would make his little joke. 'Look, Lorna, isn't that your cousin?'

I think that joke started when Mum told him how big our Jamaican family is or how small Jamaica is, how you'd be surprised who may be related to whom some way or another. His joke invariably came up when we were all in the car and we saw a Jamaican or African or any person of colour or black person in the car in front or crossing the road. *Isn't that your cousin?* It made Patrick really laugh, but we saw it upset Mum. I am ashamed to admit it but we'd giggle nervously. *Hey, isn't that one of your cousins?* It made Patrick roar with laughter, we laughed, we liked to try to be in with his jokes. It was better than being at the other end of them. Eventually Mum would snap sharply and we would all go very, very quiet and feel ashamed and awkward.

It would be the late afternoon when we finally left the thick traffic of the motorway. Then we glided through Kentish countryside, up and down the swooping hills, passing villages with strange names, farms selling fresh eggs and potatoes, *pick your own strawberries*, and winding roads with humpback bridges that made my stomach leap. Mum gasped at dream cottages covered in wisteria and tea roses. *We'll have a cottage like that, one day, when we win the pools*, she sighed. Trees canopied above us, the sky was duck-egg blue between the lush branches, as we drove past the glorious rolling green of Kent and the Sussex hills and valleys. As soon as the word 'Hastings' appeared on the road signs, we sniffed for the piquant smell of it, the first taste of salted air, eagerly searching for the line of aqua-marine shimmering on the horizon.

'I spy with my little eye something beginning with . . . sea!'

'Sea! Sea begins with S!'

'I know! Sea!'

'See the sea!'

'I saw it first!'

We leaned out of the car windows, the wind making our eyes water and our hair blow wild, opening our mouths, tasting the salt.

The house on Springfield Road was painted a pale yellowish colour. There was a pretty front garden with antique rose bushes growing in it. When the door opened the same distinct smell always hit you first and foremost, a musty combination of Lifebuoy soap, Earl Grey tea, mothballs and maybe a whiff of kippers. It also reminded me of the pages of dusty leather-bound books. The house on Springfield Road was a shrine to forgotten things. There was an old cuckoo clock in the hallway and worn linoleum on the floor. There were fireplaces, but the chimney was out of use, so instead an electric three-bar fire filled the grate. On the first-floor landing, the window was stained glass, and red and blue shafts of light hit the walls and stairs. The house on Springfield Road was enormous compared to the bungalow we lived in, with unused bedrooms, a gloomy attic and the dark and murky basement.

Grandpa George showed us up to our rooms on the first floor. Lovely, stuffy, homely rooms. The old springy beds in each room squeaked when you sank into them. A crucifix hung on the wall above each and every headboard, and there was often an old-fashioned china potty beneath. Along the mantelpieces were figurines from Lourdes and statues of saints. There was a clutter of yellowing black and white photographs of old monks, priests and nurses in frames. Also plenty of photos of us all, my brother and me as babies in that very house, in the same armchairs, but being held by people we didn't recognise or remember. And there were pictures of our mother and father when they were married and my dad as a schoolboy grinning at us cheekily. How strange that must have seemed for my stepfather to walk into this museum to our shared times past.

Looking back, Grandpa George was always very fond of my mother. He came out on Mum's side when my parents separated, harbouring the opinion that Paul was irresponsible by shirking his duties to his children and breaking his wedding vows. He rather thought it was *a great shame they didn't work it out somehow*. I remember throughout my life Grandpa George maintained a closeness with my mother, and he loved us as his grandchildren; there was a consistent and steady stream of phone calls and letters and post-cards. He never forgot a birthday and sent food parcels monthly, with teabags, bars of soap and packets of soup – he always included sticks of pink Hastings rock too.

We arrived in time for tea, and it was always time for tea, which was served in the ground-floor front room with great yet sloppy ritual. Thick slices of brown bread were carved, cut into triangles and spread with soft yellow butter and church-fête jam. Tea was stewed in a chipped brown teapot and kept warm under a burnt tea cosy, then served in pretty porcelain china cups and saucers with red roses on them. There were cakes from the bakery at the bottom of Springfield Road. That lovely tiny bakery is still there to this day, crammed with a magical selection of cakes: ice cream cones filled with marshmallow, deliciously moist bread puddings and gingerbread men.

We had tea listening to the ticking of the dark, wooden mantel-piece clock, its loud chime interrupting us at fifteen-minute intervals. The four o'clock sun streamed through the yellowy net curtains, toasting the bread on the table; the first slice was always a little stale from being left out and the milk was always a little too warm. When we visited for Easter there were hot cross buns, and always there were crumpets to be speared with a metal prong and toasted on the bars of the gas fire, as one might before a real open fire.

Grandpa George had an unusual way of eating. He exhaled noisily from his nostrils and his jaw sometimes clicked. He nearly always had cream or gravy down his tie or food trapped in the corners of his mouth. He had a very sweet tooth, like me, and loved marzipan and liquorice and fudge. I would look up at him in wonder at the way he ate sweets like me, shared them with me, and with so much delight, not in tiny bites with the usual care of adults, but hungrily, making that noise through his nose. To me Grandpa George was a testament to the fact that being grown up meant that you could have sweets, you could have your pudding for dinner and always a second helping of cake too.

As the kettle was boiled for yet another pot of tea, I was finally allowed to leave the table to go exploring. The basement and attic were my favourite places to snoop through old, out-of-date things, things that were maybe here when my father was a boy. In the attic was the room that my mother said had been Dad's, and the back bedroom that was once Uncle Peter's. I'd stand in the silence of it and imagine my father's boyhood. I looked out the window and tried to imagine being him, seeing things as he might have. In the basement I found books of sheet music that my mother said were his. I once found a tiny notation pencil in a silver tube with a lid that she told me he wrote his music with. In earnest I wrote sheets of nonsense treble clefs and semi-tones with it to try to conjure something of him.

The basement was dark and damp-smelling. Mum said there was a ghost on the narrow back stairs, and I always got a cold chill, goosebumps, walking down the creaking and dimly lit stairwell. Through the basement back door there was an outside loo that hadn't been used for decades. I'd dare myself to look into it, opening the door to see the toilet bowl was full of moss and spiders. Once I was in the back garden there was an apple tree that I climbed, and sitting in its branches, I said to myself, *I bet my dad sat up here.* He probably didn't, the tree would have been much smaller back in the 1950s, but I'd sit there and pretend anyway. Though there was the grave of his pet dog named Francis right beside the apple tree — I knew that he loved that dog. I knew that much was true.

Grandpa George

Excerpt transcribed from a recording of Grandpa George talking, made in Hastings in 1988:

'I think there should be more periods of calm and quiet. I think there should be belief and dependence on God. I get involved with questions about God and spiritual matters and of course I don't know and cannot answer . . . but somehow with God there are lots of things I don't understand but I just find I accept it . . . We must try to have quiet times to reflect. I do think that prayers help an enormous lot. I don't know how, but they do. If you ask for things that you want, sensible things, not selfish things, the answer comes somehow, in my experience. Also we should try very hard to think the best of people. All sorts of people try to irritate and annoy, but we should try to think the best and think good of them. I think one of the terrible things that I have always hated is class distinction. It is one of the things I had to put up with when I was a youth. I found the army a good experience in that direction. You were thrown together in a barrack room with all sorts of different types that, as a youth, you would not be allowed to mix with. I found that they were not so bad and they probably found that I wasn't so stuck up as they thought. I am not saying this in a communist sense, but I think there is good in all people.'

* * *

Grandpa George had bright white hair, cropped high above the collar and parted slickly to the side. Even in my mother and father's wedding photographs from the 1960s, he looked like an older gentleman. He seemed to have a lifetime supply of grey-brown chequered gentlemen's three-piece suits, which he wore fully with braces, pocket watch and waistcoat. On his head he wore a cap or a soldierly bottle-green beret. When he shaved he often missed a bit on his neck; I would spot some soap there and a few grey hairs, usually on his Adam's apple or by his ear.

When I was a little girl we would sit and chat on the third step from the bottom of the stairs and wait for the cuckoo to poke its head out when the clock chimed the hour. Grandpa George had soft pink scrubbed hands and I tried to teach him hand-clapping games.

'Who stole the pies from the baker's van? Number one stole the pies from the baker's van. One two, three, four, that means you!'

I'd sing and Grandpa George could never keep up, no matter how many times I explained the rules or tried to show him how it was done.

'Aren't you funny,' he always said to me. 'Aren't you a funny little girl?'

'Come on, try again, it's easy, just copy me.'

'You are a funny little girl, now, aren't you?'

I tried to teach Grandpa to rub his belly and pat his head at the same time. He could never get that right either no matter how much I insisted it was easy.

* * *

Grandpa George was born in August in 1916 in Peterborough. His parents met in the department store Boots, on Robertson Street in Hastings. In those days, Boots had an art department – his father was an art dealer and picture framer — and his mother worked in the silverware department. They settled in Hastings and ran a small art shop on Norman Road, a ten-minute walk from Springfield Road. The shop hardly made any money and so they also sold cigarettes, tobacco and stationery. They found they still couldn't make ends meet and so they took in lodgers and summer visitors. As a boy Grandpa George remembers losing his bed to guests sometimes and his mother staying up half the night cleaning. It is quite likely his father, George senior, may have tried to sell his own paintings too, vast landscape work, often depicting churches. There was always one of George senior's big oil paintings hanging above the dining table in the front room in Springfield Road. I recall an impressive landscape of rolling yellow hayfields and golden hedge-rows with a steeple in the distance.

When Grandpa George left school, although he was fond of aeroplanes, he got turned down by the Air Force. He did a few menial jobs in garages, until eventually he was called up in 1940:

'. . . and the next thing I knew I was on a boat to Egypt. We weren't supposed to know we were going to Egypt of course. The boat was called Sobiski — *it was a British-built motor-liner but it was Polish owned . . . It got very hot, terrible conditions, and they put us on guard, guarding strategic points on the ship. I don't really think it was necessary, just something to keep us busy. They were always trying to catch you out and give you jankers if they could. Major Gibson, he was on our side all right . . . but the ship is run by the commanding officer, so what he says goes . . . and anyway, they had class distinction with a capital C. You had to stand around and you had the most primitive, rough food . . . and the officers were up on the upper deck . . . you had to stand a few yards away from the officers who were la-di-da-ing it around, eating ice cream and jelly . . . whilst some poor blokes standing guard there, not even*

speaking to him . . . of course officers don't talk to common people. Anyway, then we went through one of the worst storms they'd ever had. The propeller came right out of the water. You'd see great mountains coming right up above the ship and then the next minute you'd be looking down into a valley. When you went across the deck you'd hang on to a rope. You wouldn't dare to let go or you'd be a goner. Anyway we were put in at Durban . . . we missed Cape Town . . . The ship was damaged and so it had to be repaired . . . Anyway we had our pep talk from one of the officers before going ashore, that we weren't to go back-slapping and familiarising with the natives and so on. If they weren't kept in their place someday they'd only . . . Talking about natives, well, the general view among ordinary troops like myself was that if a chap was good enough to stop a bullet for you, he was good enough to be treated decently. Well, I still have that view, don't you? We went to a soldiers' canteen; one of the ladies said to me it was winter weather, how could we want ice cream in this weather? And, well, that is what we wanted all right and ice cream was nice for us . . .'

During the Second World War, Grandpa George was a wireless operator on a tank in the Middle East. However to read the stack of letters he wrote his mother from the front line you would be hard pushed to believe they are from a grown man at war in a tank. George writes about the heat and thanks his mother for the Palm Sunday cross and the socks. He tells her about *a little doggy* that comes into their camp, and that he has made friends with. There are details of a beautiful Palestinian orchestra he had heard, the overtures and religious services he managed to tune in to on the wireless, and places of historical and biblical interest that he visited. But this was Grandpa George — where other soldiers might have worshipped pin-ups and had pictures of wives and girlfriends under their pillow, I imagine Grandpa George had a picture of his favourite cathedral pinned on the wall next to his bunk. It's a certainty he had a crucifix. He returned to civilian life with medals that he never ever mentioned or displayed. If he ever spoke of the war, it was only to illustrate the importance of discipline but more so the importance of manners and kindness

When Grandpa George came home to Hastings he became the verger at Christchurch, and it was during this period he met and married my grandmother, Edith Godden. It was Edith's idea that George become a nurse, and he worked at various hospitals until he retired in 1981.

Grandpa George used tools as they were properly intended, shoe-horns and letter openers. He spoke with the gentility of another time. His pockets were always stuffed with handkerchiefs, coupons and string. He loved animals and he filled envelopes to all animal charities when they knocked at the door. As he grew more elderly, his love of animals led him to products that didn't use animal testing, which seemed quite new and radical then. He loathed any form of animal cruelty and anti-animal testing posters were put up in his lounge windows. Natural lavender soaps, local honey shampoo and rose geranium bubble bath begin to appear in our Christmas and birthday parcels.

But he kept to the rules of his childhood: fish, often kippers, on Fridays, which made the house stink something awful because he had a tendency to forget about them and let them burn. He was to be found at Christchurch throughout the week and twice on Sundays. He never missed the Proms — that was when classical music would boom even louder than usual through the house. His great splash out was that he always had a season ticket for concerts by the Philharmonic society. He referred to steam engines as *proper trains*. His work in the church was a job and something he truly enjoyed. He also loved the royal family and his Queen and Country. And anything modern was described as *newfangled claptrap.*

* * *

Christchurch is a beautiful sandstone church in the centre of St Leonard's. On school holidays I'd often accompany Grandpa to church to help him change the hymn boards and replace the altar candles. We'd talk in whispers while doing these tasks. I was curious about being permitted up the narrow steps into the bell tower and backstage into the priests' musky dressing rooms, where the cassocks and robes hung like stage costumes.

I remember being inspired by Grandpa George. How one morning, when the sky was moonstone, milky as opals, I lay awake and counted the chimes of a distant clock. It was six in the morning and the house was still and quiet as I crept downstairs to the front living room. Looking through a crack in the curtains, I saw the sun was doing the God-thing, when one ray of sun beamed through a silver-lined cloud. It was as if God's own finger was that single shaft hitting the horizon.

With a framed reproduction of Holman Hunt's allegorical painting *The Light of the World* above me and the monotonous ticking of the mantelpiece clock in the background, I opened the enormous leather-bound family Bible. I had set myself the project of copying the entire Bible out word for word. That particular school holiday my fevered obsession with religion had no limits.

At night I dreamt of kissing Jesus – how I loved Robert Powell with the bright blue eyes. And how I roared my eyes out every single Easter when they showed that epic drama on TV. With a mouthful of chocolate egg I'd sit and weep, particularly in the scene when they whipped Jesus and made him carry his own cross and daubed his wounds with vinegar.

I attacked this Bible-writing work with great vigour, making my first letter bold and ornate, trying to trace over the swirl of calligraphy loops. I believed everyone – principally Grandpa George – would be very pleased that I had taken the trouble to write my own handwritten Bible. I wrote until my hands ached, until I had a red raw bump on my finger. I remember wishing the Bible would hurry up and get to the good bits about Adam and Eve but there was so much I didn't understand, before the creation of any animals or man. This was to continue every morning. I would rise each day at dawn to complete this work. However, it was Grandpa George who took me aside and told me it took monks many centuries to write the Bible out by hand. Then he patted me on my head and said: *aren't you funny?*

* * *

We rarely had photographs taken, and that summer was no exception. Perhaps that holiday there would have been pictures of Mum and Patrick playing tennis, or Gus and I playing on the beaches of St Leonard's, making new friends with other holiday children, all of us splashing each other and jumping waves. I distinctly remember when we took the cliff lift up onto the top of the East Hill, how it creaked precariously. It was a short ride, but from the top I could see the stretch of pebbled beaches, the curve of the coast and the horizon. Hastings Pier was in the distance and the amusements and arcades were below.

It was nearly the end of August, the end of the summer holiday, and I remember how we sat up on the East Hill together in a patch of daisies, eating ice creams and looking out across the cliffs towards Fairlight. Above us was a haze of cream and blue and the breeze off the sea was clean and fresh. We walked along narrow footpaths of cowslips and yellow gorse, heading towards the sweeping Firehills. Mum named flowers and insects in a dreamy voice while butterflies – red admirals, cabbage whites and tiny pale holly blues – fluttered around us.

The Heart of Springfield Road

If the heart of the home is the kitchen, then it is the soul that rules that kitchen that makes that heart beat. At Springfield Road, this was Edith Godden, my paternal grandmother and Grandpa George's wife. The stone-floored kitchen occupied the basement of Springfield Road. Even as a child, I could imagine this kitchen in its heyday; I could almost smell it, picture a hive of activity, billows of flour, the steady kneading of dough and the rolling out of pastry on the table in the centre of the room. I could imagine fat farm sausages on the griddle, the Sunday joint in the double oven, dripping and gravy in blue and white striped china jugs; a picture-book homemade pie cooling on the windowsill looking out into the yard at the apple, cherry and pear trees beyond.

Down in the kitchen there was a larder, with a light that came on when you opened the door, like a modern fridge. It was a triangular-shaped pantry with shelves filled with out-of-date tinned food. I walked inside the larder to see if the light stayed on when the door was closed. This provided a ripe opportunity for Gus to lock me in there from the outside. I soon discovered that it was indeed dark when the door was closed. Fearing the dark, the spiders and the mice, I screamed and begged him to let me out from among the dusty tins of powdered Colman's mustard, Bird's custard and Heinz baked beans. The Atora suet dated back from before we were born, because Grandpa George never threw away anything after Edith.

Edith Godden: in every one of the old black and white photographs you could see the good shining inside her. She loved children; in photos she was most often holding a child. She had ruddy cheeks, her white hair a wild mess. She always wore her apron. She was all bosom, with baggy stockings and capable-looking hands. I always pictured her with arms full of clean linen, folded to put away upstairs in one of the rosewood, mothballed drawers in the upstairs bedrooms. Clothes pegs still attached, clipped to the front of her pinny pocket.

Hastings is forever the archetypal British seaside holiday resort that needs a holiday, all faded grandeur and peeling façade. So too was the house on Springfield Road, with the walls still echoing a time when it was full of life, laughter and love. When fires burned in all the rooms, when each mantelpiece was crammed with religious effigies and fading photos. There was a time once when the bricks of the house vibrated with the laughter and tears of dozens of children who were taken in or fostered here over the years, like my dad Paul and Uncle Peter and other people who were homeless: refugees or immigrants seeking shelter. This was a house for the lost and found. Everyone who came here, it seemed, came looking for something; everyone who came here had lost pieces of the jigsaw. I imagine Edith being run off her feet but loving every minute, bossing people about, ordering and organising chaotic bathtimes according to limits of hot water. Most of all, I liked to imagine lovely cramped tea-times with too many at the table. A slather of jam and toasted crumpets. Edith probably never sat down but hovered and fussed with a crumpled tea towel in her hand.

* * *

Edith Josephine Godden was born in September in 1906 at home on Beaconsfield Road in Dover, the daughter of a submarine diver. She was a district nurse in the war. In 1930 she completed her nurse's training at Connaught Hospital for Walthamstow, Wanstead and Leyton, then went on to work in a convalescent home in Bearstead, Kent. Whatever else went on there, it was a place where they sent girls who had got themselves in 'trouble', a place designed to relieve them of their burdens, war babies, their secrets and accidents. These illegitimate bundles were then put up for adoption and sent to orphanages until, it was hoped, they found good homes. On 24 April 1941, a baby boy was born to a teenage Irish girl named Joyce Winifred Tremlett. This newborn baby was my father Paul, then named Anthony Paul Tremlett.

We will never know what it was Edith Godden saw in this baby; for all the children she helped to bring into the world as a district maternity nurse, she didn't adopt any others. Perhaps a ray of sunshine lit the room as he entered the world and something inside Edith was moved. Perhaps she saw him in a dream the night before, or in the tea leaves in her cup. I love to imagine she shared a special bond with the teen mother, Joyce, who was as young as only fifteen and may have been alone here in England. I have imagined that her Irish family didn't know about her predicament. Or that they found out and disowned her with a Catholic washing of hands. Either way, to me, it is not that difficult to picture Edith, then aged thirty-five, unwed and without a child of her own, seeing before her a young frightened Irish girl with a baby and nowhere bright for either mother or child to go. I have indulged in a scene of the two of them together, Edith and Joyce.

It is spring, a crisp late April morning. The daffodils and crocuses have burst through the grass outside and below the windows of a white, sanitised room. I see a trembling Joyce, my real grandmother, as a teenager. I see her big round eyes, the same eyes as my father's and mine, sea-green-blue, all welling up with tears. I see the two women holding hands. Tears trickle down Joyce's face and I see Edith holding her hand as Joyce might have asked in her Irish accent, *You'll take good care of him, won't you?*

In reality, I imagine Joyce probably had very little control over her destiny and that of her illegitimate son. It is a fact that the case went to juvenile court, though. Filling in the gaps in what I have been told or overheard, the real story goes a little more like this:

It is 1940. We have a teenage Joyce over from Ireland, working as a scullery or kitchen maid for a rich Kent family. She is 'seduced' by her boss, an anonymous older wealthy gentleman. She falls pregnant and is sent to a home in Bearstead, Kent, to have the baby, and this is where Edith Godden steps in and saves the day. Now, I have so many feelings about these two women. Sadness for Joyce and her loss, the fifteen-year-old Irish girl forced to see her pregnancy to full term only to have the baby given away or taken from her. I feel relief and gratitude that I know Edith was kind and good. It is a story of women making the best of a situation in a system that did not properly protect women's rights. It is a story of courage and survival and I know I am only here now because they were so strong.

It's highly likely my unnamed father's father, my true paternal grandfather, was at the very least a rogue and a coward. It is easy to imagine he was an older, married man, affluent, with a large house. He had power and a property big enough to still warrant staff during the Second World War, when rations were scarce and for most people luxuries such as servants had been forsworn. He kept his identity secret and his hands nice and clean. After the birth and adoption of my father, Joyce disappears from the records without trace. Did she go home to Ireland? Did she run away in pursuit of a new identity? Did she go somewhere far away like America or Australia? Was she committed to an asylum or hospital? Did she live or did she die? Nobody seems to know. My father longed for the truth of it; he looked for her sporadically throughout his life and always came up empty-handed, but for the titbits I can offer here. My mother has told me that my father was convinced Joyce had committed suicide, and that the not knowing, the fruitless searches, that pained him deeply. It is unfinished business, a gaping hole in the material of who on this earth you are really made of. Who made you? Wherever Joyce went, the truth of my father's birth and his true Irish ancestry went with her. But another bold truth remains: the adoption papers plainly state that as of 22 August 1941 Edith Godden was the sole parent to my five-month-old father, and that from then on he was known simply as Paul Anthony Godden.

Single mother Edith and her new son moved to Hastings and started a new life. I cannot imagine how difficult it must have been to bring up a child alone in the 1940s. In a way she may have blended in with other women, war widows also struggling as single mothers. As a regular churchgoer and Sunday school teacher, Edith attended Christchurch, that sandstone church in the centre of St Leonard's, and this was where she met and befriended the indefatigably shy church verger Grandpa George. They grew closer and closer until 1952, when Edith and George married – both for the first time and quite late in life. (Later still, in the late 1960s,

Christchurch is where my mother and father were married too.) I really couldn't tell you how they went about courting each other. I imagine they shared a love of dogs and music, evening walks and concerts. During these early years Edith ran a nursing home with her sister Helen and brother-in-law. When they wed my young father would have been a boy of around ten or eleven years old. In the wedding photos my father is in a blazer and cap and looks very much the cheeky schoolboy. After the modest wedding at Christchurch and a honeymoon in Buckfastleigh, George and his new wife Edith and new son Paul made a home in the house on Springfield Road in the year 1952. And so here is the beginning of the story – another beginning – though Grandpa George never legally adopted Paul, and my father's name remained Godden.

Edith was a member of the Mothers' Union and took in various children who needed care. Soon the house on Springfield Road was filled with temporary foster children, some from London, others local, all allocated to Edith through the church and the union. These included Uncle Peter, who was just a few years younger than my father. I imagine there must have been a cacophony of teasing, tears and laughter, of instruments being played, homework slaved over, the chaos of meal and bathtimes and in every room another story, another heartbreak or triumph. I am idealising it, of course I am, but it seems to me the house was run by good intentions, kind and generous souls who took strangers in. Grandpa George said it wasn't always a happy ending: for example, there was a child called Donald who was always in trouble for stealing. Edith was convinced Donald had some good in him because the dog always went mad with delight whenever he saw him. One of Edith's litmus tests was how kind people were to animals and how animals were to individuals. Donald wound up in borstal in the end. Maybe he wasn't a bad person, just good with animals and good at getting caught.

I still have a brown leather case that belonged to Grandpa George; it is battered and barely closes. Inside it there are birth and marriage certificates, ration books, food tokens and a day-pass giving leave from army barracks. There are picture postcards of the old Hastings clock tower and the Hastings tram running alongside it. The messages on the back of these postcards start *Dear Mother* and then talk about the weather and end with *lots of love, God bless, George.* They are dated 1955 and 1956 and sent from London, where George was completing his nurses' training, and they are written to Edith. It seems even Grandpa George called her 'mother'.

Grandpa once told me:

'I was working at the hospital. It was December 20th 1972. I can remember that date all right. It was in the evening I was doing a late turn. I was working on the male block of the hospital. It was the 20th, so just before Christmas, there was a lady who asked me if I would have a drink with her and I was having a drink and chatting to her . . . then a staff nurse from the other block came over to see me and said, 'There's a policeman downstairs, he wants to see you about your wife,' and she said, 'Terrible,' so I went downstairs to the office. The policeman was there. The staff nurse said, 'Here he is,' and then she said, 'Shall we tell him or shall he just sit down?' So he said, 'Make him sit down.' She said, 'Shall we, give him something?' and she got some brandy out of the drug cupboard and said, 'Shall we give him this?' and the copper said yes or something like that and then he told me and I couldn't make head or tail of it. I knew she was dead. The police took me down to the police car and drove me to Royal East Sussex Hospital where I had to identify her. I will say this about the police, they were extremely kind. I said to one policeman, 'I have said things about the police but I take back what I have said.' I stopped at home the next day. The man who ran over Edith was very young . . . it happened on the

95

Green, just at the top of the road . . . The week before, I had been to a medical lecture in that same room they held the inquest in; it all made me feel very peculiar. I don't know how I felt — it took me several years to adjust to it. I am still not quite adjusted.'

It was Christmas 1972 when Edith Godden was killed in a road accident at the top of Springfield Road. In George's old brown leather case there are dozens of letters and flowery cards kept safe and bundled up with ribbon from people who remembered her: nurses, patients, churchgoers and friends. It seems Edith touched people; they all echo the sentiment that *Edith was so good, it was like it shone out of her.*

In the basement kitchen the heart of Springfield Road stopped beating once Edith was gone. Grandpa George never moved or changed anything, nothing at all, after the day she died, and forever more, the basement became a damp, cobwebbed shrine, stocked with pre-1972 tinned goods. Dust covered the boxes of buttons, her handwritten recipes, her meticulous housekeeping accounts, sewing silks, thimbles and packets of dress patterns. Her fine china crockery faded, silver cutlery grew tarnished. I was fascinated by it and would go down there just to look at things, I'd find newsletters about forthcoming fundraisers, jumble sales and coffee mornings scheduled for 1973 and stacks of old *Reader's Digest*s with recipes she had marked for later. Her cooking pots rusted in neglect. But the light still blinked on when the pantry door was opened, as though Edith had just popped to the corner shop at the top of Springfield Road for a pint of milk and she would be back in a bit.

At the time of her death I would have been only six months, in my cot. Now, as I write this, it dawns on me that this was my brother's first loss. Grandma Edith doted on him, she enjoyed spoiling him. I imagine him knowing something was missing, realising that Edith was gone. Perhaps Mum and Dad explained it to him quietly together when they saw Gus running around the house calling her name. Perhaps my brother thought she was hiding and went and looked for her in the kitchen, in the back garden, before it was explained to him that she wasn't there anymore. Gus was a sensitive and bright little boy. He must have understood something of what had been lost and mirrored our parents' and Grandpa George's grief.

At Springfield Road, I always listened for the heartbeat while I played with lost things. The pieces of a life, evidence of love, left by Edith and my real father and all the people that had once been here: pencils, thimbles and coins. I'd pick at a crumbling bit of wall with my thumbnail and imagine Edith's ghost passing me on the stairs. Her chubby arms full of clean laundry and linen, her cottony white hair, her apron pockets bulging with clothes pegs. Edith's ghost left a steaming apple pie cooling on a windowsill – just a feeling, an image in my mind that wasn't ever really there, but I could still taste it.

The heart of the home, Edith Godden, Springfield Road

The Wendy House

During the late 1970s, money became really tight and things got tougher. Once I was settled into school, my mother had to start looking for a new job in Desborough. These hardships were echoed in the outside world; on the front cover of newspapers I remember men in donkey jackets, miners in a furore over cuts and union strikes, angry picket lines and race riots. Closer to home, the closure of the nearby Corby steelworks put hundreds of people out of work and this included my stepfather who was made redundant, losing his job there as a statistician. Even as children we were aware of this upheaval; we were all anti-Margaret Thatcher, and when our free milk was taken away, we marched about the playground and sang with vitriol: *Thatcher, Thatcher, the milk-snatcher!*

I was at Loatlands Primary School full-time and old enough to walk to and from school alone when my mother took a job at the shoe factory. Northamptonshire is famous for the shoe-making industry. This was toxic labour, and Mum's hands became hard and scarred from a mixture of the chemicals and the leather glue and the stress she was under. Meanwhile, my stepfather went into a retraining programme to become an accountant. In the beginning I had an after-school babysitter called Mrs Bright.

She was like the lady who lived in a shoe, with so many children she didn't know what to do. She lived just down the hill and I'd go to her house after school and play there until Mum came home from work and picked me up at teatime. I remember that Mrs Bright's garden was a chaos of toys and children from the neighbourhood. Then one day one of Mrs Bright's little girls, Charlotte, got her finger trapped in the back door. Mrs Bright fainted at the sight of all the blood. I was the eldest, the little kids were crying at the sight of Mrs Bright collapsing, and so I dialled 999 – something they had taught us in Brownies. However, after that, none of us had Mrs Bright to babysit us after school. Following that incident, after school every day, I'd go home to find the plastic bottle of orange squash and malted biscuits my mother hid in my Wendy house. The Wendy house had been given to me one Christmas by Grandpa George. It was permanently erected under the mossy, corrugated plastic porch down the side of our house. It was yellow plastic, with a red sliding door and aluminium poles to hold it up; a blue plastic roof, a green rug on the floor and two see-through plastic windows. It was, essentially, a small colourful house-shaped tent. I loved it and made curtains for it. Inside, there were two card-board boxes: one was a washing machine and the other a cooker. I had drawn on buttons, dials and gas rings and cut holes in the front, a circle for the washing machine and a square for the oven. In the summer sometimes I was allowed to have a school friend to sleep over in the Wendy house, but when it was cold and wet the wintry wind and rain licked up the sides, making it flap open. I tucked the walls under the base poles and wished my mother would hurry home.

* * *

Occasionally I'd walk down across town to wait for Mum outside the red-brick leather factory. To me the old factory smelled so good, leather and glue, and I liked the noises that came from inside. I imagined engines whirring, gigantic sewing machines, roaring furnaces. The windows were prison-like, small and sooty, barred and high. I'd sit on the railings, hook my legs over the bars and hang upside down. The lower steps became my beam and I rolled over the poles into somersaults. When I grew bored, I'd go to the corner of the car park where the wall had collapsed. Beyond the bricks, the junk, the shopping trolleys and industrial bins there were bramble patches and twisted gnarled trees in a wasteland, where I'd go scrumping for crab apples, sour plums or blackberries.

Then when the bell finally rang shrill and the doors opened, there was a waft of warm air, hot leather and new shoes. I'd sniff and look for my mum among a clatter of gossip, headscarves and a blur of blue matching overalls.

'What are you doing here, cheeky monkey?'

The factory ladies smiled down at me and I'd find myself staring at the corner of my plimsoll and the kerb. My mother would look worn out, exhausted, but happy to see me. After a very long goodbye and a gossip and fags, we walked home together and I'd tell her about my day at school. There was an ulterior motive for meeting my mother from work, of course – if it was a good day, we'd stop to go shopping, and I could help choose the groceries, keeping a steady eye on the cheesecakes and yoghurts in the fridge. If it was a really magic day, I could cajole her into stopping at the newsagents to buy me the latest *Tammy* or *Twinkle* comic. While she paid for it I'd sneak a flick through the slightly older *Judy* or *Jackie*, which had love stories with real kissing at the end.

Kiss Chase

There was always something magical and beautiful about those first days of spring when the world was snowy with blossom. When new buds were sticky and strawberries appeared, tight and pale green, waiting to be painted red and sweetened with warm sunshine. Asparagus was purple in the fields, and in the far-off distance there was a sudden wave of oilseed rape crops, bright and yellow on the horizon.

When the scent of freshly cut grass reached our senses it was a green light. We knew when the school bell rang we could at last break away from the tarmac of the playground and finally run free on the lush school playing fields. Break-times at school became a terrific festering itch of grass fights. We made dens of cuttings and hedgerow camps, prickly with hawthorn. Girls sat in soft cooing circles making daisy chains. They flipped into handstands against the classroom walls, a line of pretty pink knickers, all with the days of the week in *Strawberry Shortcake* or *Snoopy* cartoons. Girls counted in cartwheels and chalked up squares of hopscotch. The lines of the netball pitch marked out territories for the tag-team games of catch and British Bulldog, that brilliant boisterous game which involved tackling each other rugby-style. Coats became goalposts and cardigans were spread out on the ground for beds in the make-believe rooms of houses, hospitals or castles. With the springtime bird chorus and the first cuckoo came the sing-song of skipping ropes and the stamping rhythm of rhyming hand-clapping games. We caught furred caterpillars and they'd tickle us as they crawled over our cupped hands. As girls we were particularly gentle with caterpillars; we tried to feed them leaves, amazed, in awe at their nature of becoming butterflies one day.

Meanwhile, boys were maniacs. They ran wildly with their coats on back to front, with the hoods up covering their faces, blindly colliding into each other and roaring like bears. They tortured daddy-long-legs and kicked the bins until wasps flew out angrily.

Oranges seemed bigger then, huge and tight. Sometimes it took almost all morning-break to meticulously peel away all the white pith to reveal the perfect orange segment.

The longer light, the heat and the dandelion seeds in the air were a call for robust games of kiss chase and war. Charging across the plains and fields, I was a lion and the boys were antelope stampeding. I played rough, I leapt and flew, bundled and tackled boys to the ground. I stuffed grass in their mouths and down the backs of their shirts. We gathered and called other girls to unite with us, marching around the playground screaming *We want the girls! We want the girls!* until we made a string of ten or twenty girls, holding hands in a chain. Then we charged across the playground, up the bank and onto the playing fields, into an equal number of boys lying in wait like soldiers in grass trenches, their back-up troops at the top hill behind them. With an exhilarating roar our two armies ran at each other. We grappled and fell, the wounded crying out.

'I've been shot!'

'You can't shoot me anymore, I'm already dead!'

'I can too, I can make you double-dead!'

'That's not fair!'

'Well, I just threw a hand grenade, that means you're deader than me!'

We rolled on our backs like puppies, with the smell of fresh-cut grass stinging our nostrils. Spring was like too much sugar, a drug that made us laugh so much and so hard we almost wet ourselves. We chased and grabbed and squeezed at each other's parts, boys slobbered kisses on the cheeks of girls who squirmed and squealed in a mixture of delight and disgust. We formed packs and hunted boys, intentionally taking the weaker ones for our own purpose. We chased them, we took them prisoner in epic hedgerow camp games that took weeks of break-times to conclude. We ordered our boy-servants to fetch and carry for us in our houses in the under-growth while we squashed berries with sticks on dock-leaf plates.

There were compelling games in the long grass, the first blooms of *show me yours, show you mine.* In a fuzz of golden hay there were delightful flashes of truth-or-dare kisses. Suddenly, we had a good reason to like school. Winter was a grey memory, abandoned like our woollen bobble hats and gloves. Everyone suddenly looked different: there was a spate of new haircuts and growth spurts and gappy smiles as we were all losing our milk teeth.

My appearance changed dramatically too. I'd had my ears pierced for my seventh birthday and I wore gold stud earrings. This was to compensate for two loathsome facts: first, to my disgust, I now had to wear blue NHS glasses in class for reading and writing. I thought they made me look ugly. Second, my mother, now working and not having the time to help me in the mornings, had cut my long, beautiful but unmanageable curly hair off. I now had a short boyish haircut, which she insisted was called a lion-cut, but which grew out fast and erupted into unruly afro-frizz.

However, that spring we grew more confident, as we became aware we were not the youngest babies in the school anymore. We had a new uniform of green grass stains on our elbows and knees. We felt lighter coming to school in just gingham summer dresses and the boys in those short grey shorts.

* * *

In our last golden term in the infants, the new boy arrived in our class. He had eyes like the sea, dark green with blue flecks. He was tanned, with auburn hair, brown freckles and very pink lips. He could run fast and had been to Disneyland. He had moved into the new house on Braybrooke Road opposite the sweet shop. Our teacher Miss Barclay chose me to show him around for his first breaktimes. That's how I got to meet him first and how we became friends.

That first day, he lifted up his shirt and said, 'Punch me!'

When I punched his stomach he said, 'Harder! Look! See, it don't hurt! Look look, see . . . Do it again!'

He punched his muscular torso with his own fist. He was a seven-year-old with a six-pack and I loved him. With the arrival of the new boy that week I was distracted in class. I wriggled in my seat, staring at him when Miss Barclay read us our afternoon story. Miss Barclay wore dresses with low necklines. She was pretty, with bright blonde hair like Debbie Harry, and when she leaned over we could see she was wearing a black bra. We giggled and nudged each other, fascinated by the otherworldly black lace cupping her bronzed bosoms. A fly banged against the classroom window lazily. We were milky and soporific with afternoon daydreams. My frizzy hair was knotted with grass. I undid a button on my summer dress and slipped it off my shoulder to rub my bare cheek against it while looking at the new boy. My naked shoulder was shockingly smooth, my cheek was hot against it. Watching him hurt my stomach. I had butterflies with teeth. I stared at the beautiful new boy, twiddling with my curls. Miss Barclay's voice was lulling and soft. I stroked the cool skin in the hollow at the backs of my knees. I drew a scratched love heart on the back of my hand with my fingernail only to quickly lick it off, jumping with the sudden sound of the end of school bell.

The new boy – I will call him Mark – spoke fast and excitedly, his eyes wide and sparkling. I remember he wore a silver boxing-glove charm on a silver chain around his neck. He showed me a grey piece of lead, like a charcoal-silver freckle, under the skin by his temple and said it was where an electric pencil sharpener back-fired and could have blinded him, 'could've killed me if it had gone into my brain . . .'

I sighed like I was being shown a hero's war wound.

After school I walked him home the long way around. Mark's house was huge compared to our bungalow. I became shy and polite when I met his mother, a pretty lady with short red hair. In his bedroom upstairs there were *Star Wars* models and pictures of him snorkelling in America. He told me what it was like to fly on aeroplanes. Best of all he had a new purple Chopper, the coolest bicycle I had ever seen, and he let me have a go riding it. He gave me backies too; we laughed riding it dangerously fast downhill.

One day after school Mark and I were out walking together. We were by the humpback bridge and the bricked-up train tunnel at the back of the school fields. The sky had become dark with storm clouds and it started to spit with slow, fat drops of rain. We were talking about James Bond and that's when Mark looked at me mischievously and said that we should stay out in the rain and get drenched on purpose. He persuaded me that if we got wet in the rain his mum would make us take a bath together like in James Bond. He told me that we should tell his mother that we got lost down the lanes and that we got caught in the storm accidentally. Mark had a wicked glint in his eye when he said this, and so instead of turning back to go home, like a dare, we stood there watching the rumbling black sky unfold above us. Thunder rolled and the lightning cracked. We looked at each other and simultaneously began to run. We sprinted fast and hid beneath a tree, jumping with each flash of lightning and calling out with each roar of thunder. Then the fast summer rain bucketed down; it poured and poured and soaked us through. We tipped back our heads and caught the drops from the branches above in our opened mouths, I span with outstretched arms and leapt about.

In my remembering, that moment will always smell like summer rain on cowslips and hawthorn. With the chestnut tree blossoming above us, this memory shines like the raindrops in his eyelashes, his eyes bright, glittering and laughing. We splashed and kicked in puddles at each other, wetting each other's legs and clothes on purpose as we raced each other along the lane through the downpour until we were out of breath, soaked through and back at his house. As soon as we got in the door his mother made a fantastic fuss. Just as he had hoped and predicted, she said we'd catch our death, and she ran a bath for us. However, while I soaked in the bath, Mark sat on the floor in the stairwell and talked to me through the locked bathroom door.

'What are you doing now?'

'Washing my knee.'

'I can see you.'

'Then what am I doing now?'

'Washing your arms.'

'Am not.'

'Washing your tummy?'

'Nope.'

Mark's mother and my mother became great friends. They'd laugh about how we were dumped in the bath together after the rain, but it wasn't true: for the record, we didn't have a bath together. I did not *take a bath with my first puppy love*, as my mother teased me for the rest of my life. However, in the days after the thunderstorm, I lay awake in my bed and played out daydreams where I impressed Mark with my super-fast running and cartwheels. We were like Batman and Catwoman, or James Bond and one of the beautiful spies. In my dreams we waded through wheat fields of yellow and got caught in thunderstorms and I saw the rain on his long eyelashes, our clothes soaked see-through as we held hands and ran like we were bionic: we were Steve Austin and Jamie Sommers.

✳　✳　✳

Once Mark dared me to kiss him. We were in the building site by the side of his house and we had crawled into some unused concrete pipes. Inside the pipes it was secret, shadowy. We closed our eyes tight, held our breath, scrunched up our faces, puckered and pecked lips. That first kiss was quick and ticklish. I covered my face and cracked up laughing and he waited for me to stop and then leaned towards me and we did it again and then a few more times. Each time lingering a little longer, sitting side by side. Then Mark dared us to kiss with open eyes. At first I kept giggling and it was an embarrassed mess of slobbering and a clashing of teeth, but I remember the heat of another mouth being so close to mine, and the feel of it on my cheek when he exhaled through his nose. Then he dared us to kiss in the open air. I took some convincing. I was afraid of being seen as we stood on top of the pipes and kissed under the naked sky, in full view of all the birds and the trees. We kissed with the teatime sun burning above us. God and Jesus and anyone else could have looked down and seen us. My cheeks flushed, the hairs on my arms and neck stood on end and my heart pounded in my chest.

That summer afternoon we locked ourselves in his dad's shed with the lawnmower, plant pots and the spades to play James Bond. The game was to act out the part when James Bond kisses Miss Moneypenny. Mark asked me to take off my cardigan so I could be more like Miss Moneypenny. We both agreed that she would take off her cardigan to be kissed by James Bond. Then he lay down and asked me to lie beside him on the floor of the shed. We kissed as we had seen adults do in films, with our lips glued and our heads turning slowly at different angles. We were in a movie of our own and he was the hero, the handsome James Bond, and I was the beautiful girl wrapped in his strong arms. We put my cardigan over our heads and in that hot pitch blackness, we sank into our own school cardigan world of soft first kisses.

I ran home then, when I thought I might explode and when I could take no more kissing. I ran faster than I ever could, all the way up the hill and home. The steep climb didn't even hurt my legs as they pumped on the adrenaline of kissing and the fire of the secrecy surging through me. The neighbourhood kids, my classmates, were playing and racing on their bikes out on my street, it was still early and light, but I ran past them. I burned and I couldn't bring myself to speak to them in case they saw it in my eyes. I was afraid that I had been doing something wrong and that it was there for all to read in my face. I wanted to be alone to replay every moment, to make sure I remembered the kissing, every sensation from beginning to end. While it was still light outside, I got into bed and lay there, listening to the birds' evening songs. I had a book open in front of my face but the words swirled on the page. In my head I could imagine I was kissing him again and again. I was fizzing like a bee in a jar.

Then at school the next week, my next-door neighbour Kathy was Mark's girlfriend and declared she was the first to kiss him. I was outraged and broke my silence to announce that actually I had kissed him first. Oddly enough nobody believed me, and Mark flatly denied ever kissing me. So every day I suffered my first bitter sting of jealousy, watching them holding hands and being soppy together at breaktimes. They were much more public than Mark and I had ever been. I felt betrayed, and as distracted by seeing them together as I had been by keeping the secret crush. I decided there and then that boys and all that kissing was much more trouble than it was worth. Boys were more useful for fighting, to make tree camps with or to beat at running races.

Throughout school life Mark would still come up to me and rave about *Rocky*, while skipping about on the spot with his fists in front of his face. He'd pull his shirt up and ask me to punch his stomach. I'd punch him and he'd pretend it hurt him to make me laugh. Then he'd make a miraculous recovery, say *gotcha* and we'd chase and race each other on the school track. He told everyone I was *the fastest girl runner for our age in the school* – quite a statement, and rarely disputed. Though I wanted to be the fastest for our entire year, faster than even the boys too. I wanted to be truly bionic. My brother took Mark under his wing and took him to his boxing club with him. They started going training together every week. Our mums went to aerobics together sometimes too. Once in a blue moon, I have dreamt about hazy fields of yellow and thunderstorms, and I still have that silver boxing glove, somewhere.

Mrs Tiggy-Winkle

Mr and Mrs Sharkey were a friendly elderly couple who lived a few doors down from us on The Ridings. When we were roller skating, hurtling up and down the pavement clinging to hedges and fences, Mrs Sharkey would pop out and we always had time for a little chat at her garden gate. There she'd stand in her floral apron, her cheeks a powdery peach and pink, her hair silver-white and pinned in a bun. If Mrs Sharkey had time, she'd even invite us inside to sit at her kitchen table for a while. I loved to watch her doing her dishes or baking, sometimes she'd let me help peg the sheets and tablecloths on the line. Then she would grin at me and pause and say, 'Cakey?'

It was our little joke, how I would pretend to think about it for a while and take ages to say, yes, please. Then she'd chuckle and go to the cupboard in the corner where she kept the tin filled with her homemade cakes.

I can still taste them now, delicious buttery currant buns in white paper cases with pink rose patterns. They were golden, moist with sweet plump currants and sultanas and sometimes cut glacé cherries. Heavenly. If Mrs Sharkey was in a rush and only had a minute to spare, she'd give us a bun each to take away with us. I'd eat mine so slowly, walking down the road at a lovely idle pace. I'd pick out the cherries and fruit, nibble the cake from under my fingernails, scrape the bun remains off the empty paper with my bottom teeth until it was clean, then chew the paper wrapper until it was soggy and disintegrating and swallow it.

Mrs Sharkey's husband was a lovely chirpy Irishman. When we played out in the street after school we would see him down at the bottom of his drive with the doors to his garage wide open, busying himself there with his lathe and all his dangerous-looking oily-black power tools. One summer he made me a skipping rope with wooden handles and a long orange rope. I played with it in the street, cantering like a pony along the pavement. Then he made one for everyone else in the street. He measured the rope lengths to our different heights and then he carved our initials into the wooden handles so we wouldn't mix them up.

I remember Mr Sharkey often called out to me across the street because I walked looking down at the pavement. I would be peering for lost things in the gutter or scuffing up my ugly, sensible shoes against the kerb. Mr Sharkey would catch me and wolf whistle.

'Hey! Salena, head up! That's right, always walk proud with your head held high. That's it, chin up, that's-a girl!'

Mr and Mrs Sharkey watched out for me. I realise now they must have seen me wandering around waiting for my parents to come home, lost in daydreams, running my finger along railings and the tops of fences. They'd always have a friendly word and a cake for me.

During those hours waiting for mother's factory shift to end, I can remember being closer to the ground; I jumped cracks in the pavement and I poked in between those holes with sticks and put stones down drains to hear them plop into the water; I'd sit on the kerb making obstacles for ants; I looked up at sunlight through the membrane and veins of leaves; I counted out pockets of polished conkers in a line along a wall; I filled jam jars with rose petals to make perfume; I looked down into the fuchsia jaws of snapdragons; I'd shake blossom trees to make it snow, hanging upside down off the branches, twanging and shaking the petals. I remember I liked to pretend I was blind. I'd dare myself to walk down the road with my eyes shut tight and my hands outstretched. It was a surprise to lose the ground beneath my feet and fall off the kerb or feel the thud and shock of walking into lamp posts. I'd say sorry, but it was just a telegraph pole and I'd laugh and look about me hoping nobody saw me. And I'd go on the swings in the nearby park and swing with my head thrown back so the houses were up and the clouds were down.

When Mrs Sharkey was busy, she'd say, 'It's lovely to see you but you'll have to come visit another day, dearie.'

I didn't want to ever exhaust that kindness, so I'd run off saying, 'Oh, it was windy, I just thought you might like help with putting your washing out, that's all!'

I'd never admit the truth: I'd never tell her that I was cold, lonely, hungry or I'd run out of friends to call for.

When my mother was late and it was getting dark, I'd sit and wait on the back doorstep and tell myself fantastic sad stories. I would make believe that my mother had been in a fatal accident. I'd make myself cry. I'd go through every moment of the accident, her last breath, her death, right up to the police coming to find me to put me in a children's home. I would picture this horrible orphanage and an Oliver Twist life and I'd plan how I would run away and where I would go. I would roll with this tragic story, until I was so miserable and convinced it was all true, the sound of her footsteps and her appearance at our garden gate would quite surprise me. I would be so relieved to see her, my eyes would sting.

I'd want to throw my arms around her as if she'd returned from a war or great adventure, but instead I'd snap at her, 'Where've you been, Mum? You're late! I've been worried sick.'

Princess Leslie

Every Saturday morning I'd walk to gymnastics alone. I remember a flat white sky, as plain as a chipped china plate. I remember early mornings taking my time to dawdle down the hill, past our school, all dark, empty and silent and along the lane, trudging to get to the other side of town. As a creature of habit, I always took the same route along the high street, and I saw the Indian restaurant had wooden chipboards over its front window again and vile racist words and *Go Home* scrawled in paint. There was also graffiti on the wall of the bus shelter opposite, an A in a circle and black letters: THE WHO. I was pretty sure it had a lot to do with the glue-sniffers and the skinheads who wore parka jackets and Dr Marten boots. I also thought it was something to do with the film *Quadrophenia* that Gus was raving about.

During those solitary morning walks to my gym class, my head would be soft as cotton wool, reliving my dreams from the night before. As a child I had recurring dreams of being a superhero-athlete and winning gold medals. In these vivid dreams I could do a row of one-handed back flips and hands-free somersaults, sailing through the air and landing in the splits. In these wonderful, egocentric dreams, I wore a royal blue leotard, like they wore in the Olympics. I often dreamt that I could fly – I soared above my house, my school, to the seaside. Sometimes I would hover above my sleeping self, or sit up in a tree overlooking our back garden and watch our bunk beds through my bedroom window. I dreamt I was a superhero with special powers. I had a cupboard in my stomach where I kept favourite and necessary things like bananas and ray-guns for fighting the baddies. My boyfriend was a combination of Elvis and Jesus, he lived in a shed in the clouds and had heaven-blue eyes. I would continue playing out these epic stories from my dreams as I walked to pass the time, indulging in images of breaking world records in athletics. I prepared speeches for when I met the Queen as I precariously balanced along walls, as though they were a gymnast's beam.

I had really wanted to go to ballet classes; like most little girls I wanted the pretty ballet shoes with pink ribbons. However, there were no ballet classes in our village and it would have meant travelling alone by bus to the nearest town of Kettering every week, which was too far for me to travel alone. I always wished I had a better leotard: mine was a size too small, a washed-out green, with a girly trim of skirt attached and short sleeves. I remember a couple of girls who would screw their faces up at me every week in the changing rooms.

'Urgh! That's a ballet leotard!'

'Why are you wearing a ballet leotard to gym?'

'It can't be a ballet leotard because it isn't pink!' I'd say in a pale defence but I suspected she was right because she was so perfect.

* * *

I was often wounded and sorely troubled by spoilt and more privileged girls, finding them clever and bossy. However, their bribes of shiny and sweet things were too alluring for me to pass up. These girls had ponies and took gym, ballet and tap classes, but they could never climb fences to get their own ball back.

On Saturday mornings after gym, I would go from door to door until I found a playmate and often I called for a girl called Leslie. She was two years below me at school. She had flushed cheeks that got redder when she was in a temper and she threw quite spectacular tantrums. Leslie's mother was glamorous, blonde with bronze skin, like she had just come back from holiday even when she hadn't. She wore black eyeliner like Catwoman. Leslie didn't have siblings or a dad. We made up plays from story books. Her mum encouraged us and applauded, clapping with her gold jewellery jangling. To my absolute delight, she said I could do a really good Coco from *Fame* and we'd always end up jumping and dancing about to 'Hi-Fidelity'.

Looking back, Coco from *Fame* was a hero and inspiration. It was huge when Coco burst through the TV and into our lives in her full glory. The theme tune was sung by Irene Cara. She was such a star and it was exciting to see such a beautiful black woman owning the stage and screen. In playground games and role-playing, for the first time in my childhood I was designated a role I actually liked and wanted to play. In games of Fame and make-believe I was always Coco. I know I was so young, but even back then I knew this representation mattered and had an impact on me.

Princess Leslie. I didn't know what it was about Leslie. She was like a princess who has everything, but I felt sorry for her. I never played with her at school. She was an only lonely child and her father had died at sea. On the living-room mantelpiece there was a photograph of a handsome, important-looking gentleman in a naval suit by a ship with the letters *QE2* on the side of it, like the

QE2 my dad was on. I never voiced this but I entertained the thought that our fathers might have met, or might even have been friends somehow.

Leslie had the latest Barbie mansion and stable. She had the new Plasticine Barber Shop, where you had to turn the handle and Plasticine comes out like hair and worms from holes in the doll's head. She had a beautiful Victorian doll's house that she never played with and an almost life-size rocking horse. In the garden she had a swing, a paddling pool and she always had bubbles all year around.

The thing about Leslie, though, was that she sometimes made me kiss her. I had no idea why I had to kiss her, but usually when her mum was out of earshot or down the other end of the garden she'd lisp, 'I know, let's play Sleeping Beauty. You be the prince and . . .'

I knew what came next.

'. . . kiss me.'

She lay back on her bed with outstretched arms, her hair feathered on the pillow. She looked up at me, then closed her eyes and, in a faraway voice, whispered, 'Kiss me. I have been asleep for one hundred years. I pricked my finger on the spindle and now you have to come and kiss me . . .'

I stood awkwardly by the bed with my hands in my corduroy pockets, looking around her room cluttered with glittery pink things. Under the button-eyed stare of the rainbow-coloured fluffy teddy bears and dolls crammed along the shelves, she told me again to kiss her. She lay there on her pink Walt Disney bedcover, which matched the curtains. I looked away at her sparkly angel wings and ballet things, a china unicorn with a silvery horn; there was a musical jewellery box which you could wind up and it played a tune while the ballerina inside turned around. Falling out of their Weeble tree house were her vast collection of Weebles — *Weebles wobble but they don't fall down* — and hanging above my head was a mobile of fairies. Leslie opened her eyes and looked up at me directly.

'If you kiss me I'll ask my mum for you to stay for tea and you can watch *Jaws* with us.'

It was a fair trade, but it was strange kissing Leslie. She made me lie on top of her and say, 'I am the handsome prince and you are the princess', while she wriggled beneath me. She liked it very much. Her skin flushed and she was overly warm and clammy. She smelled of milk and something sweet. Once the deed was done and she felt I had kissed her sufficiently Leslie ran and asked if I could stay for tea.

Her mother smiled. 'Of course, but be sure to ask your mum if it's OK for you to watch you-know what!' And she sang the *der-der-der-der* theme tune to *Jaws*.

At Leslie's house we ate in the living room off the coffee table, and we were given delicious sandwiches with crisps on the plate and cocktail sausages, fizzy SodaStream in orange or cola. We'd have chocolate Wagon Wheels and bowls of ice cream and a squirty syrup called Ice Magic that went hard once it hit the ice cream. Best of all was the privilege of watching television. There, lying on a pile of cushions on the floor, I watched all the good Saturday stuff: *Wurzel Gummidge*, *The Bionic Woman*, *Wonder Woman* or *Charlie's Angels*, followed that night by *Jaws*. All three of us were wearing funny cut-out cardboard 3-D glasses that had been given away for free in cereal packets that didn't really work. I remember that the opening scene of *Jaws* began with a boy and a girl kissing on a beach, and there was a nervousness in the room. This was only heightened then as the music started — we giggled, clutching pillows, and held hands, squealing; Leslie's mum played along and screamed too. We covered our faces in a pillow at the first sound of the *der-der-der-der* and the first sight of the shark's fin cutting through the dark surface of the ocean.

❊   ❊   ❊

Another Saturday afternoon, Leslie was in a particularly demanding mood. It was raining and we had to stay inside. She kept complaining even when I let her win at card games. We had wandered into the conservatory when she decided to go through her mother's gardening tools. Picking up some garden pliers, she passed them to me then lay on her belly and asked me to sit on top of her. She then told me to pull out hairs from her head with the pliers. She put her head on her arms while I sat on the small of her back and sighed as though I was giving her a relaxing massage. She encouraged me and spoke in that whispering lisp, the *kiss me* voice.

'Could you just pull out my hair with the pliers . . .'

I took some hairs in the pliers and pulled gently.

'Are you even doing it?' she lisped cattily. 'I can't feel anything.'

'Yes, I'm doing it.'

'Harder then, pull harder, pull my hairs out one by one.'

I gave another tentative tug, then she leaned up on her elbows and, looking at us straight ahead in the reflection of the glass conservatory wall, said in this affected, toffee-nosed voice, 'Come on! Just do it! Just get on with it! Pull my hair out of my head!'

She haughtily exhaled through her nose as though to say, is it too much to ask? I didn't like her horsey tone of voice at all so I took a good few strands and pulled sharply. As though I had flipped a switch, Leslie screamed, one long pure note. Her mother ran in to find me sitting on top of Leslie with pliers full of her daughter's hair. How could I explain what I was doing? Leslie put on a magnificent show. She roared with tears, and even started saying *Mummy Mummy* which I knew was for maximum effect – as kids we said 'mum' and only said 'mummy' if it was very serious and we wanted to get full-cream attention. Leslie's mum looked at me with astonishment and said maybe I should come back to play another day, but it was best that I went home now. As I closed the front door behind me I could hear Leslie howling and coughing. She was being exactly like the *Just William* Bonnie Langford character from TV. I knew she would *squeem and squeem and squeem* until she was sick. I turned out of their drive and walked miserably to the street corner. I stood and looked down at my shoes. I felt dreadfully ashamed and the worst part was that I think I made her head bleed a tiny bit.

Spaghetti Legs and Curly Top

Standing on the street corner I heard my name.

'Oi, curly-top!'

I looked up and saw the gaping, toothy grin of Tara Collins on the corner. Tara Collins had a long face – in fact she was a very long girl. She was the tallest girl in our school, and taller than most of the boys too, apart from Darren White. She towered over us in netball, effortlessly slam-dunking goals. She had a big broad smile that was all teeth and she had long spaghetti legs like a baby giraffe. This afternoon, she was wearing striped knee-high socks, plimsolls and roller skates. She had spit-stuck a rose thorn between her eyebrows and she had strawberry lip-gloss on.

I was kicking stones down a drain with the toe of my shoe when Tara asked, 'What you doing?'

'Nothing much.'

'Where are you going?'

'Nowhere.'

'Where have you been?'

'Erm . . . dunno really, round there.'

I pointed to Leslie's house and shuddered guiltily.

'Wanna come skating?' she asked.

I noticed her brother and a few boys with skateboards outside her house, which was set back off the road at the bottom of a steep sloping drive. The uneven plastic wheels of her roller skates scratched across the surface of the bumpy concrete pavement, first one foot, then the next. I brightened up and told her, 'There's some new smooth tarmac on my road, they've just done it this week.'

'Brill! I'll come with you to get your skates then . . . weeeeeeeahhhh!'

Tara scooted towards me and hooked her arm through mine. Us kids were always looking for new smooth bits of pavement to skate on. The council was slowly doing up all the roads around our way, the potholed old streets becoming sheer, sleek and black with gleaming yellow lines, as smooth as ice to skate on. We were all hoping for those new yellow and blue roller boots with stoppers for our birthdays and Christmas, but for the time being most of us made do with skates that fastened to our shoes. They had laces and a buckle and hard uneven wheels; if you undid a nut at the bottom you could slide them to fit your growing shoe size. They were handed down from cousin to cousin and sibling to sibling; they seemed to last forever.

'Come on, I'll come with you to yours. Let's get your skates and then we'll come back round here to mine and smash our heads into the garage door. We've been going so fast. Look! Come on! Watch! We've been taking it in turns on Dad's crash helmet . . . Do you want a go?'

She pointed to her brother. Marcus Collins was wearing his father's shiny black motorbike helmet, which nearly swallowed his shoulders. He was sitting on his skateboard with his knees drawn up to his chin. He put the visor up and gave us a thumbs-up, then he put it back down again and gripped his skateboard, ready to launch. Tara burst into applause as we screamed a countdown: *Ten, nine, eight . . .!* He had been pushed and was already gone, zooming down his drive. There was a thunderous crash as he hurtled head first into the garage door and fell off the skateboard. The boys fell about laughing.

'Brilliant!'

'I want a go on the crash helmet! Do you?'

'I do!'

'Ace!'

Seeing Tara laughing with her strawberry pink lips, watching her clinging to the lamp post, all spindly arms and legs, I felt that all was well with the world after all, and the guilt and shame about Leslie began to fade. I heard the tinny music of an ice cream van in the far-off distance. It was just an ordinary Saturday afternoon in Desborough in the late 1970s. Above us a mild and ordinary sky we neither noticed nor cared about. It was the neither season – neither winter nor summer. I knew when I popped in at home to get my skates, my stepfather would be watching the football on television, my mother would be in the kitchen, sorting out the washing or cooking.

There were glow-in-the-dark stickers of the Hulk on the bib of my skates. I sat on the kerb carefully lacing them up and Tara held out her hand to help me stand up. Later that same afternoon, we'll go and have a turn on the motorbike helmet; and we'll scream a countdown and speed down her drive, bashing head-first into her garage door and making an almighty crash.

But first we are here – we are holding hands, our wheels vibrating on the rough road until we hit the new oily black tarmac and glide smooth and as elegant as figure skaters. With outstretched arms we hold each other by the wrist and spin dizzily in a circle, the lovely sound of innocent laughter and the rumble of our skating wheels rolling across new tarmac.

Once in a Lifetime

I was wearing my favourite summer dress. It was pale turquoise cotton, with a pattern of tiny yellow primroses and blue forget-me-nots scattered all over it. It had powder-green ribbons at the front and pearl-blue buttons up to the neckline, and dainty puff-sleeves also trimmed with ribbon. It came all the way from America, a hand-me-down from my cousin Kathie in New York. I thought it was so beautiful, and that summer I'd finally grown into it. It was a Saturday, a sunny day, my stepfather was out at the tennis club and Mum was sitting at her Singer sewing machine. St Giles church fête was that day and I was looking forward to singing in the choir. There would be a coconut shy, bric-a-brac stalls, home-made jams and cakes and a myriad of other fun things. I could hardly eat my cornflakes I was so excited. I chattered incessantly, pestering my mother to do my hair for me. I wanted everything to be perfect and this included my hair. I often wanted it to be twisted into buns like Princess Leia, and I couldn't do that on my own.

It was just the three of us having breakfast and a pot of tea together, sitting around the dining table. Half of it was cluttered with Mum's mending and cottons – she made me dresses sometimes, recycled out of the material of her old clothes. Gus and my mum began reminiscing about our father. It had been a while since we had mentioned him.

'I remember when he taught me to pour a pint,' Gus said and laughed.

'Oh yes, he took you around the other side of the bar and lifted you up. That was funny, you must have been only two or three. That was in Ramsgate.'

'And when we went go-karting . . .' Gus continued, and I wished I had a memory of my father of my own. I had nothing but a shape of how our life was before and these inherited stories, a still photographic image of him. I laughed, copying them, my eyes glassy as though I was remembering these times too. It always felt good when we talked about my real father like that, the three of us together.

By the time Gus and I got to the church it was a warm lunchtime. The gardens were strewn with flags and balloons, the trees and hedgerows decorated with streams of colourful bunting. There were doily-covered stalls of cakes and books and tables of jumbled clothes. There were games, competitions and raffles with fantastic prizes. There was a one-pound note for the person with a hand steady enough to follow an electric wire with the hook of a bent coat-hanger without it buzzing. I met classmates and fellow Brownies, all with hair tied prettily with ribbons in bunches and swishing ponytails. We had a run-through in the cool of the church, then marched with a clatter of Sunday best buckled shoes in twos, down the side lane and into the centre of the gardens. The music started and we performed songs that had choruses of *laugh, kookaburra laugh* and *soldier soldier, won't you marry me?* My cheeks ached from grinning. In the audience I could see Sunday school teachers, Brownie leaders, the vicar and all the mums and dads cheering and applauding. My mum wasn't there, but Gus was.

With the sky perfectly blue above us, we tore around the church grounds. We hid in the graveyard behind the tombs and raced across the back fields, playing hide and seek, with countless new places to make camps and ambushes. We were given chocolate cornflake cakes, we had cherryade moustaches and water pistols. New white socks crumpled and wrinkled below grass-stained knees. Chubby boys sweated, tying their best shirts around their waists. I sat up a tree with a girl called Rebecca. We had disappeared together, claiming the tree as a safe place, *home*, where we couldn't get tagged. Rebecca was a pretty blonde girl who chased boys all the time and who the boys chased back. Jealous girls called her a flirt but I liked that about her. On this day, though, she was upset, and we lowered our voices as we spoke and patted each other's hands, as we had seen our mothers do. We were sitting opposite each other on a branch, in the hollow heart of the tree, as deeply engrossed as teary aunties on the gin in the kitchen at Christmas, confessional and whispering. Our faces were hot and sticky, our legs were scratched from the tree bark and whipped with running through the rough wild grass of the back fields.

Up there, in the soft green rustling leaves, Rebecca started to cry. 'My mum and dad are getting divorced, nobody knows, but I do . . .'

I touched her hand as Rebecca continued. 'My daddy's not going to live with us no more now. I don't know when I'll see him.'

She was crying quietly, holding in any noise. She looked down at her fingers, fumbling, tearing at a twig, ripping the bark off it with her dirty pink nails. Her big hazel eyes reddened and her blonde hair had fallen out of its French plait into gentle, silky curls around her oval face.

I told her, 'My mum and dad are divorced. My mum says it's for the best. We have to live with her new husband, my stepdad,

127

but we do have a real dad and he's a musician. My real dad plays on the *QE2* and that's the Queen of England's own ship, *Queen Elizabeth*. And he's cruising the world playing in the band and Mum says that's why we never see him.'

I gulped, the words stuck in my throat.

She sniffed and replied, 'My dad works in Market Harborough.'

'Well, at least you can see yours. That's not very far away, is it? Dry your eyes, Rebecca, don't cry. Come on now, silly, it will be all right, don't cry.'

We sat in that tree, muttering details of our parents' divorces. I bragged about my father. I told her he was funny, like when he taught Gus to pour a pint of beer, reiterating the morning conversations with my mother and brother from breakfast. I made Rebecca chuckle through her tears until she snorted and blew a snot bubble, which made us both laugh. She wiped her nose on her cardigan sleeve and dried her red face.

Suddenly Anna Parris shouted up, 'Salena, your dad's here.'

'What dad?'

'Gus said to come and fetch you, your dad's come for you.'

The idea of my stepfather being here at the church fête surprised me, but I thought he might be with Mum. Maybe they had come to see me sing after all? They were late, but I could show Mum the makeshift stage where we had performed. As I climbed down the tree I saw my brother running towards me. His eyes were lit up and urgent, and he held out his hand to take mine. I knew then it must be something important – my brother and I were long past the age of holding hands.

'Dad's here! Come on . . .'

'Dad?'

'Yes, Paul! Come on, Salena, hurry up. Come on!'

His voice was excited, wavering with soft and strange love. There was a kindness in his face, like he had a wonderful surprise, something beautiful to show me.

I scrambled out of the branches, trembling in my limbs, and I looked at Rebecca and Anna. 'Paul's here.'

'Who?'

'Paul! My real dad, Paul, you know, the one I just said about, he's only flippin' here . . .'

My brother took my hand in his and led me up through the church garden to meet this man I had never known, the man who was my real father. We hurried. I skipped to keep up with Gus's longer stride until all of a sudden I could see him. He was striking, tanned and wearing mirrored shades, a black shirt and dark blue jeans. He stood nervous as a groom at the front entrance to the church. In my memory of that day, he looks like a rock star, and my first impression was a swooning feeling. This was followed by a compulsion to make a good first impression. I hoped my hair wasn't too wild so I patted it, feeling wayward frizz at the top. I pulled up my white socks and smoothed the front of my dress.

In those first few seconds I was on full alert to remember the smallest details. My world went into slow motion, as though these minutes meant life or death, and it did, it meant everything to me. As I walked towards him I studied him, how he looked in the churchyard I knew so well, how he stood as we approached, how his shape grew bigger as we got closer. I listened to hear his voice for the first time. I was the most awake I could possibly be but I felt like I was sleeping, as though I was in a dream. I could not believe he was really there, that it was really him.

There was a surreal quality to those first minutes. Time poured as slow as golden syrup, in the amber light of a perfect afternoon. The balloons softly bumped against each other in a slight breeze, the mottled shadows of the bunting and old tree on the paving were littered with soft, trodden cherry blossom and old confetti. The sounds of the fête and other kids playing and the music slipped away. The only three people on the planet were my brother and me and this man of mythology. I could feel my brother buzzing too, as his hand left mine and the skin on our arms touched briefly. We were both feeding off this first moment, two chicks in the nest both wanting the worm at once. I searched my father's face, looking for clues. I yearned for him but I also wanted to know the truth.

Where have you been? Who are you? Who am I to you? Do you think I am like you? What do you know about me? Are you proud of me? Will you come and visit us again? Why have you not been to see us ever before?

There was a sense of relief, and also an urgency: a need to be reassured, to be liked — more than that, to be loved. I was aware of my great neediness. A need so big and so hungry, I realised I had been starving for that moment all of my life.

I want you to see me in you, to see we are the same. I want to say that word, your name: Dad. *I want to call out the name* Father *and for it to be ours and for it to be true. My real dad. I want to be held in your arms and for you to tell me stories. I want you to talk to me and to tell me that all of this has been a test and we passed it. That this is like that story, where a king comes to find his long-lost children to take them to his palace to live together. Then I want you to say you are sorry, I want to hear how you are very sorry you took so long to come to see us. Promise you will never disappear and go away again. How we waited for you, we blew out birthday candles and wished for you. We called for you in our sleep and in our dreams hoping this day would come. That you would come one day, one perfect summer's day, exactly like this. Finally here you are. I want you to say that now you have seen us and what you have been missing that you want us in your life, say you want to make up for lost time and cannot believe you haven't been to see us before. Say something about how we have grown and that you'll look out for us now. Say you missed us. Say that you love us. I need to hear that you love us. Whatever the reasons and excuses for not coming before, I don't care, because you are here now and that is all that matters. You are my real dad and you are here and I love you. I'll say it first if you like, Dad. Now you have to say it, say you love me.*

We were awkward as strangers, nervous and self-conscious. We walked side by side into the church. We stood at the altar and admired the golden eagle Bible plinth. The sun shone through the stained-glass windows and made rainbows on the floor, puddles of gold, red and indigo. I tried not to stare at you, Dad, but I couldn't help it. Then we showed you the church gardens and the stage; I told you that you missed me singing. You said you were impressed by that, you said you would have liked to have heard me singing. You asked me if I had been nervous and I said I had butterflies and you smiled at me like there was nothing wrong with getting nervous. You told me you got butterflies when you went on stage too. I remember thinking, *we both like music, Dad, see, we have so much in common.*

I felt so proud when you took my hand. We looked at the stalls and the cakes, and you offered to buy me something, but I didn't see anything I wanted. I didn't want anything because you were holding my hand and that was all I ever wanted. I had everything I wanted walking beside me in the church gardens. I pointed out classmates and teachers. I kept thinking, *look, I am holding hands with my very own real dad.* Your hand felt big, soft and warm. Mum had told me you had piano-playing fingers and now they were holding my hand.

We got to the electric wire and coat-hanger game and you asked me if I would like a go. I had been eyeing the one-pound note prize all afternoon. There was a series of loops, bends and S shapes to weave in and out of with a hook without touching the wire. I tried for you, Dad, I tried so hard. I could feel my cheeks burn as you watched me. I could feel you watching me and I wondered what you could see. I was trying so hard and thinking how I must do this well so you would think I was clever and good. What steady hands you would say. I didn't want to disappoint you, Dad, I wanted to make you proud. I made it only halfway and then the wire beeped. I was crushed, I trembled, but then I looked up and you smiled beautifully with a genuine warmth and you said, 'Don't worry, Salena, it's just a game.'

When you said my name and you said it softly, I felt a jolt of familiarity. When you said my name, it echoed over and over down a long tunnel of memory. The way you said *Salena*, it sounded like something more than my name, like a lovely song I once knew. Then you had a go. I watched your hands, they were shaking, much more than mine, and the machine beeped.

'Looks like we're both not very good at this,' you said and patted me.

Every time you touched me my heart pounded. Both of us are the same, I thought, both of us are not very good at this game. I was giddy with you, to be with you. You made me laugh. I said something cheeky and I managed to make you laugh too.

The three of us left the church and you asked us if we'd like to go to the park. On the way you bought us both orange ice lollies. Gus and I didn't really play on swings together any more and we certainly didn't usually get taken to the park by an adult, but we understood that this was one of those making-friends exercises that grown-ups do with children. We went on the slide, my brother and I, and from the top of the slide we looked down at you. You looked small, thoughtful and quiet. You were smoking and wearing your sunglasses. Gus and I looked each other in the eye, unspoken questions that neither of us had the vocabulary for, and Gus shrugged and nudged me as if to say, go on, go down.

I went down the slide on my stomach and head first: the brave choice. You watched, sitting on the park bench in your dark sunglasses. You seemed so distant over there and almost sad. I wanted to know what you were thinking and what you saw. What did we look like to you, my brother and I, playing nicely together, going down the slide bravely on our bellies, backwards and upside down to show off for you? Did we look like the kind of son and daughter you'd like to have? Gus and I exchanged looks, but we kept acting like kids, dumb cute kids who play nicely together at the park. After the park, we went back home and I ran in to tell Mum I had you with me. She already knew you were here, of course, and she'd told you where we were. She had seen you earlier, she said, you came to call for us and she told you we were at the church. Now, I think she knew you were coming, that's what all the talk had been leading to this morning. It was meant to be a surprise, but I was not equipped for it – how could I be?

You had a cup of tea, Dad, and I sat on your lap. We were all in the white living room and there I was sitting on my very own real dad's knee. Mum told you about our schools, she told you that I was in the Brownies and that Gus was in St John's Ambulance. We were happy and the sunshine seeped through the venetian blinds in stripes of orange-coppery light on the white walls. It was all so easy and I felt so happy to be so close to you, Dad. I looked at you intently, the tiny hairs on your knuckles. I noticed the way Mum was smiling too and being different somehow. She was smiling and sitting up straight, attentive. Her eyes were shining.

Then, as you sipped the last of your tea I sensed you preparing to leave. That part wasn't ever going to be easy. As you stood up I saw you and Mum exchange a look. I told you I wanted to come with you. I needed to hear you swear you'd be back again and very soon.

You asked me, 'Hey, have you met Henry?'

I could see through this trick to take my mind off you leaving, Dad, and I started to cry. I wanted to go with you and I asked when we'd see you again, and you said soon. Then Mum joined in with a great big stupid smile on her face, which irritated me, as she repeated, 'Who's Henry, Salena?'

I clearly remember thinking, *I don't care who Henry is, I just don't want you to go, I need you and I need more.*

I started to cry and Dad, you said, 'Ah, well, if you don't want to meet Henry, then I'd better tell him to go!' Then you gave me a winning smile.

So I played along and said, 'Who's Henry then?'

'Please!' Mum said.

'Oh, OK, please! Who is Henry, please?'

'Oh! No, no, no, you didn't want to know before, so I won't tell you now!'

You teased me, you did, my dad, my lovely real dad teased me and I giggled through hot tears.

'Please can I meet Henry, Dad! Please!'

'Oh, you want to meet him now, do you, Salena?'

'Yes, please, Dad! Please!'

'Come with me.'

You winked at my mum and took me to your car and gave me a huge stuffed dog, a teddy bear that was a dog, not a bear. It was half my height, with a big floppy red tongue and ears. I hugged him.

'I love him! Thank you.'

I squeezed Henry, and Gus looked on, and I could see through the blur of my tears that he wanted something too. I could sense my brother watching me hug this huge Henry dog-ted and I wondered if you had something for him too. Then you gave him your sunglasses. Gus loved flying, he loved books about Biggles. The sunglasses were the kind pilots wear, they were really cool aviators, and he was thrilled.

Now that you had taken off your sunglasses I could see my reflection in you; when you crouched down to say goodbye, I recognised those eyes. For a second as you held me I recognised something in the feel of you, the shape and the smell of you, your hair, your neck, your skin. Something I thought I had lost was now close to me and so familiar. I don't remember what promises you made as you stood up, I don't remember your exact words of comfort as you said your goodbyes. I started crying again and you told us to be good. Gus cried too and you hugged him and you promised you'd be back another day, wait and see, soon. We cried as we heard you turn the key in the ignition and back up out of the drive. We cried and watched you drive slowly away.

I searched everywhere in the universe and in everything you touched in my world for your scent, for flakes of your skin, for the strands of hair, of each minute of that one afternoon. Every tiny triviality, like water retaining memory, seeping through each crevice of those few hours we spent together. That afternoon became a shrine, a cave. I stroked the walls of those few hours with all five senses, second by second. I took a stick and scratched our names there and every minute detail I daubed and highlighted with paints. I felt the coolness and the heat of those walls against my cheeks. I can still smell that day; when I think of it I inhale some form of dust, it sticks in the back of my throat. I can still summon the sensation of waiting for you, Dad, of having you and losing you. Those few hours are an animal carcass. I devoured all its tender flesh. I boiled the bones to make a glue soup to keep us together and I slept in the hide of the beast to dream of you. All we had was that one day when you appeared from nowhere and then you went again. For those moments I looked into your eyes, I saw something I now understand was regret or guilt.

I also believe I saw love, and that was all we ever had, Dad.

AUTUMN

My mother

The Other Woman

Excerpts taken from my diaries, London, 2009

The manuscript has finally arrived, but as I turn the pages my heart sinks – it has been almost five months since I submitted the latest draft, what takes these people so long? And now this version is way too far the other way; it has been stripped of love and humour, warmth and kindness, this miserable edit is hard as a black snowball, I do not intend to throw a black snowball into the world.

I switch off the phone and unplug the internet to be alone to re-read and rework the new harsh edit. I weep all weekend. It's as though I'm going backwards all over again, covering the same hurt and frustrations. I give myself a very hard time, I am crippled by fear of failure and fear of the dark.

Outside my window, as I write this, I hear the wind and the rustle of dry leaves, the death rattle of autumn at the end of such a high summer. I am crashing, coming back down to earth with a hard bump. I always did hate the end of the party, the end of the summer light. Now here is the early dusk, and dirt in the corners of my rooms, the kitchen floor needs mopping, everything feels grimy. The rent is late, and God only knows how I am going to find it this month. The fridge is empty, humming away with nothing to fill its cold belly. I feel utterly empty too. And this book is a big, mean, black dog digging me up, digging up the past and gnawing on my bones. There is nothing I can do now, though, but dry my eyes, roll my sleeves up and go through this book from the beginning all over again. There's no going back, there is no unwriting this, there is no unremembering it all – it's started now.

On Monday I had no choice. I had to get away from this black dog and the past, put on the lipstick and heels and go to do the gig – the Book Club Boutique at Dick's Bar, Romilly Street. This week's theme was 'Smash the System', an anarchic gig with the boys from *The Idler*, with guests Tom Hodgkinson and Penny Rimbaud. When I arrived at first the world seemed very sharp, jagged and loud. I felt small and introverted. However, there is nothing like the adrenaline of a gig to pull me back into the present. And a decent martini or three. We had a packed house and there were lots of friendly faces.

During the interval I was on my second espresso martini, smoking outside on Romilly Street when she walked towards me. She looked out of place among the usual BCB crowd; she was trembling and shaky. A woman in her sixties, well-heeled, with sleek, bobbed hair. She approached me and said, 'Are you Salena Godden? I knew your dad, Salena.'

Here we go: the past smacked me around the back of my head with a cricket bat. Just when I was back in the present, here I was being dragged back into this book. Who was she, but an old lover of my dad's. Is this normal? I mean, do old lovers of fathers often come out of the woodwork to seek out their children thirty years later? She told me she had found me on the internet. She apologised for shocking me and showing up out of the blue. I could see she was quite surprised herself to be standing there. The book isn't even published, but I was now meeting the woman who possibly contributed to the end of my parents' marriage.

She seemed kind, I mean harmless enough; she was oval-faced with a freshly bobbed head of blondish hair. Shorter than me, homely, soft features and very curious, round shiny eyes. So then what could I do but offer her a drink? I asked her if she liked wine and then led her to the upstairs bar where it was quieter. She was with a friend, presumably for back-up. (Where was my back-up?) I could see she had done her nails and put her best blouse on. I could tell she was very nervous to meet me. But I still didn't fully understand what her intention was. I was wondering if there was something important she needed to tell me. She clearly felt compelled to make contact with me. She made a joke, she told me she wasn't a mad stalker, she smiled, she was happily married. But she told me she had sneaked away and her husband would kill her if he knew she'd come to see me. It was then it dawned on me that she didn't know about Dad.

She asked, 'Was it alcohol-related?'

I heard myself reply, 'Well, you don't do something like that when you're stone-cold sober, right?'

As she probed for details, she produced out of her handbag photographs of my father and herself from the mid-1970s. She placed these images along the bar like playing cards. I recall the barman, Dick Bradsell, served our drinks and wiped glasses, looking on concerned, nonverbally checking if I was okay.

In these photographs Dad was wearing *that* sheepskin jerkin I have seen him wear in photos of him holding my brother, with my mother, and at home in Hastings. If this was a game of poker, she had a full house.

There was one photograph of my father taken sitting on a bed on the *QE2*. She even said something like *this one is your dad on the* QE2.

I now know that when my mother told us our father was at sea, he really was at sea, but now I picture him at sea with this woman. So this is where my father was, who he was with, when my mother was struggling to clothe and feed us. These were the missing images of my father during those lost years. Then she produced poetry and letters he'd written to her. Hard evidence, with the dates – 1975, 1976 – on the top. I recognised the green ink and the handwriting. I know I would have been three and four years old, my mother a newly single parent on benefits, struggling working part-time stacking shelves in a Co-op supermarket. How much stinky truth can I take? How much should I take?

'You should have this,' she continued and handed me a book that she said she had always meant to give to Dad: an old collection of poems by Francis Thompson, with ragged yellow pages, musty and old, perhaps a first edition. She said she'd always kept this book for him, that Dad loved this poetry, and I should have his book. Wasn't Dad's dog called Francis when he was a boy? The dog grave in Grandpa's garden?

As I write this, I look at the photocopied letters and poetry she gave me. These are not like the sweet letters I've read, the ones to Edith, from a young man coming of age, perfecting the trumpet and about to be wed. These words are written from a depressed and darker version of my father. They have tones of self-loathing, self-sabotage and regret. Maybe there is the possibility of another sibling? Or am I reading too much between the lines?

She sang from the same song sheet – she told me my dad would be so proud of me, she told me I was just like him, I reminded her of him. Her eyes misted over as she announced he was the love of her life.

And all these things I have heard before from my own mother's lips. This woman said she could never forget him, she couldn't stop thinking about him and that she was compelled to come and see me. But why now, and after so many years? What could I offer her? Maybe she just simply wanted to visit her old flame? As she spoke, I decided I wouldn't run and ring my mother to tell her she had come to see me. At least, not for a while, not until I had figured some of this out all for myself. My poor mum has been through enough trying to protect me from exactly this. I told the woman she was brave and bold. I shook her hand and I meant it, because we all mean to have certain conversations but often never have the balls to do it. We tell ourselves to let sleeping dogs lie, we tell ourselves to let sleeping dogs lie after lie, but we all make mistakes. Everybody has apologies and peace to make with some-body – we are all someone's last thought before they go to sleep.

And as I shook her hand she looked at me searchingly, she looked into my eyes, my father's eyes, and before I knew it, I gave her what I believed she had come for; I hugged her. I held her close and felt she was small and a little afraid.

So I was to be the strong adult. And it was as though she could somehow touch my father through me. For a split second, I felt I was passing on my father's love and that he would have wanted me to hug her. He would have wanted me to be kind. This soft thought was swiftly followed by a cold and horrible sense of duplicity – I was holding the enemy in my arms. On the phone in the morning would I really say: *Good morning, Mum, I gave Dad's old mistress a big hug last night?*

We separated from that hug. I drank, I swallowed fat gulps as she nervously talked me through the photographs. There was one of a pub landlord and his wife. I forget their names, but she asked me if my mother ever mentioned them. Then she told me what a good baby I was, and how they'd put me to sleep in a room above the pub. This was painful, the way she remembered my father putting me to bed — *what a good girl she is . . .* she said he said. So where was my mother? Working? Dancing? Picking potatoes in a field for 50p? While this woman was there, in the background of the pink house, the shadow in a rose-tinted dream. I now have an image of my father and this woman looking over me as I gurgled in a cot and as he dandled me on his knee, she is there too.

This morning, I receive emails and more photos of them and then. I did give her my email address. I thought I could handle it, I thought I needed to know more, but today in a harsh and sober daylight I am not so convinced I want to or need to know any more — not for this book, and not for research, and not for me or my mum.

In these pixelated shots, Dad is wearing the same neckerchief and smile I've seen in photos of him when we were a young and happy family. Am I clinging onto fiction? I am certain there was a once upon a time, in a kingdom far away, when my mother and father were very in love, but now it's all scrambled and confused. Reading her email, I feel a creeping but familiar sense of betrayal and I'm dealing with the same old abandonment issues again. I might not have taken all of this so much to heart if I hadn't been in here, rewriting this book, again, if I wasn't back in the jigsaw puzzle filling in the missing pieces, again. But then again, she might not have found me if I hadn't been writing this book in the first place and sending ghost smoke-signals. Is that what this is? What is this? Coincidence or fate, or the threads that connect us all? Did I somehow summon her and her version of my past? Did we ask for this? I now picture the launch for this book and a queue of women of a certain age all clutching poetry and old photos of my dad. Perhaps I did, I asked for this. I poked the skeletons in the back of the closet and now I have to watch all the maggots squirm and wriggle.

I will always be in love with him, she said, *he was the love of my life.* The love of my life.

Bonfire Treacle

Home and school life continued much as it had before. That one visit, that summer afternoon with Dad, was stored in our memory; we'd got carried away with hopes, and our high expectations were like stubborn stains from blackberries as the summer drew to its close and we heard nothing more from him. During those long, dark evenings of the winter months my brother and I were like cellmates in our small, shared bedroom. Sometimes we'd do homework or read and sometimes we'd play cards or board games. When we were extra-bored we'd string a net across the bedroom and tap out games of table tennis without a table, with just ping-pong bats and a ball. We'd also quietly play records on an old mobile record player that was stored as a box; when it opened the lid became the speakers. We would sing along to our limited record collection, which included the vinyl of *Sesame Street*, *Mary Poppins* and *The Jungle Book*, The Beatles' *White Album* and an epic album titled *A Farewell To Kings* by the 1970s Canadian prog-rock band Rush which we knew off by heart. This was where I first learnt of Xanadu and Kubla Khan. Rush took lines of poetry and set it to experimental and orchestral progressive rock. I recorded this song 'Xanadu' onto cassette from the vinyl and would cycle around the neighbourhood playing it on my tape recorder while singing loudly of feasting on *honeydew* and *the milk of paradise*. I believed I was conjuring a spell, I believed the words meant something magic and powerful. It was a many years later I learned the words and visions that I was obsessed about were written by Samuel Taylor Coleridge.

Every year around Halloween my brother and I made our own bonfire toffee — a slab of brick-hard black treacle and syrup, which was so indestructible we'd need a hammer and chisel to smash it up to share. It was sucked until it was as thin as glass and just as sharp on the roof of your mouth. We polished and skewered conkers and had conker fights in our bedroom. Gus showed me how to take aim and get a good lick as the conkers smashed together. Champion conkers were named after how many wins they achieved. I always flinched, afraid Gus was aiming for my knuckles on purpose, and more often than not his hundred and twenty-fiver obliterated my fiver.

I recall how we stood in the dark bedroom to watch distant fireworks through the window. I was keen to observe the changes in season, the leaves turning saffron and the flocks of migrating birds. How these autumn evenings glow with a fiery orange in my remembering; I was at that age when I was as toothless as the gappy grin we carved into jack-o'-lantern pumpkins.

On Sunday evenings it was bath night. Afterwards, our bedroom was silent but for the quietest fizz of Gus's radio playing the Top 40 below me, and I'd lie on my belly on the top bunk and sort through my pencil case and new felt tip pens. With all their tops on, my pens were like soldiers in helmets in a row along my pillow. When a felt tip was fading I'd lick the nib to make ink come out; it tasted like plastic but was not altogether unpleasant, even sweet. If I were to lick a felt tip now, that inky flavour would be a corridor leading me to then, the first of the dark school evenings and that feeling I still always get at that time of year. Although autumn felt like a beginning, as it was the start of the new term, it was the end of the idyllic summer and the freedom of long, light evenings and rising my bike and playing in the streets.

* * *

My mother called me from the kitchen. The windows in there were steamed up and she was scribbling on a notepad as she asked, 'Darling, will you do me a favour? Will you go to the shops for me?'

She was leaning over the kitchen counter, trying to remember something. Her writing was curly, joined-up with loops, and it read: *SALAD CREAME, WHITE CABBIGE, CARROTTS.*

'How do you spell cucumber?' she asked.

I began to say, 'C . . . U . . .' as my mother wrote, *QUE, MARROW FAT PEAS, POND MINCE, CIGGYS.*

My mother is dyslexic. It's November 1980, and this was a word we didn't understand or know how to spell. Now, though leaning over the kitchen counter, she nibbled the pen as I watched her write. She sighed and said again, 'Hang on, hang on, lemme think . . .'

She was in no mood for a spelling lesson but I couldn't help myself blurting, 'Mum, it's cabbage with an A, not an I. See? You wrote cabbige.'

She shot me a look, annoyance twinned with embarrassment, and then she scribbled out the A so it now read CIBBIGE.

'Oh, what am I doing? Stupid woman . . .'

She corrected herself and rewrote it to now read CIABBIGE, then she exhaled and scratched that out and wrote the whole thing again in slow loops before saying in a small, weary voice, 'I get so muddled up sometimes.'

Her face crumbled, her features trembled as though she might cry.

'I know. It's OK, Mummy, I know what you mean anyway, don't I?'

I did know what she meant. And I knew how, as a girl, her father bullied her over her lessons; he was so domineering he put her off learning to write and spell altogether. She told me how he'd ripped poetry books out of her hands so the pages scattered around the room. She told me how, when she was eight, he made her struggle with Shakespeare when she longed to read *Alice in Wonderland*.

'Where other children had Pooh Bear, Noddy or the Famous Five I had to read Shelley, Keats, Wordsworth and "The Lady of Shalott". I did love "The Lady of Shalott", though. I would lie in a field, in the long grass, and read. Sometimes I'd just hold the beautifully bound book and watch the clouds. That's why I want to make sure you kids have what I didn't – I want you to enjoy being children.'

When my mother got in from school, her father would make her do her homework in front of him every night. He would lean over her, scrutinising her every letter and number, contradicting what the teachers had taught her. By the time she got to school the next day she'd be so confused and tired that her school lessons went badly. One day, she just shut down: that's how she always put it.

'I just shut that learning part of my brain down.'

Once, my mum sent my brother to school with a sick note saying he had to take his *tables* twice a day instead of his *tablets*. We laughed about it, me and Gus, as we imagined him either doing his twelve times tables or condemned to eat classroom furniture, twice a day. *Funny Mummy.*

Spelling may have baffled her, but my mother was a brilliant athlete at school. By the age of thirteen she broke the school sports records by jumping her own height of five foot one, then she went on to come second in the All England Championship. In her mid to late teens she was going to try out for the Olympics – which she reminded me was a massive achievement for a black woman in the early 1960s – but she told me her parents wouldn't let her go to the try-outs, because they were in another part of the country or because of money or because it just simply wasn't meant to be. The truth was much darker. Years later my mum told me she didn't make it to the Olympic try-outs because her father beat her too badly to go.

When I remembered things like this I could only try to hug her around her bump. She was round with pregnancy, with pale lavender shadows smudged beneath her eyes. She was so tired, she cried easily, even at simple things like if you told her you loved her, which made her well up behind her round glasses. We had to be gentle with Mum; she had miscarried and lost a baby before. I made sure to cuddle her often but carefully. Also I had seen pictures and films where women in labour sweated and screamed in childbirth; on programmes like *The Waltons* or *Little House on the Prairie* it looked violent, bloody and traumatic. No matter how many times my mother assured me that the pain was worth it once you had the bundle in your arms, I didn't believe her and I still don't. I was afraid for her and of this vulnerable state of being pregnant.

My mother gave me the shopping list and she looked at me through those round spectacle frames and said, 'Now, listen, when you go to the butcher's be sure to tell him you want a pound of mince, and not a pound in weight but a pound in money's worth. Be sure it's minced beef, OK?'

'But it feels horrible and there's drippy blood.'

'Then ask him to put it inside two doubled-up plastic bags so you can't feel through it, all right? That's a good girl . . . And don't forget to get some soapy water and wash that glitter off before you go.'

'Aw, but Mum!'

She looked at me over her spectacle rims and held a finger up in warning.

As I laced up my shoes I heard the car and announced, 'Patrick's home.'

My mother did not turn around; she was partially deaf and didn't always wear her hearing aid. She told me this was her father's fault too; he had pushed her through glass French windows once when she was a girl. I hated being reminded of these stories about my grandfather's violence.

'He's home, Mum!'

I nudged her and repeated, then bent to tie my shoelaces. Mum heard me the second time and a resolve flashed across her face, something that could only mean *I have a bone to pick with him*. She looked at me and arched an eyebrow. She stiffened when Patrick appeared at the door. Funny thing was, he was in a very good mood, with a dirty lopsided grin. He kissed Mum on the cheek. Mum said nothing. She pulled on her yellow rubber gloves and turned on the hot tap. He was leaning into her neck and looking at her and grinning. Mum refused to look at him; she watched the running tap and the washing-up liquid bubble up, and there was an awkward pause.

'What?' Patrick finally said, with a sideways smile, looking amused, looking at the dishes in the soapy water and then down at me. I looked up at him behind her back and shrugged ever so slightly, as if to say, *Don't ask me what she's upset about this time.* I didn't mean it. I hated that I shrugged, I felt duplicitous, and Patrick began to make fun and laugh at Mum.

'See ya . . .'

'Where you going? Where's she going?'

'Shop!' I said to my stepfather, opening the kitchen door,

'Money! Wait! The list . . .' Mum shouted, dragging off her wet yellow rubber gloves and looking for her purse in the front pocket of her apron.

Patrick picked up the list and started laughing. 'Pond mince?'

'Oh, shushhhh up.'

'Pond mince? Pond mince ha ha ha . . .'

'Oh, stop,' Mum said, snatching the list from him and giving it to me. 'And don't you forget we've got a family meeting tonight,' she snapped, brushing past him to get her handbag from the other room.

During my mother's pregnancy we had to endure these excruciating 'family meetings'. They were meant to occur about once a month, to clear the air and share time. The four of us would sit awkwardly in the living room together as a 'family' for an hour after dinner with the television switched off. We didn't know what to talk about at first. Patrick would make glib, snide jokes and try to pull serious faces as Mum recited catchphrases that sounded forced, like they came from a *Woman's Own* magazine – she would keep saying, *Isn't this nice, this is family time* – then we'd talk uncomfortably about our day and finally various chores were dished out. I had to clean the bathroom every weekend and polish Patrick's tennis trophies. I had to sweep the leaves in the driveway in autumn and help shovel the snow in the winter. We also had to wash Patrick's car, do the dishes, polish our shoes and tidy our room. The notion of pocket money always came up and was scoffed at. Patrick would get dead serious and launch into the budget and pontificate about how we got through so much food. He'd complain that we all had to pull up our socks and tighten our belts. During one such meeting, my stepfather made a rule that we would shop only once a month from the new massive supermarket out of town. He had an unpleasant military approach to shopping, bulk-buying tins of cheap baked beans and marrowfat peas, massive boxes of own-brand cornflakes, huge tubs of greasy margarine, cheap frozen fish fingers and thin beef burgers. At the end of the month Mum had to be inventive; if we ran out of anything, we went without. This always came up at the family meetings, before negotiations inevitably broke down into serious arguments with Gus about his looming mock exams and school reports. Then, after homework schedules and chore rotas were drawn up and the meeting was concluded, and once the laughter or anger had subsided, Gus and I would be sent back to our bedroom while Mum went into the kitchen and Patrick lit a fag and sank back in front of the sport on TV.

Now, leaving Patrick and my mother in the kitchen arguing about the cost of the grocery bills, I walked to the shops that evening to buy *pond mince*. Crisp November skies and northerly winds meant it was time to wear winter coats and tights again. I felt the cold against my cheeks and my knees, but I felt important walking to the shops with a folded five-pound note inside the palm of my glove, my hands driven into the bottom of my coat pockets.

I saw something glinting under the leaves. I stopped and I bent down to examine it and found it was an untouched bar of chocolate. I got under a streetlight to look at it. The paper was damp but the foil new and unopened. I knew there would be trouble if my mother thought I had bought it, and if she knew I found it in the gutter, she'd make me throw it away. Either way it had to be my secret chocolate bar. I put it in my coat pocket and planned to hide it at home under the blanket in the doll's cot at the end of my bed. I kept quite a larder there; under the doll's bedding were jam-smeared Jacobs crackers wrapped in tissue, a piece of old Easter egg, some chipped Hastings rock, a pinch of desiccated coconut to reflavour old bubblegum, and now there was this damp chocolate bar. I kept this secret stash for when I was sent to bed without any tea – I was a true Brownie guide, always prepared. I hid the chocolate bar deep in my pocket. The dusk light was a dusty mauve, the plum and damson colours you get at the end of the year when the nights draw in. Breathing in the smell of bonfires and wading through dry leaves, I heard the odd whistle and bang of fireworks. And my duffel coat felt familiar, but tighter since last winter.

Doughnut and Lolly

One of my happiest memories of Guy Fawkes night was when we went to stay with Aunt Doreen and Uncle Laurie for the whole bonfire weekend. They were best friends of Mum and Patrick from the tennis club, not blood-related, but favourites of Gus's and mine. They took us to a bonfire, to see the Catherine wheels and rockets, colourful showers of stars exploding and falling into the night sky. They gave us our own packet of sparklers, not just one, but a whole packet. Afterwards we went to a fairground, which was always more exciting at night-time with the flashes and buzzes, the smells of popcorn and hot dogs, the thrill of all the noise and laughter. I was allowed both candy floss and a toffee apple, but most of all I remember how we went on a steam engine carousel, up and down and around I went, dizzily laughing and holding on tight to the reins, the chintzy organ music and colours all swirling before me through the smoky air.

When we stayed with them we never wanted to come home. I remember calling them Auntie Doughnut and Uncle Lolly and laughing and watching *Jason and the Argonauts*. I played with Uncle Laurie's hair for hours, sat up on his shoulders, and he kept saying to Doreen, 'She finished yet? She done yet?'

But I was never finished playing with Laurie's hair. He had a good head of silky hair, but more so I remember it was nice to be allowed — he was one of those rare adults who let you play with them. He tickled our feet, and Gus and I wrestled and climbed all over him. We had a play fight with all the cushions and then we fell in a pile on the rug in front of the fire, all three of us laughing and laughing.

That particular visit, we went out to get some air, leaving the Sunday roast cooking slowly in the oven. There was a dense fog as we took a walk that afternoon across a rugby pitch. We could have lost each other; we couldn't see our own hands in front of our faces. Gus and Uncle Laurie walked slightly ahead, slipping in and out of sight, obscured by the veil of mist, though I could hear their voices. I held Auntie Doughnut's hand. She told me all about 'Broomy', the secret magic flying broomstick she kept in the shed that could do spells.

Maya Angelou once said: *I've learned that people will forget what you said, people will forget what you did, but people will never forget how you made them feel.* I understand what that means when I remember these good times we spent when we were staying with Doreen and Laurie.

Not long after that, Uncle Laurie had a heart attack and died in his sleep. I think it was around the same time that Elvis died — I know as a child I put them together in my head. My brother cried for hours, lying face down on his bunk and sobbing into his pillow. I swallowed all my tears up, but he let his all out and once you let one lot of crying out, there's more to follow. I didn't know how to react. I teased him to try to make him stop, which made him worse. I remember there was a part of me that was convinced Laurie would be back; I still hadn't quite grasped the finality of death. We all loved Uncle Laurie so very much, he was the most loving and gentle man we'd ever known; he was our favourite, a father figure.

As the years passed, I would still stay the night with Aunt Doreen, but usually visit on my own because Gus grew out of sleepovers. I liked to watch as she pinned her hair into a croissant shape at the top of the back of her head, in a sweep of soft spun silver like a Hollywood film star. She had great style and glamorous outfits and ballgowns. She once made me a tennis outfit, an ensemble out of one of her 1950s dresses: a mini-tennis dress with a jacket to match and a longer skirt of the same material to wear on top for cool evening wear. It didn't make me a better tennis player, but I thought I looked the business.

In the evenings Aunt Doreen would teach me to play poker, chess and draughts. She made cocktails in proper martini glasses, her glass of course filled with the real deal, but mine made with ginger ale and topped with a cherry. We'd pretend to get tipsy, like *Dumbo*, and I would hiccup and tell her I could see pink elephants. I remember us both cackling with laughter; she always had such a wicked sense of humour and a contagious laugh.

Aunt Doreen kept me on my toes constantly by testing my spelling, stretching my vocabulary and general knowledge. We had terrific debates — she told me that the moon landing was a hoax because there was no breeze on the moon and the American flag was flying as though there was wind, and this baffled me for years.

Most of all, she encouraged in me a playful sense of humour and mischief. She once told me that the best part of the Second World War was that women got do men's work and that her sister was lucky enough to drive a red double-decker bus. I was fast and I seized this kind of opportunity by retorting, 'The Second World War? Why, Auntie Doreen, I know you're making things up this time, you couldn't have been born then . . . you look like you must only be twenty-one years old.'

'That's it, kid, you're learning! That's my girl ... keep them coming! Flattery'll get you everywhere, kiddo!'

Then she'd chuckle, we'd clink glasses and she'd reward me with a shiny fifty-pence piece.

Black Ice

One autumn morning, I was late for Sunday school. Usually we'd all get there early and play outside, kicking balls about on the gravel until it was time to go in. Then when we got indoors we'd mess about in the toilets with the taps while the teacher put out chairs and tables and handed out pens and Bible story quiz sheets. There was something weird that morning, though. We were told to be quiet, please, to sit in our seats and pay attention. I was sitting next to Anna Parris. I poked her and she leant over and whispered in her most serious voice, 'Have you heard?'

'What?'

'Tara Collins was in a car crash last night.'

'What?'

Anna repeated herself, hissing in my ear, but I could not hear her. I was so busy poking her and mouthing *what?* and trying to get Anna to repeat herself that I missed the very beginning of what the teacher said. Anna hit my thigh, frowned and mouthed *shush* at me. I crossed my arms and thought *bossy boots* as she pointed at the teacher to make me listen. I caught words like *tragedy* and *accident* and the tail end of a sentence that ended . . . *sadly, boys and girls, Tara Collins's mother died.*

There were gasps as the sentence sank in. I looked down at my fingernails, coloured in with felt-tip, and listened intently. I was unsure what facial expression was appropriate and looked down the row of seats and saw how everyones faces were in shock; they looked like fishes' mouths. We had all imagined our mums dying. It was the one thing that you could not bear to imagine, though. It was the one thing that would make the world utterly black. When the teacher finished speaking we turned to each other. Different versions of events were passed along the rows in hushed whispers. Sunday school that day was sombre and strange. Those of us who knew Tara formed a silent alliance; some who didn't know her acted like they did. We were closer somehow, and we flocked like twittering little parrots repeating the sympathetic statements of the adults.

'I just wish there was something we could do . . .'

'Poor Tara.'

We were well behaved, and we didn't laugh at the teacher when she dropped her book. We didn't point and giggle at the deaf old lady in the pew in front of us when we went into the church for the family service. And when the priest said, *let us pray*, we prayed properly and hard, eyes squeezed tight shut and no peeking. Some girls were crying when the priest said Tara's name. Anna Parris's mum gave me a lift home and all our seat belts were put on, even though it was just up the road. I said goodbye and thank you and then I ran as fast as I could. I ran around the corner, past the sweet shop and down The Ridings and I flew around the house and into the back kitchen door. She was there. My mum. She was there and she was alive at the sink, the windows were steamed up, and I could smell Sunday dinner, roast chicken, and hear vegetables bubbling in the pots. She was my mum and she was wearing her blue and white apron that looked like Wedgwood china. She was finishing a ciggy, her head tilted back and her fingers still wet, as if she'd put it out in a bit, after this last drag. I felt a rush of relief and threw my arms around her round waist and began to sob.

'What's all this?" she said, holding her hands up. She extinguished the cigarette in an ashtray and I held on tighter.

Gus came in behind me and whispered something above my head and she touched the crown of my head and listened. I loved the way she was touching my hair and listening. As though any minute she'd say something like: *oh, don't worry, we have a bandage for that* or *all you do is soak it overnight in a little warm salt water and it'll wash out in a jiffy.* Gus gave a blow-by-blow account, his own cold, action-packed version.

'They hit black ice and apparently they swerved and . . . wrapped around a tree and . . .'

I cried the way children cry, I bawled, confused and shocked by death and its final meaning. When we grow up we are surprised when we catch ourselves crying like that, finding there is so much howling inside. Sometimes there is a reservoir of tears, and once you let go, you feel lighter and wonder why you carried all those tears for so long. It is just like laughing; sometimes crying is like when you cannot stop laughing.

Gus was still giving his sensational, comic-book account, speaking fast, without taking breath.

'. . . apparently, they were only going about fifty or sixty, Mum, but the fog was so bad last night, remember, Mum? It was a deadly and fatal combination of black ice and thick fog. It took ages for the ambulances and the firemen to come, Mum, apparently, right, they had to cut them out with chainsaws and use winches and everything! The worst accident on that road in history! We all reckoned, yeah, they must have been going sideways for about a quarter of a mile 'cos there's glass and skid marks all the way down the road and then they must have started rolling, faster and faster, and once they started rolling, well, you imagine that, hey, Mum, hey guess where it is? It's about halfway down the hill just before the . . . you know, where the farm is, yeah, you know? On the steeper bit of the slope on the road to Rothwell, you know, where we went strawberry-picking once, yeah? There, it's just before the strawberry farm. You should see it, Mum, we all biked up the hill to have a look, and the car, you should see it, Mum, it's hanging in the tree, practically in half. Lucky there were any survivors at all, they must have crashed through the fence, gone over the ditch, through the hedge and then hit the tree. Totally wrapped around it, Mum, and the car, the car is almost split down the middle where they must have sawed them out and then . . .'

'I . . . loved . . . strawberry-picking . . . there!' I spluttered and stammered and cried even harder into my mother's apron, I could feel Mum nod, motioning to Gus to shush, and he left us and took his shoes off and went off into our bedroom.

'Blow your nose. I cannot hear a word you say when you cry like that, love.'

But I wouldn't let go of her, I spluttered, I wiped my nose on the back of my sleeve.

'Mum, listen, Tara's mum is dead . . . really dead . . . and they don't know if her dad is going to be OK. Her mum died . . . Imagine poor Tara . . . imagine? Poor Tara's mum! We have to do something Mum, Mum, you and me, we should go around there . . .'

With tears rolling down my cheeks, I began to try to persuade my mother that we should go to Tara's house. I believed we should make up beds and peel extra potatoes. I was also convinced that they could stay with us and maybe we could even adopt Tara. My mother listened as I talked and it was comforting. I felt like we were hatching a plot and conspiring. I waited for her to reply, which she did, carefully, with big pauses between each word. She had a plan, I knew it, and I was ready to cling to every word. I knew she would come up with something really brilliant. She wiped my tears and asked me if I was listening and she said *blow* and I blew my nose.

'Now, listen carefully, are you listening? Tara and her brother will be very, very sad right now and they need to be close to their family because when people pass on it's a quiet time. If you really want to do something . . .'

Enraptured, I nodded my head.

'If you really want to do something, what you should do is—'

I couldn't wait to hear. My heart raced at the thought that there was one thing, one brilliant, thing I could do to make it better.

'Salena, what you should do is you should make her a card and put it through her door so—'

'No, but, Mum, we should go around to their house together and take them some books and sweets and nice yoghurts—'

'Listen. Listen. Listen.'

But I didn't listen. I kept interrupting and she repeated that one steady word.

'Listen . . . Listen . . . LISTEN.'

Mum deepened her voice and looked me right in the eye. 'Listen, I know you're very sorry for Tara but she will not even be there. She's probably still at the hospital or with her family. It's family time and she'll need to be quiet . . . Listen! What you could do is make her a card and pop it through her door so that . . . so that . . . when she does come home she'll know that you're there for her. It's QUIET time and you can't just go around there and—'

'But, Mum—'

'No, Salena! How many more times do I have to tell you? It's QUIET TIME! *QUIET TIME!*'

With my mum yelling *quiet time* in my face I knew I had lost the battle.

'OK, OK, what shall I write in the card?'

'What shall you put in the card?'

A project, a task, was being set and a determination took over as Mum answered slowly.

'Let me think. Just put that you are sorry and—'

'I know!'

'Put that you are sorry and that—'

'OK, I said I know.'

I cut her off and ran into my bedroom on a mission.

Late that dull Sunday afternoon I walked solemnly under an unremarkable sky. When I got there all the curtains were drawn and the house was in silence. Nobody was home. The bikes weren't out. The car wasn't there. *Of course the car wasn't there.* The drive was very steep, and I thought of the crash, and of the crash of helmets against the garage door and us all laughing. I didn't want to disturb anyone, not even the neighbours. I didn't know how to look or how to explain why I was there, at the house where death just happened. I felt like a trespasser. I nervously crouched at the back door. It was glass, the swirly glass of bathroom windows, with a brown wooden frame. I pushed my lumpy envelope through the letterbox at the bottom of the door. It was hard to get it in, bulky. I had put loads of things in the envelope for Tara, things she might need: my lucky conker, a real American one-dollar bill, a plastic joke ring that spurted water and a rubber eraser that smelled like Coca-Cola.

The envelope wasn't fitting, so I held the stiff flap up and poked it through with my fingers. I was just getting scared that it was stuck or that it would trap my finger when the packet shifted, I heard it thud heavily on the linoleum floor on the other side, and for a split second I froze, thinking I heard movement inside. I jumped and quickly backed away as though I was doing something wrong: a chill feeling as though I was being watched.

I walked back up the steep drive and turned left down the hill towards our school. I walked with nowhere particularly to go and nobody in particular to play with. Dusk had fallen. The orange streetlights flickered on. I wandered slowly, untangling these new emotions, melancholia and dreadful fear. I stopped to tie up my shoelaces and sat on the kerb for a while to think, nervously biting the skin off the side of my thumb. Then I walked down the lanes and to the fields on the edge of town and climbed a gate and sat on it. I called to the matted old brown horse and offered it bitter crab apples. Its breath was a warm steam into the chill evening air, and after I patted it my hand smelled of horses. I imagined being Tara and I felt so sad for her. I felt as though my package was a litany whispered into the wind or a message in a bottle thrown into the deep sea, but it was the best I could do and it was all I had to give her.

Tiny Tears

It was a bitterly cold day when my mother was rushed to hospital to have the new baby, prematurely. I remember being excited to have a new baby sister or brother, but I was desperate for my mother the ten days or so she was gone. She had miscarried a baby before this new child and so I was very afraid to see her broken like that again, to find my mother in darkness, her eyes red from crying, her small voice. I never forgot it.

My brother and I were left to fend for ourselves. We went to and from school as usual and helped ourselves to cereal and toast in the mornings. The house was empty without her, silent and loveless. The idea that this could be permanent was too horrible to contemplate. After school I shivered and waited, sitting on the back doorstep in the gloom and dusk, fearing the worst, waiting for my stepfather's car to light up the drive.

There were complications with the birth. We had a new sister, but she was fragile, tiny and blue. She was in an incubator and there was a blood transfusion. This was all I knew and a horrible dread consumed me. During those long, dark February nights I steeled myself for the possibility that my mother might die. In the books I loved to read this happened all the time; the stories of

Hans Christian Andersen, the Brothers Grimm and Charles Dickens were filled with stories of orphans whose mothers died in childbirth.

I was anxious, I was waiting, always waiting, for news, for my mother to come home safe or for Patrick to come to let me in after school. To pass time I started walking, circling the neighbourhood, blowing on my cupped hands to keep them warm. It had started getting dark and was spitting with rain when I knocked on Mrs Sharkey's door. I wanted to be less pitiful, but the sight of her kind face and the gush of warmth at the open door made my eyes hot with tears. She was wiping her hands on a tea towel and I could see she was about to say she was busy and about to send me away. I was hungry and cold and as my eyes filled up I looked away and down at my shoes.

'What's wrong?' she asked.

I looked at her and then down again into my upturned scarf, and I felt my lip quivering. Through a blur of hot tears I saw her face change and she asked me inside. I was grateful but awkward because this time it wasn't a game, this time I felt I needed her. Once inside I began to cry, regurgitating the things I had been told but didn't fully understand. I told her that my new sister was smaller than a doll. I told her that I was scared.

'She's in an incubator and my mum's really ill and . . . and what if . . .?'

Mrs Sharkey put her arm across my shoulders and listened and assured me that my mum would be all right. She made me dry my eyes and gave me a handkerchief, then took out a pot and heated milk to make her special milky coffee. She made me a ham sandwich, the most delicious sandwich I had ever eaten, neatly cut into four quarters, on moist white bread with creamy butter and soft pink ham that was ever so slightly salty. I found it difficult to eat carefully and with all of my manners. I was self-consciously hungry and I ate too fast and the sandwich stuck in my throat. I tried to sip hot coffee to dislodge it. Mrs Sharkey watched me and told me to slow down and take my time. Then she walked to the corner cupboard in the kitchen and her grin made me chuckle as she said her lovely catchphrase.

'Cakey?'

She asked if I would like to warm up by the fire and led me into the living room. I thought I must be a very trustworthy person to be allowed to sit in the proper front room and eat my cakey and drink my sweet and creamy coffee. I felt shy and awkward; I hadn't sat in there before, and our chats were always at the kitchen table or by the back doorstep. Mrs Sharkey told me to take my shoes off to warm my toes and this embarrassed me, making me feel like I was really welcome to stay for a while longer. I was grateful and in no rush to sit on the cold doorstep at our house anymore. I fumbled nervously with my laces, acting as though I had somewhere else to go in a bit, as though I thought she was the one who might want some company — because asking for comfort when you really need it is the hardest thing.

The blue glow of the electric fire was warm and inviting. Mrs Sharkey switched all the bars on high, until they glowed orange and red beneath the coals. I took my shoes off and, suddenly aware of my odd grey boy's socks, I tucked my cold feet under me. She put a tartan blanket on me — she had bought it on a caravan holiday she'd had in the Highlands of Scotland, she said. The room had two armchairs but we sat side by side on the big green sofa. There were lace curtains and doilies on the glass coffee table, my coffee cup sat neatly on a *Cork, Ireland* coaster. She told me about Ireland and about her family pictured in gold and silver oval frames above the mantelpiece; she told me the names and ages of all of her nephews and nieces who lived in the long ago and the faraway.

As Mrs Sharkey explained her family tree I pretended to go to sleep for a joke and snored loudly. She played a lovely game with me, pretending to be offended. She said, 'Oh, how rude to fall asleep when I'm in the middle of telling a story . . .'

I snored on and she held me, enveloping me in her arms. Then she pretended to fall asleep too, and snored even louder. With our eyes clenched shut, we peeked at each other out of one eye and then belly laughed as we whistled, snorted and made pig-snuffling noises together.

'Well, well, what a big snore for such a little girl,' she said, blowing a raspberry on my neck to wake me up, making me laugh and wriggle.

With Mrs Sharkey holding me by the fire, we became still and gentle. Eventually I let myself go and drifted off for a little while. I was so comfortable in the glow of the fire, the soft heat of her arms, I fell into a lovely warm haze. I did not dare move, just so she'd hold me safe, for just a little bit longer.

* * *

When they came home, my mother and sister were doing fine after all. It wasn't until much later my mother told me about all the drama, that she'd had nightmares in the hospital and got up to sleepwalk the corridors in the night, dragging her drip along with her.

I remember now how we sat on the bed and whispered to each other and watched my newborn sister sleep. Jo-Ann was very small, a living, breathing doll, with black silky floppy curls. I measured her against my Tiny Tears doll and Jo-Ann was smaller. Her skin was the colour of my palest inner wrist and she had a penny plastered over her belly button. When Patrick was home I was

169

discouraged from picking Jo-Ann up to cradle her. When he wasn't home, though, I could help out and kiss her all I liked. Patrick started coming home from work with chocolate bars for my sister. She was barely off breast milk. I watched the new baby slobbering, her miniature fist clenching carefully cut-up chunks of melting chocolate and caramel. I would salivate and pretend to help her, wiping her face with a napkin while I stole a tiny piece of chocolate.

Sometimes in the evenings when Patrick and Mum were watching television I risked sneaking into their bedroom to her cot-side. I had to be ready to dive out of there pretty sharpish though in case Patrick caught me. If he found me with her, he'd accuse me of waking her. Even when I told him I was trying to make her go back to sleep he'd tell me off.

'No, you weren't, you're keeping her awake. Now get to your bedroom and don't you ever let me catch you in here again.'

I would risk it and sneak back in to see my sister, stroke her hair and soothe her as she cried. I sang to her: *Goodnight Mister Moon, come again and see us soon* . . . I liked the way she grabbed my finger with her tiny hand. Jo-Ann cried a lot, but when I was with her, she'd go quiet and be happy and peaceful. She always made me feel as though I was her special one.

Stepbrother

I remember a family day out much later that same year, 1981. We were visiting my stepbrother and walking along the seafront in Grimsby. The seascape was cheerless; the tide was out, the sea a murky slurp of grey in the distance. We walked along the out-of-season beach, past shuttered ice cream shops and rides. There were fading signs, arrows shaped like orange carrots read *Donkey Rides*, and it looked like it was going to rain.

We only saw Tina and Graham, my stepfather's two real children from his first marriage, perhaps three times a year: Easter, Christmas or occasional birthdays. Patrick sometimes went to Grimsby on his own at weekends to visit them. My mother pushed the tan-coloured corduroy pram with baby Jo inside. I held the pram handle, while Gus lolloped separately along and ahead a bit; he had grown tall and his legs moved in long gaping strides. Meanwhile, Graham kicked a stone along the edge of the pavement and kerb, with his hands shoved in his pockets. We hadn't seen him for a while. He had a gruff and hoarse voice that was breaking, and his Lincolnshire accent lilted up and down at the end of every sullen sentence. If you could get a whole sentence out of him, that was. He was very pale, almost bluish, with a splatter of fat freckles. When he laughed he hid his mouth with his hand. Gus and I liked him, but he was very shy until he got used to being around us again. It was all quite awkward, with the adults making strained efforts to make it a *good visit* and everybody playing at happy families.

Gus and Graham got on best; they were closer in age, played ball games and had similar interests. My stepbrother had all the latest electronic computer games. One summer the boys made a tent and camped together in our back garden. Gus told me they stayed up making shadows with torchlight, burning moths on candle flames and pulling the legs off daddy-long-legs. I was the youngest and Graham was sometimes a bit rough with me. He'd laugh and swing my dolls by the hair and catapult them across the room. Once, after we watched *Star Wars* at the cinema, Gus and Graham made me cry when they took an ankle each and held me upside down, banging my head on the floor, playing out a scene from the film.

Graham's sister Tina was older. Of course, I liked it best when Tina visited too; the boys wouldn't pick on me so much then. She was pretty, with auburn freckles on her nose and reddish hair with flicks hairsprayed into her fringe. She wore black eyeliner and skintight jeans. She let me brush her hair and told me secret, grown-up things. One visit, Tina showed me a passport-size photograph of a punk-rocker with a skinhead and whispered *that's my boyfriend.* He looked like a glue-sniffer, his ears were pierced and his eyes were dark and dangerous, but I told her he looked very nice. I liked the way she had whispered that secret to me.

I can remember that seafront, that cold November day in Grimsby. It was a depressing sight – we were pedestrian and ordinary, and all a bit bored of walking. The car was parked miles away down a side street, a free parking space to avoid paying for the car park. The sky was a flat slate grey. It was raining out at sea, but we were to make a day of it. Mum kept saying things about the view and how *taking in the sea air and a bit of exercise won't do you no harm.*

I watched Patrick making a fuss of Graham, roughing up his hair, putting his arm around his shoulders, being affectionate. He was leaning down to Graham's ear for nice chats that only they could hear. I got jealous in waves; I wanted to be my stepfather's shiny one too, to make him notice me. I loved to see my stepfather when he was like this, when he made a point of being lovable and loving. Even if it was not a direct hit, even if it was not for my benefit, I inhaled the fumes like his secondhand cigarette smoke.

It's grim in Grimsby, I thought over and over. When I said it out loud Mum shot me a look to say, *don't go spoiling the day.* I said I was only kidding around, thinking, *don't you get it? Grim in Grimsby, why is it called Grimsby? Because it is so grim and . . . What shall we do then?*

Nobody said any of this. We just thought it and walked separately along the dull seafront. A brackish stench rose from the dark brown sand and an olive-green scum and froth had washed up with the tide. The railings were salt-tarnished and weatherworn, metal hinges were rusted to bolted doors and locked-down shutters, the deckchairs were padlocked and the posters of the summer seasons were all torn and rain-battered. There were smashed beer bottles in bus shelters that smelled of wee. Mum kept calling this *exploring* and honed in on the benefits of getting some sea air into us. She kept up this banter and gave us Polo mints she found in her coat pocket. We were being careful to act cheerful and as though we were all included for a day, included in a thing that didn't really seem to exist. We were all involved in this united nothing, we were forcing something, faking it without even knowing its name. It was tense, draining, silences were punctuated with Mum's noisy deep intakes of breath and repetitive clichés about the fresh air.

173

The boys kicked a pebble to each other, shouting *goal!* At first it was half-hearted, and then they started running, racing each other, as the pebble rolled off the pavement and down the steps onto the sand. Mum said we couldn't take the pram down onto the sand. I couldn't ever run fast enough to catch up or get a kick of the stone. I held back: it was not about me, it was not my special day. Behind us on the distant promenade my mum sat and smoked a ciggy and rocked the pram. In the other direction, the boys and my stepfather were miles away by the edge of the tide. There was no distinct horizon, just a grey fog of indeterminate mist blending sea and sky. I crouched with a rustle of my red cagoule over a puddle of crab pools and poked at sandy worm shapes. There was a dead starfish on the sand, seaweed knotted in washed-up objects, plastic and rope. I wished we were allowed to take our shoes and socks off and paddle. I wished it was summer.

Afterwards we went to a sea-view hotel and restaurant and were seated in the window. There were chocolate-brown velvet curtains and apricot tablecloths and napkins. There were different condiments in sachets in a silver basket in the middle of the table.

'What is tartare sauce?' I asked.

'I know! It's like salad cream with bits in it.'

We had been promised fish and chips but this place was classier than our usual chippy. We had run into the first place that was open when the rain started pelting down. The menus were in red leatherette-covered booklets. We sat up and kept our hands in our laps and elbows off the linen cloth. It was an alien experience, being a family in a restaurant. My baby sister was at the head of the table in her highchair and we all looked at her as she banged her plastic tray with a spoon. We focused on her every dribble and gurgle. I wondered if our stepbrother would love his new sister as much as I did.

'See, she always does that,' I told him. 'She likes it when you do this, blow on her hand, see, she likes it . . .'

I was aware that they were connected in a way I could never be with my stepfather. I was wary that they were blood brother and sister through him, and I really hoped Jo-Ann would not like her brother more than me when she got older.

Patrick asked Graham, 'What do you fancy?'

My stepbrother chose scampi in a basket. I didn't know what a scampi was and wondered why it came in a basket. We read the menu out loud and made shushed comments about the prices. Graham said he'd eaten lobster before and he liked it; we saw it was the most expensive thing on the menu. Gus had chicken and chips and I had sausage and chips and we all had a fizzy orange. Outside the front window, rain slurped down the weighted canopy; a man was poking it from the underneath with a stick to drain the water. It was bucketing down, coming in at a slant, obscuring the horizon.

My hands smelled and there was dirt and gritty sand under my nails, so I asked to go to the bathroom. It was on the other side of the lobby, through the posh restaurant and down some gilt stairs. I walked slowly across the plush red carpet. I sucked the inside of my cheeks so it looked like I had cheekbones and pushed my chin up. I imagined I belonged there. I saw a piano in the corner or the lounge and bar area and I imagined that my father owned the place and that I was going to the lobby to meet him for luncheon. We'd probably call it luncheon, my real dad and I, and I'd say something like, *shall we have the lobster, Papa?* I went into the grand and marbled bathrooms and washed my hands with the pink soap and dried them on pink napkins from a dispenser that said *towelettes* in curly writing. Watercolours hung on the peach walls, a painting of two cats in deckchairs dressed like humans. Dry petals filled a glass bowl and there were plastic flowers in a vase. Old-fashioned tea-dance music was coming from somewhere. I took it all in and looked hard at my reflection and watched my pupils dilate. I leaned closer and watched them for a while. I wasn't happy. I stood in the quiet of the toilets for a minute or two, sulking, watching my pupils growing and shrinking as though they were breathing.

When the food arrived, the slick grey-haired waiter was flirty with Mum and we all laughed over-politely. When he had gone Patrick poked fun at Mum and the waiter and laughed about his bow tie. We ate fast and hungrily, filling the holes in our stomachs and the gaping pauses. There were some jokes made about the size of Patrick's cod and the huge amount of chips we had to get through each. Scampi in a basket was, I discovered, like nuggets of fish finger and I tried one. Graham squeezed ketchup and tartare sauce all over them. Jo-Ann made that face, with her out-of-focus eyes, and we laughed, the tension coming out, our lips all grease and salt and vinegar. Jo cried out and Mum nursed her away from the table, saying she needed changing. We held our noses and said *poo-ey!* Graham giggled with Gus and me about Jo-Ann's stinky nappy.

Throughout the meal Patrick spoke to his real son. I heard him asking him about school and sports and how his sister was getting on with her exams and then I heard him ask, '. . . how do you feel about coming to us for Christmas this year? It will be special because it is Jo-Ann's first ever Christmas.'

Gus and I sat quietly in front of ketchup-smeared plates and cold leftover chips. We slurped our fizzy pop through straws. The waiter returned and cleared the table and asked if we wanted dessert or coffee. Patrick asked Graham if he would like a Knickerbocker Glory. The waiter brought over plastic picture cards of all the desserts. This was a pivotal moment – we knew if my stepbrother said no, we'd leave now and skip pudding. I twitched and Gus nudged me under the table. I looked at the photographs of luxurious ice cream creations with names like Choc-Mint Magic and Toffee Bonanza. Gus leaned in and pointed to a photo of a tall glass of gooey brown chocolate and whipped cream. He licked his lips and whispered, 'Hmmm, Chocolate Fudge Sundae . . .'

'Hmmm, Banana Split more like!'

I pointed and whispered back.

Patrick looked at his watch and said we could always get one from an ice cream van. My heart sank, imagining us all in the boring car, sheltering from the rain, licking 99s, looking through rain-splattered windows at the dull grey sea. The waiter lingered, waiting for a decision as Mum returned to the table. Jo was cradled in her arms in the sleeping position – it was a bad sign, she'd want to get going. The waiter gave us a moment and then Patrick said, 'OK? Let's go! Maybe we'll get one from the ice cream van.'

On the journey home it was quiet in the car except for the squeak of the windscreen wipers. I watched the rain make trails down the window, my eyes following individual drops until they joined with other drips. It wasn't ever really about whether we had ice creams or not – I was nine years old and beginning to be more aware of feeling as though I was outside looking in, observing my family going through the motions and wishing things were different.

WINTER

Christmas, late 1970s, Desborough

Wish Upon a Star

The snow came in the night, falling thick and fast. By morning, there were deep snowdrifts in the narrow country lanes and jagged icicles hung like fangs from guttering. We were astronauts walking on a crunchy moon on the first day of proper snow, preparing for our expedition to planet school. Bundled up in mittens, hats and scarves, we met each other in the middle of the road, a brave new world, the white world. We wore plastic bags on top of our socks inside our wellington boots. We had eaten sticky thick porridge for breakfast, believing it would glow blue like low flames, central heating in our bellies. We puffed and stamped our feet through frozen puddles, and left our mark, dirtying the fresh clean snow of garden lawns with footprints and names. In gangs we rolled massive snowballs until they were boulders and too heavy to push. These would become the round bodies of snowmen, with pebbles for eyes, carrots for noses and sticks for arms.

'What did one snowman say to the other snowman?'

'Don't know? What did the snowman say to the other snowman?'

'Can you smell carrots?'

We threw snowballs all the way to school. The first one in the back of my head surprised me with that sudden thud and sting.

I retaliated, skidding and chasing around the shapes of cars. Then we scooped big handfuls of clean soft ice cream to eat.

'Eating snow is dirty.'

'No, it isn't! It's only frozen sky! It's natural.'

'Urgh, you ate yellow snow!'

'Did not! It was clean from that wall!'

'Yellow snow, yellow snow, you ate yellow snow . . .'

Boys mercilessly rammed snow down the backs of necks and rubbed it into faces, making them red and rashy. We slipped down the hill to school, claiming the middle of the road as cars were few and far between. We sucked icicles, our free ice lollies. We goaded each other that school would be closed for the rest of the week and that there would be a blizzard.

'It's going to drop to Ice Age temperatures – that's below minus zero!'

'No, it's gonna be colder than that, more like minus below twenty!'

'There's no such thing as minus below, it's below zero.'

'It's called sub-zero minus actually!'

'Sub-zero minus, whoopee! Ice Age!'

'It's going to be below sub minus zero!'

'Hooray! Ice Age means no more school!'

We told each other fantastic horror stories – that a car had been found in a ten-foot snowdrift with its passengers frozen solid inside. We insisted that woolly mammoths were coming back. We talked about avalanches and Antarctica and played at being great explorers searching for the North Pole in a world inhabited by giant polar bears. A rumour spread that the river was frozen over and we made plans to go ice-skating, although not one of us owned ice skates, and ice-skating would have been more a case of ice-skidding in our wellington boots. We spread tales that the teachers were snowed in and described how they were starving grotesquely to death in their homes. On days like these, many children were kept home, especially kids from the farms and more remote areas, so we held high hopes that the class numbers would be too low to even bother opening the school gates.

School was a ridiculous, glittery chaos that close to the Christmas holidays. Our teacher read us Christmas stories and watched over us as we industriously made Christmas cards, card-board stars and papier-mâché snowmen, the desks a mess of glitter-glue and crêpe paper.

I remember enjoying preparing for our annual school nativity plays. I always landed the role of either shepherd or one of the three kings, which were really boys' roles. Each year my mum made my costumes from old cotton bedsheets from home. I had a brilliant time, though, once I stopped being envious of the pretty angel – traditionally that part was always given to the cute blonde girl in the school, and they stood her on a table and dressed her all in white with a halo and silvery wings.

Each year during those last weeks of term, the school dinner ladies came around each class and every single child had a turn stirring the Christmas pudding mixture. This cauldron of gloop and currants, sultanas and plum, the sickly smell of brown sugar, figs and sweet rum was wheeled around the school. When you stirred it you had to make a wish. Every year I looked into that vat of goo for the sixpence and with my eyes closed tight I made the same wish I still always make.

It took ages to undress from our winter things when we re-entered the classrooms after breaktimes. We blathered and fussed with talk of chilblains and frostbite, blowing on our hands and rubbing our frozen feet until we could feel them again. There was a constant distraction of snow gently patting the windowpanes, like a sparkly friend tapping on the glass. We always said *God is shaking out his eiderdown* or *the angels are having a pillow fight*. We did our lessons in our socks, with damp hair, runny noses and flushed rosy cheeks. Clothes that had been caked white from rolling in the snow dripped and steamed on classroom radiators. The worst casualties of the snowball wars were sent to the school secretary to get ill-fitting, musty-smelling clothes from the lost and found. When it snowed, the girls were permitted to wear trousers instead of skirts – an amazing freedom that evened out the snowball chases and fighting odds.

So sweet was that sound of the early home-time ring of the school bell. Always a couple of hours early due to the weather and the dark. We skidded and slid deliriously into the fields, making plans to meet at the top of the steep hills at the back of St Giles church with makeshift sledges – a black bin bag stuffed with an old pillow, tied and bound with string and tape, or sometimes we just sped down the slope on old tea trays. The fields were white as far as the eye could see, with black matchstick trees in the distance, an undulating cotton sheet, an expanse of endless sand dunes, as deep and untouched as the craters on the surface of the moon.

* * *

On Christmas Eve, 1981, I was with Anna Parris, her brother and her father, walking their two Golden Labradors. It was late in the afternoon as we walked towards Rothwell. We crossed meadows, frozen streams and frosted woodland. The sky was an apricot hue, laced with a fine mist. It was like a painting with the smoke-grey hills in the distance and the branches bare as bones, like charred skeletons. Our noses were red and runny, we carried sticks and called out to the dogs to *heel* and *walk on. Merry Christmas!* we called out in chorus, happy to see someone, anyone, approaching so we could yell it again.

'Happy Christmas!'

'Ho-ho-ho to you!'

Mr Parris was a lovely dad. He had a peppery beard with ginger bits in it and golden-brown eyes like Anna's. He was the headmaster of a big school in a nearby town. He seemed to always find time to help build things with his children and their friends. Once I went to play there and found them all making a real igloo out of snow. I'll never forget that; it was big enough for all of us to get in. We sat in the round centre of it and I remember finding it warm inside.

I also recall one summer Mr Parris made an obstacle course down the centre of their long garden and he and Anna taught me how to ride a bike proficiently. He built a rope ladder and a swing in their apple orchard, and we spent hours swinging on the rungs of the ladder and eating unripe apples. Anna was my most sensible and bookish friend. She taught me how to hold my breath and swim underwater, she tried to teach me to play *Cats* with her on her piano and she introduced me to the Brownies. My Brownie uniform was a second-hand brown tunic that was too short for me, with a yellow tie and a brown leather woggle. I wore my Brownie bobble hat ridiculously balanced on my afro. It looked better if you had straight and silky hair like Anna's. She was a tomboy too, with a bob of honey-coloured hair, sandy brown eyes and pale freckles across her nose. I pored over my Brownie manual, and together we competed over badges, both aiming to achieve two full sleeves; to us these sewn-on trophies not only symbolised that we had passed the tests of semaphore, cooking and first aid, but that we were smart and we could solve anything, that we could survive in the wild and live in camps and tree houses.

So that Christmas Eve, we ran through the sludge with the dogs leaping excitedly and barking. Then we stopped and called the old brown horse to come to the fence to eat snowy, muddy grass from our red palms. Standing on the gate railings, we shouted, *here boy.* Our fingers were cold and dirty; we cleaned them inside our mittens. The sky was sweet above us, swept with the colour of rhubarb and custard penny chews, Fruit Salads, pink and yellow.

'Do you get butterflies on Christmas Eve?' Anna asked.

'I do!' her brother replied.

'I've got butterflies in my tummy already, Dad, I have,' Anna said softly, taking Mr Parris's big, gloved hand.

'Me too,' I said, shoving my hands deeper into my own pockets and tucking my chin into my scarf.

The four of us fell quietly into step as I began to think about my own dad and the letters we had written to him that week. That year Mum had asked us to write to our father and say what we wanted for Christmas. I didn't know what to write; we had never asked for anything or written to him much before. I'd found the letter difficult. More than anything, I wanted to ask for something to give him a clue who I was and how I had grown up. Mum suggested I ask for a vanity case, but I didn't know what a vanity case was. Mum told me it was a case for young ladies, with a mirror and a manicure set, somewhere to keep precious things and jewellery. To me it sounded like it would make him picture me as a pretty young lady.

So that Christmas, I wrote to my father asking for a vanity case and I couldn't wait to see what he'd send and what on earth a vanity case looked like, but because it would be from my real dad, I suddenly wanted one more than ever.

The icy grass crunched under our boots. There was a lavender mist across the dusky fields in the distance. The dogs padded by

186

our side, and as we came back into town pretty Christmas lights in house windows winked and blinked on and off. Chimney smoke wisped into the evening. We caught a lovely little smile playing on Mr Parris's lips underneath his bushy beard as he listened to us talking about Father Christmas. We were discussing how Santa could get to us even though our bungalow didn't have a chimney.

We felt the magic of Christmas Eve all around us, sparkling in the frost. We were content that tomorrow would be the best day of the year. And as we said goodnight to each other the North Star was twinkling above us. We kept yelling *Happy Christmas* until we were out of sight of each other and I was walking alone. A street away, I could still hear Anna Parris shouting into the peaceful Christmas Eve, the silent night, the holy night, all is calm, all is . . . *Merry Christmas, Salenaaaaaa . . .*

Christmas

Memories of childhood at Christmas blur into a montage very much depending on my mood and the hunger I felt then, and also now in the remembering. The last weeks of December, those last evenings of the year, often remind me of the magic and warmth of home fires, of the familiarity of a sing-song of chattering voices above my head, the voices of my step-grandparents, Nanny and Grandad, or visiting friends like Auntie Doreen. Once the novelty wore off and I'd stopped jumping on knees, I would settle and curl up, lazily flip the pages of a *Beano* Christmas annual. The adult talk was tipsy, fuelled by hot toddies and mulled wine, and cackling laughter came from the kitchen where the women fussed over the grease and jelly of the boiled ham, while the men poured whisky or rum and stood with their hands in their pockets, rolling on the balls of their feet, chewing fists of peanuts. With great ceremony, they'd uncork Mum's homemade rocket fuel, the damson gin, and sometimes let me have a taste as they all clinked glasses and said cheers and talked loudly over each other and over Mary Poppins on TV singing 'A Spoonful Of Sugar'.

I remember well the rose-lit, tinselled living rooms of my parents' friends, with the comfortable cacophony of those competing voices. I recall straining to comprehend the hush of talk between adults. I sat underneath tables or behind sofas, out of sight, so content with my newfound wealth of gold chocolate coins, colouring in with a packet of new felt-tip pens. I remember moments at Christmas when we were like a real family, the ideal family, like the adverts showed, all shiny chocolate boxes and crackers, sausage rolls and Twiglets.

Then there are also memories of times when I found Christmas strange, depressing, stifling, disappointing. There were times when Christmas was painful, when there was preferential treatment of favourites and jokes about Scrooge were made through gritted teeth and forced smiles. There were moments when I'd mope off and hide from my alien family and lock myself in the bathroom, convinced I must have been adopted. I remember one Christmas my brother Gus and I rolling our eyes at each other as we watched our step-siblings unwrap their gifts from Patrick, the latest top-of-the-range electronic games and such, while we opened a present to find we'd been given one chocolate bar each. What did we expect? I suppose in these moments I believed that if the step-siblings were opening these showy and shiny gifts, then maybe, just maybe, I'd get that Barbie or writing set I had my heart set on. I had a head filled with advertising and playground boasts and the lists we'd been told to post to Santa, and I wanted the same presents my classmates and siblings were asking for. Then that gluey knot in the belly when we looked back at the tree and all the gifts were gone. It was all empty shiny paper and going through the motions of what Christmas is and never was.

There was one year, though, a time when we were rich and my stepfather was unbelievably generous, something to do with him being made redundant or a tax refund. It was early on, before my sister Jo was born. The happy Christmas, a white Christmas –

I felt I must have been the best stepdaughter and luckiest girl on the planet, there were so many presents under the tree. That may have been the year we played Monopoly and watched television all day. Was that the last Christmas we all got on happily? Or perhaps that was the same year when Mum found me quiet, wondering why there was no package from Springfield Road and Grandpa George. I recall how she laughed that they were forgotten and hidden in the shed. Then when she appeared with cold damp boxes, I tore into one addressed to me, and found I had been given the most beautiful play china tea set, decorated with roses and gold lacquered edges.

There were times when we had our stepbrother and stepsister to stay. A Christmas when they stayed always meant Patrick being particularly playful and loving. We'd all sit in the living room together, *The Wizard of Oz*, James Bond or *The Three Musketeers* on the television. We could smell dinner cooking slowly for hours, and we were allowed to eat all together at the dining table and have a glass of wine with our dinner. One year there was a box of Liebfraumilch and I distinctly remember feeling giggly and bold and loving everyone and finding my family the most hilariously entertaining people I had ever known.

It's that one white Christmas I remember most clearly, though. The feel of that day when we were close, when everybody was happy. We had glasses of fresh orange juice for breakfast and warmed croissants with real butter. That was the year it snowed thick and fast. We took a walk on Christmas morning while the turkey cooked on a low, slow heat in the oven. Bundled up in mittens and wellington boots, we walked around the country lanes towards the town of Market Harborough, and the four of us, Gus and me and Mum and Patrick, we had a snowball fight. The sky was ice-blue with bright wintry sunshine reflecting off the snowy fields and hedgerows. That's my happiest childhood Christmas memory: that snowball fight on Christmas morning and laughing like we were a real happy family.

* * *

Christmas 1981 was my baby sister's first Christmas and both my step-siblings came to stay. I remember watching Patrick take photographs of just the three of them, just his three real children. I wanted to be in the picture. I wanted to be in the gang. That Christmas I remember Mum being really tired and baby Jo-Ann teething and crying. Most of all I remember that was the Christmas my mum had asked us to write to my real father. Perhaps it goes without saying that the gifts never arrived, and there was no word from our real dad. Mum made excuses about the Christmas post, and Gus and I were told they just might arrive in a later post after Boxing Day or in the new year – but the truth is we didn't understand why we were asked to write to our father that particular year, and it wasn't until later that we discovered why.

The End

Gus and I hoped that we'd see our father again. We now knew that he lived in Bristol and that he had remarried. I privately entertained the idea of running away to see him, or imagined that maybe he'd come and fetch us when we were older. We lived with the sensation of waiting, though to say any of this out loud felt to me like a betrayal of my mother and her choices. It was a loyalty I was afraid to break. It didn't even occur to me that he might not want to know us or that he might have made a new life. I made up romantic excuses for his abandonment. I also believed that my stepfather didn't want my mother's ex-husband coming to the house to visit and so I blamed Patrick too.

The truth is, as long as you have the perception of an achievable dream, you can keep surviving. Meeting our father, getting to know him and having him in our lives one day seemed obtainable; we truly believed that one day the privilege of knowing our father would be ours.

When Mum called my brother and me to her side, she was unwell and pale, with dark circles beneath her eyes. We three were seated in the living room. It was an overcast and ordinary day in the bleak

February of 1982. I sat on her left and Gus sat on her right. Gus and I looked across from each other and smirked a bit. Our mother began to speak in such a serious tone, in a low and deep voice, that it made us nervous, restless.

Mum said, 'I have something to tell you both.'

We pulled faces, larking about and laughing at her. She was building up to something but we were not totally listening until she completed her speech with these three words:

'Paul is dead.'

'Pardon?' my brother blurted, and we looked each other in the face and then burst into peals of laughter. It was our mother's face; it was so strange and so serious we laughed and then slowed to a snigger. I looked at Gus: he tried to take control so I tried to mimic his features, which made him chuckle and that made me giggle. I looked at my mother: she was between us, stroking both our backs with the palms of her hands as you might a baby. Feeling this soothing gesture and catching my brother's eye, I started roaring with laughter again, which set Gus off. Gus and I laughed, we laughed until it hurt, we belly laughed. The more I laughed at Gus, the more he laughed at me, out of control. Away from our mother's hands, we fell off the sofa and were face down into the carpet, hysterical. Gus looked at Mum and kept catching his breath and saying, *It's her fault, she keeps making me*, which sent us both into fits of laughing again. I have never laughed so hard in my life. There were tears on our cheeks, then suddenly Gus wiped his face and croaked, 'Salena, stop . . .'

In slow motion, I saw my brother's face change. First, his dark eyes went glassy, then his mouth turned down at the corners and his brow knotted. As though a cloud had passed over the sun, a shadow crossed his face as something registered. He couldn't see the joke anymore, though I was still frozen in smiling. I thought the cloud would last a moment and then normal service would be resumed and we'd laugh together again. But the more serious he looked, the more nervous it made me.

Mum said, 'I think she's in shock.'

Gus's eyes were out of focus and filling with tears, but I didn't want the laughing to stop. I tried to laugh some more. I forced out a fake laugh. Mum held him, and he was making a noise, a low wail that I had never heard him make before and which wasn't laughing. I didn't want the laughter to ever stop. Their shoulders were shaking now, they were both weeping.

'Paul is dead, Dad's dead, Salena.'

Then my mother made a long sonorous cry, a single note that resonated through me. It rang underneath and inside and throughout her and into and through me, it was a howling, it was my mother crying and my brother crying, the two of them in front of me. I couldn't take it all in and I mean I didn't want to and then I started to cry too.

Mum told us he took his own life. That was the bit that was hard to understand. Mum told us he was very, very sad. She said he ran out of choices and the only choice he had was to end it all. We asked how and she wouldn't tell us exactly. I was nine years old and I was trying to imagine being so sad you would kill yourself. With this I wept harder. It was the fact that he was very sad, that one day our dad was sad, unhappy enough to kill himself. I had never heard his emotions discussed before, I never knew he could be sad. I wanted to go to him, make him happy. I heard my brother and my mother crying, his head was in her lap next to mine, her hands on our heads; she stroked our hair and we cried together.

Mum told us quietly that he died before Christmas. Before Christmas? He committed suicide on 11 December 1981. He was already dead, long dead and long gone. It was February, two months after the event. There was no funeral, no goodbyes to say or respects to pay. This was the end. Those letters we wrote and posted, mine about the vanity case, they were written and posted to a dead man already long cold in his grave.

The Silence

Silence. It was very silent all of a sudden. The rage was silent and the grief was deep and dark. There was a black and cold hole inside me and I fell into it. If I could have, I would have given up speaking forever. I reduced my language to polite monosyllables at school. I could not find any words to say what I was feeling. I know I felt like a fake because I didn't know my real dad, not really, did I? I didn't live with him or get to visit him, did I? It was not like Tara Collins, who lived with her mother and knew her, and in any case that was an accident. Her mother would still be here if she had the choice. It was Dad's choice that I was struggling to come to terms with. My father didn't die from an illness or an accident. He killed himself on purpose.

I give up and sit by the kerb and flick ants down the drain using bits of dirt. I climb inside the wardrobe and sit on the shoes. I inch the door closed and stay there for a while. I am in the dark, you cannot find me here, you cannot see me, you cannot hear me. In fact, I am not really here at all.

I rode my bike on my own, intending never to turn back, to run away from home. Up and down steep and winding country roads I cycled for miles, wet inside my cagoule with cold and furious sweat. Eventually I stopped and sat at my favourite spot, on the yellow, rusting frame of a broken-down tractor on the very edge of town. I climbed into it and hid, miles away from home. I had cycled so hard I was shaking and my legs were weak. Around me, bleak brown fields, black hills and grey roads like dull spaghetti stretched into the distance. The trees had ashen branches and there was no birdsong. I hugged my knees and shivered, damp in my rustling plastic coat. I got lost staring up into the flat dull sky. With my head tipped back I opened my mouth wide and cried, soundlessly at first.

It was dark when I returned home. My hot head was throbbing and aching and I crawled down to the end of my bed, with my feet on the pillows. In the dark and under the covers I wondered over and over, *what if one day I just give up like that? You did it, Dad, you did it. You're my dad who killed himself.* I had learned something new, that sensible grown-up people, with cars and houses, with family and friends, adults with children and responsibilities, kill themselves.

Without words Gus and I called a truce. There was no speech or handshake, but a concrete feeling of uniting in this shared grief. It solidified us as brother and sister and was absolute. It was a pane of glass we carried between us for the rest of our lives.

At night, in the silence, I'd replay that moment when we realised our shared dream was smashed. I saw my reflection in my brother's eyes; they were black as teaspoons of treacle, dark and shiny. I was looking into two black pools and seeing the twin of my own pain. I remembered his face as it went from hysterical laughter to clarity, to shock and finally that long scream and loss. We mirrored each other, sharing that unforgettable second when the penny dropped, the branch snapped, and we fell through a jagged sky to the hard ground. I rewound it and felt my own heart breaking in slow motion. I saw it again and again in my mind; my brother's eyes when he first really heard the words *Paul is dead* and I watched his face, his disbelief and the excruciating sting of the meaning of those three words. I watched my brother breaking, then I felt my own heart splintering, shattering, both of us, together at that minute. It was a hard slap of cold granite, a metallic taste of fear, of terror and a thumping in the blood.

When birth and death came screaming at me, all I could do was throw my head back and scream along. Death and birth screeched and crashed into my nine-year-old head. With the birth of my new sister and the death of my father in the same era, things were changing inside me, and outside I felt my shell harden.

It was the word *choose* I have always had the most difficulties with. I struggled with the fact that, you, Dad, would rather die than ever see the sun shine again. Or share love, laughter. Or, more to the point, see us, your children, ever again. More practically, you would rather die than see if you feel differently in the morning. For the first time in my life I grew silent. I read even more books, and in the quiet turning of pages, I started to imagine blackness, nothingness, I started to picture what suicidal could possibly feel like and mean.

If this were a comic book, the graphics would be black and red now. After hearing of Dad's suicide, the rainbow technicolour pages of my childhood, my fields of gold, sky-blue summers and daisy chains, became monochromatic drawings with long charcoal shadows, and I withdrew.

I know I stopped dreaming I was a superhero. I did not fly above churches and forests and fields, I no longer dreamt I was kissing Elvis in Hawaii or that I had a cupboard in my belly with bananas inside. Instead in my half-dreams I'd see my father.

I'd see you there at the end of our bunk bed, watching us sleep, standing over us, an illuminated figure in the bedroom. I'd lie in my bed as still as stone and watch you looking down at my brother.

There was a bluish light around you, as you slowly turned your head to look at me, and I closed my eyes so you would think I was sleeping. My heart pounded in my chest but I was not scared, not of you or of your ghost. I was expecting you to visit. I knew they wouldn't let you into heaven because you killed yourself. I knew they wouldn't let you into hell either. Where did you go? Did you come to say sorry? You looked at Gus as he slept and when you turned to look at me I closed my eyes, and when I opened one eye I saw you had gone. I knew you would be back, though. I felt you watching me. I have always felt you watching me in the dark.

It is probably no coincidence that my father killed himself around the same date as the anniversary of his mother Edith's death. As I grew up, the more I thought about it, the more it made sense. My father knew how it felt to seek his beginning. He spent much of his life searching for his natural birth parents and he suffered and grieved when he lost Edith. Now with the knowledge of that pain and emptiness, that waiting and seeking, it was as if he passed all that sad weight on to his children, so now we would also know that loss and we might also always miss something we never had. So that we might also grieve a father we never got to know. This was our shared inheritance. His second wife and new family must have been devastated too, beyond devastated. Mum, Gus and I did not go to the funeral. Looking back, I think the adults thought as kids we would have found his funeral highly traumatic. Apparently, this was a decision made by all the adults involved and all with the best intentions, but because of it there were many unanswered questions – my brother and I never knew the man when he lived, nor the whereabouts of his final resting place. We could not say hello to the living or our last goodbye to the dead.

I was convinced that if we had been allowed to be even a small part of your life we would have been one more reason for you to hold on, Dad. One more loving and happy memory to make you stronger, to make you want to live. As a child, I thought we had a wonderful time that one afternoon, I felt a bond, and your one visit kept us living in hope for years. Maybe if you had known us you could have waited to see whether you felt a bit better in the morning. Mum always said sleep is the great healer.

Sleep well and goodnight, Dad.

Fishing

Not long after we found out our dad had gone, I can remember my mum asked Gus to take me fishing. These two events may be unrelated but it is what was left unsaid and the feeling we shared that day that sticks in my memory. Gus had got the fishing rod for a birthday present in March and I'd been pestering him to let me have a go. At Mum's insistence he relented, but I could see he didn't want to take me to his secret place. Nevertheless, we packed jam sandwiches and orange squash mixed in a plastic bottle, while Mum made us take cold boiled eggs. We hated cold boiled eggs.

We walked across dewy fields, through wet grass that came up to my waist, and climbed over stiles heading towards Rothwell. It was spitting lightly, and I struggled to walk so fast, my corduroys damp from the reeds and long grass. He complained and ordered me to hurry up, we begrudged and bickered at each other, then eventually we walked in silence, me jogging ten steps behind, trying to keep up.

Finally we got to *the* good spot, according to Gus. I couldn't see anything more remarkable about this place than the stretch of river behind or ahead of us and I grumbled as much. Gus tutted and started work, feeding his line through the loops on his rod. I watched, feigned interest, trying hard to enjoy my first fishing trip. We sat on cold, damp grass. I looked at the dun, muddy water and waited for something to happen. Gus had maggots for bait, which revolted me. I couldn't take my eyes off the sickening sight of poking the worm guts through the hook. Gus cast his line and settled. There was only one rod and I very rarely got a turn to hold it. When I did, I invariably did something wrong – wound the line too tightly so it snapped the line or let it out too loose so he'd have to reel it all back in – and that annoyed Gus further. So for the most part, I sat in my red cagoule with the hood up, elasticated and tight around my face, padded out by my fat, curly hair. I absentmindedly lobbed cowslips into the river.

'Don't do that, you'll scare the fish,' Gus growled.

'What fish?'

'Shush, don't talk, you'll scare them away.'

'Scare who away?'

'The fish! Now, like I said, shut up.'

'But, Gus?'

'Just shut up, will ya.'

I was about to launch a volley of *shut ups* right back but he gave me the look. Since I had insisted he take me in the first place, I knew my best bet was to shut up when he gave me *that* look. Gus began quietly lecturing me that fishing was a relaxing pastime for people to get some peace and quiet and that fish can sense predators and hear noise above water – but I was ignoring him. I couldn't see any fish, the water was murky and there were no other fishermen. I reckoned fishing was a load of boring rubbish and I said so, under my breath.

Time passed so slowly. It seemed we had eaten our jam sandwiches hours ago and we were beginning to get hungry. I looked at things floating in the water, plastic bags and other rubbish. Then

I busied myself picking flowers for Mum, but there were only dandelions and cowslips. Gus said they were weeds, so I cast them aside and stared gloomily into space.

When Gus and I recall this fishing trip, he thinks we probably caught a minnow. I do not remember the thrill of a single bite or a catch. We both remember that I was annoying him, though, and that we were cold. Sitting on that bank, on a mulch of damp sameness. We were quiet, the sky was darkening and I could see a sheet of slate clouds in the distance, rain heading in our direction.

Then, with nothing else to do, I studied my brother, his habit of intentionally biting the skin on the side of his nails and spitting out the chewed bits. I watched him for the first time in a long time, taking in the new fuzz of his moustache, his bony and long legs, his coarse hair in need of cutting. But more than that, I saw his eyes had no light or twinkle. I looked upon my brother as though I were seeing him for the first time, as an outsider, the way you might look upon a stranger. He was hunched over; his mouth had none of the usual curl of smiles playing at the corners. Gus was never one to talk much, but for the first time I could see a new melancholy in his demeanour. I wanted to touch him, reach out, I wanted to talk to him but I didn't know where to start. I could see he was sad and trying to be brave. I could see his pain, but I tried hard to stop thinking about talking all the time so much, something I have always found difficult. We sat moodily apart and together. I started shivering, concentrating on staring wordlessly at the brown motion of the muddy water. After a long pause, Gus finally looked over at me and we caught each other's glance and shrugged.

He said gently, 'You all right, sis?'

'Yeah.'

'You sure?'

'Bit cold.'

'Yeah, it's getting nippy.'

'Gus?'

'What?'

'Doesn't matter . . . nothing.'

Gus nodded at me, lifted his chin as though encouraging me to continue. Both of us knew there was something to talk about but instead I just said, 'M'ungry . . . You?'

'Starvin' Marvin.'

Then we remembered the eggs. We opened the tin foil they were wrapped in and the stink was foul. We were hungry, but these eggs were really unappealing. Out of boredom I peeled one and saw the yolk was grey as the sky above us. We threw them in the river and watched as they floated away downstream. I watched the bobbing eggs, food for the fish, and twenty years passed until we hugged each other and finally had that conversation.

Golliwog!

I soon read every book in the library at my primary school. The headmaster joked that they had to order in new books just for me. When I had read all the books at the school library, I became a proud public library member and I started borrowing books by authors like Dr Seuss, Enid Blyton and Judy Blume. I devoured big sturdy books by the Brothers Grimm and waded into hefty compendiums with titles like *A Thousand Adventures for Girls.*

On the walk to the public library I passed through the older part of town, the factories and the council estates. Some of those houses still had disused outdoor lavatories in the stone backyards. They were industrial boom houses, built from dark, sooty slate and brick when Desborough was a roaring leather and shoe-factory town. I usually avoided those streets, the windows hung with St George flags, the growling dogs, the child-lynching mobs I tended to attract. They'd tease me, telling me that their dogs were ex-police dogs that were trained to bite *Blackies*, *nig-nogs* and *golliwogs* like me. They called out these names the moment they saw me. In gangs they took up chase with their dogs snarling, hounding me across the back of the new estates and muddy building sites, caterwauling.

'Golliwog! Golliwog! Get back on your marmalade jar!'

Once in the safety of the library I immersed myself in books. Among the encyclopaedias and atlases there was a heavy biology book I peeked at on each visit. It had fascinating pictures of a snake dislocating its jaw to eat a whole frog and bare-naked African and indigenous tribespeople. There were illustrations that showed how apes morphed into cavemen, children changing into hairy adults and vivid spaghetti diagrams of the insides of women where babies came from. Most often, though, I turned to the centre, a double-page spread of a bloody baby, mid-birth, with its head coming out of a hole. The caption below the picture read *The Miracle of Life* and to me it was the goriest thing in the whole library. It was dusk, closing time, and I was nearly the last person in the library. This part wasn't unusual; I would often get lost in all the books I wanted and be so indecisive, knowing I was only allowed to choose four.

Outside, I heard the dogs barking. I glanced out of the window and saw six or seven itchy, snotty-faced kids with bikes and dogs waiting for me outside. They looked bored; they chewed gum with slack jaws. I recognised at least two of them from my school, a vicious girl with a long greasy fringe that always hung in her eyes. Smithy. She was tough, one of about eleven brothers and sisters, with a rusting car in the middle of their front yard. Next to her stood a boy – I knew him too, he had a girlish name, something like Marion. He was albino, with white fuzzy baby's hair and sharp pointed teeth due to some calcium defect. He looked like a vampire's baby. They were with bigger, older punk kids, though, and loitering. I knew they'd try to take my books off me and that they'd call me names and their dogs would snap at me and chase me all the way home.

They were swelling in numbers and blocking the entrance

when my hero was on his way down to the boxing club and he saw the gang. He knew they had no use for books. My brother appeared at the entrance to the library and I beckoned madly and waved. Gus saw me through the glass in the doorway.

'You all right, sis?'

As I checked my books out, he waited for me, then we walked through the swinging doors together. Gus looked down at me, he didn't take his eye off me once, holding both my shoulders and asking gently if I was all right.

'Did anyone hurt you? Which one was it?'

My knees were weak. I was trembling. They jostled, bristled and called us niggers. With this, quite suddenly, Gus swivelled from the waist and threw a direct punch at the biggest of them, hitting him in the face with rapid precision, twice, then three or four swift jabs, bloodying his nose and knocking him clear off his bike and onto the ground. It was so fast nobody had time to blink, even the dogs barked too late.

'Leave her alone! She's still only in juniors,' Gus swore at them. 'You're all older'n her. Leave her alone unless you want more!'

Marion jumped on his bike. He wobbled in his hurry to speed off as fast as his thin white matchstick legs could go. From the safety of the other side of the street he yelled, *nig-nog golliwog!* and something about getting his big brother, but Gus brushed that threat off like a fly. The punk he had punched sat cradling his face with cupped hands, blood dripped through his fingers from his mouth and nose and down the front of his slashed Iggy Pop T-shirt. Gus stepped over him, hoiked up a good thick greeny from the back of his throat and spat.

'Don't go near my sister again.'

He swore and then he took my arm and walked me across to the zebra crossing opposite the library. Gus looked down at me and told me with an assuring authority, 'You're all right, sis now go straight home.'

And as I started hurriedly up the hill, cuddling my stack of books to my chest, he called out, 'Oi! Salena!'

'What?'

'Don't tell Mum.'

The Day the Joke Glass Broke

War broke out the day the glass broke.

I was inside, in our bedroom on my own, and it was winter. I was reading a book when I heard a knock at the window – it made me jump, but I was relieved to see it was Gus. The doors were all locked and he asked if he could get in. I opened the window and then closed it before he could climb in. I laughed and teased my brother as he ran around the outside of the house trying all the windows, which I kept opening and closing. He was getting annoyed with me, which made me do it more, and I laughed as I just managed to get the dining-room window closed before he could get his arm in.

'Stop messing about! Let me in or else!'

I started juggling fruit. Then I peeled a tangerine slowly, doing a silly dance, eating the segments with my mouth open so he could see the chewed-up orange mush in my teeth and tongue.

He yelled, 'Hey! You're gonna get done for that.'

'Mum said I could have one.'

'Where's mine then? Come on, gimme one. If you can have one, then so can I.'

He stamped his feet, blowing on his hands; his nose was red

and running. Eventually, of course, I let him in, opening the dining-room window so he could climb through as the front and back doors were all locked to keep out strangers. Gus came inside and said *you took your bloody time*, but his anger abated as he ate a tangerine.

We were bold enough to wander around the whole house, to snoop about and look in our parents' wardrobe, to hang out in the living room. We turned on the big stereo in the lounge and listened to music on the radio, loudly. Elvis was on, I distinctly remember that. We played cowboys through the swinging saloon doors, and when we were shot we collapsed across the lounge and threw ourselves backwards over the couch. We started playing with things on the shelves. A miniature barrel that looked like a beer barrel but had nothing in it and a soda fountain that made a whoosh noise when you pulled the handle.

But it was me, I reached up and I picked up the glass and started pretending to drink from it and that's when it snapped at the stem. The glass that broke wasn't even glass, it was made of plastic. It was a trick, a joke glass of brandy you tipped to your lips and nothing came out, the liquid trapped in a double layer of plastic. It was quite realistic, though; Patrick had got it in a joke shop, maybe one summer in a Hastings gift shop. I remember my legs went to water and my heart leapt in my throat as we stood in horror with the broken joke glass in our hands. We tried to reassemble it. The stem had snapped, but we balanced it against the wall so it looked like it was OK from a distance. Patrick hadn't paid much attention to the joke glass for a long while; it was a bit dusty and we thought he wouldn't notice – at least until we could get our hands on some glue.

Sheer and horrible panic engulfed us both then at that exact moment, when we heard the car coming up the drive. So they wouldn't see us through the living-room window, we dived behind the sofa and snaked across the lounge to switch the radio off and then crawled on our stomachs, opening the door a crack to slither through the hall and back into our bedroom. We didn't have time to make sure the sofa was smooth and unruffled and the pile of the carpet was swept straight. I was shaking and my brother lay on the bottom bunk pretending to read. We waited silently, listening for the inevitable, my heart thumping in my chest. Once, when we were in trouble like this for breaking something, I tried to drink a bottle of Indian ink. I only managed a sip, but I would have rather died of ink poisoning than ever face my stepfather's wrath.

The blood was trembling inside my veins. I paced the bedroom, waiting to see if we had got away with *it* or not. I couldn't stand the waiting; I went into the kitchen. My baby sister was crying, red in the face and shrieking. Mum said it was cold outside, that it might snow, more to herself than anyone. She was seeing to my sister and disappearing into their bedroom, leaving me loitering by the kettle, and I pretended I was there to make us all a pot of tea.

'Salena?' Patrick bellowed my name, towering over me.

'Is Gus in the bedroom? How did Gus get in?'

I was cornered. I looked at the kitchen floor as I told him I let him in through the window, and above my head I felt him look down at me with such furious disgust I wished the ground would swallow me up. He opened the very window in question and closed it several times, as if checking the hinges still worked. Then he leant out of the window and inspected the walls, outside and inside, the white carpet, the windowsill, the window ledge, the skirting board for any dirt or damage, for shoe prints or marks, all the while yelling, 'What's the matter with you kids? Are you stupid? Are you stupid or something?'

Whenever he lost his temper, his face flushed reddish and his mouth twisted ugly. He opened a packet of cigarettes and went to put the cellophane in the bin and then he saw the tangerine skins. Two crimes, two huge and terrible crimes. One: climbing in windows. Two: taking fruit. It didn't matter how much I hung my head and began to protest that Mum had said I could have one.

'Yes, one! One! How many did you take? Can you count? Are you stupid?'

Gus was called, and we stood side by side in the living room. As was customary we were told to put our hands outstretched in front of us. My stepfather had his stick, a piece of willow switch. Patrick was also prone to clipping us around the head, which left a horrible stinging in the senses and a sharp heat in the ear.

'What have I told you about taking things without asking?'

I was crying while my brother Gus bit his lips and looked at his shoes.

'Look at me when I am speaking to you.'

My mother stood beside her husband. We were told that we should appreciate the fact that we had a beautiful home, a roof over our heads and food on the table. We were told that Patrick worked very hard to provide for us and my mother told us she was tired of all these fights. She said that we should all try harder and stop making it all so difficult, that we needed to have more respect and gratitude. We were given a couple of whacks across the knuckles with the stick for taking a tangerine and climbing in and out of windows, and were just about to be sent to our rooms without any dinner . . . when Patrick saw the broken joke glass. I froze. Patrick went into a frenzy. He inspected the lounge for other misdemeanours, checking and feeling the back of the television to see if it was hot. Then he felt the back of the stereo and found it warm where we'd been listening to the radio. He noticed everything, that the sofa was ever so slightly off-centre and that a tennis trophy had been moved an inch. He questioned us about a kink in the blinds, a scuff in the white carpet and a mark on the paintwork. Lengthy and terrible tirades inevitably followed.

'Are you stupid? What were you doing in the living room? Why weren't you in your own bedroom? Why did Gus come inside in the first place? Why did you let him in the window? Are you stupid? Where had you been, Gus? Why did you touch my glass? Are you stupid? How dare you play the stereo! Do you know not to touch my things? Are you stupid? Well, are you? Gus, where were you today?'

'The Rec,' Gus said

'The Rec? The Rec? What's its real name? Huh?'

We didn't know the answer and Patrick scoffed and hit us and said, 'What is Rec short for? Are you stupid?'

'Recreation ground?'

With stinging palms and ringing ears, my brother and I were sent to our bedroom in disgrace without any dinner. I seem to remember he set us the task of writing an essay on why it was called the recreation ground. Meanwhile, the row continued burning in the lounge between my mother and Patrick that night. My mother has since told me that they had the biggest fight when she told him he was being petty, that after all it was only two tangerines and a plastic joke glass that was just collecting dust. They fought. Then, when my mother told him he was going over the top, she slapped him, he gave her a good slap back, and all hell broke loose. All we heard was screaming, yelling and then the most awful, deafening, miserable silence.

Lying on his bunk with his back to me, my brother told me it was all my fault. I knew he was right and I was so sorry. Gus hadn't told Patrick it was me who reached up and got the glass down off the shelf, Gus shared the blame. I was weighted, the pockets inside

214

my head rattling with the loose change of guilt. Nobody spoke. There was nothing but the wretched stink of guilt and silence, interrupted by the distant television cheers of Saturday football. I knew Patrick would be slouched in front of the television while Mum slammed pots and pans in the kitchen, both silent and furious. Gus lay still, facing the wall, also silent. I stood in darkness behind the closed bedroom curtains, pressing my nose against the cold windowpane, watching for night and snowfall. My stash of chocolate bars and crackers in the doll's cot at the end of my bed was already depleted. I was hungry, my belly rumbled, but I knew we wouldn't be allowed any dinner, so I filled my hunger with regret. Besides, I felt I deserved to be empty because I was bad. A bleak darkness fell and the bare tree branches made the intimidating shapes and faces of monsters against the inky sky, while black ice coated the roads.

Swings and Slides

At the age of nine, I rehearsed a new sentence: *My father committed suicide.*

When the other children finally found out and asked me how he died, my honest answer slapped the air. I could feel each of them rehearsing that sentence in their minds, fingering the material of those two unfamiliar words: *Committed. Suicide.* A phrase so heavy with purpose, its final meaning, a piece of information that kills conversation, words that meant something difficult and final was committed and done with intention – it was a sentence you couldn't take back or change. I heard the other children whisper *Salena's dad killed himself* and I wished they wouldn't. It was the topic of lunch-break and we were sitting in a huddle. Sheila Sparks touched my arm, and I looked into her round freckled face, at the hollow blue shadows that lived under her eyes. I shook my head. I knew I shouldn't have said a word to anyone – for weeks this was a private conversation I had been keeping with ghosts, with shadows, nightmares and clouds. I was regretting it now. It was as though my classmates were poking about in the private shrine in my head, moving the flowers and knocking over the candles.

It was windy and Sheila's blue eyes became glassy. I focused on her single fat teardrop like a sliding window and through it I could see her brown freckles. Then I patted her patting hand back, sniffed hard and stood up too. What had been a silent sadness was thickening and becoming some new emotion I had no words for. As they discussed my father's suicide, I believe I began to grow angry. News like this was like fresh bait; it reminded me of seagulls swooping down on bins and tearing old chip packets open. A brassy girl called Joanne Brown looked like her mother down the factory; all she was missing was a fag drooping from her lips. I distinctly recall how she folded her arms as she said, 'You'll be all right, girl. Know what? Us lot, we never even ever knew our dad. Know what my mum calls him? She calls him a bass-stud! He is one too! He did a runner as soon as my mum got herself pregnant with my youngest sister. My nana says men are all bass-studs . . . she says it's so!'

I flinched at the way Joanne said bastard, as though it was made of two words: bass/stud. I was also very impressed at the way that word came out of her mouth with such vitriolic ease. We all repeated that magic word and it sounded good in our young mouths and to our soft ears. And the first hard scabs formed inside me and over my raw wound. As the bell rang for the end of lunch break, Kate, another girl in our class, announced spikily, 'What about my dad! Good riddance to him, he may as well be dead, he was a right bass-stud.'

As we walked across the playground Sheila confided, 'We never hear a word from our pa, Mum says our pa was a right bass-stud too . . .'

'My dad was just really unhappy . . .' I began to say.

For a while my classmates tiptoed around me. I am sure they let me win at things, pretended it was my turn when it wasn't. They shared their crisps, fed me segments of oranges and KitKat fingers. I was rarely left alone at breaktimes, I was interrupted when they caught me staring skywards and making out shapes and faces in the clouds. The truth is, we all seemed to have parents who were in some way or other absent and we all had parents who fought. We all lived in a mess of stepfathers, stepmothers and split-up families. Now, looking back, perhaps Anna Parris was my only close friend who had what I considered a sensible and normal family. She had her two real parents who were solid and together, and to me that was the most enviable thing in the world.

* * *

Sheila's mother was a silver-haired firecracker, a tiny woman with a wheezing laugh that ended in a machine-gun cough. She was a fine example of how much fun it can be to have a single parent and she was older than all our mothers. She seemed to have a very different way of doing things from other mums, an old-fashioned way. She washed Sheila's hair in the kitchen sink and let her stay up until past midnight. Mrs Sparks was a chain-smoker who regularly gave the pair of us money to go to the smoky working men's club to get her fags. We loved it in there, nestling up to the boozy bar to buy fags. They sold sweets and pop, and we would loiter there as long as we could without getting noticed, sucking cola bottles, inhaling the stale boozy aroma, blue smoke, foul language, taking in the sight of toothless old men coughing and swigging ales.

Then, with our loot of sweets we would retreat to Sheila's bedroom to make radio plays. I remember having to press the record and play button at the same time as we recorded our harrowing horror stories. The plot usually required an orphan receiving a beating and so we'd create these sound effects by whipping a belt on the bed or slapping our hands together before the microphone. Once finished, we'd hear ourselves on tape and laugh because Sheila did the same voice for all characters, but for the male parts she'd pull a different face, which obviously could not be translated onto audiotape.

I can picture us now, down the park, standing upright on the swings, bending our knees and swinging in unison. And how on warm days we'd spin upside down on the roundabout, sucking on two pence Mr Freeze ice pops as long as our arms, the raspberry flavour dyeing our tongues blue. We'd play *dare, truth, kiss or promise*, taking it in turns to knock on doors and run away or go under a jacket with one of the boys. We kissed boys in the dark orange, furry underworld of their parkas. And we'd kiss them up the top of the slide but only to the count of ten – any longer than that count to ten meant you loved them and you'd have to get married.

Coffee and Sherbet

It was the half-term school holidays and I was passing Tara's house, hurtling down the hill on my bike. When I got to her driveway I felt odd as I remembered I hadn't been there since *that* grey Sunday. The early morning sunlight glinted on the wet black tarmac as I screeched to a halt outside her house. It looked normal: the curtains were open. *Well, since I was here and was passing I thought I'd call for you.* I practised it again, *I was passing on the bike and just thought I'd see if you wanted to come out to play or something,* and then I planned to yawn like it was no big deal if she was busy or if she had plans and I'd leave again.

Nervously, I knocked on the low letterbox of the glass door. It took a while for anyone to answer, then Mr Collins surprised me by coming to the other door, the kitchen door. He looked different; he had longer hair and sleepy eyes. He was in a hurry, grabbing a slurp of coffee, late for somewhere – work? He looked surprised, he knew my name, he acted almost happy to see me. He invited me in and asked how I was and would I like a coffee?

'Coffee?'

Then Mr Collins called Tara, who came in smiling and in her Mickey Mouse nightie. I was suddenly aware of the time. It was way too early for visitors – perhaps both too early after her mother's funeral and too early in the morning – my brother and I went out first thing in the mornings during the school holidays, as if we had school to go to. Most kids didn't come out to play until after *Why Don't You . . .* and the mid-morning cartoons had finished. I felt like I was intruding and I wished I had gone for a nice long bike ride first and killed an hour or two.

'Thought you might wanna visitor today or something . . .' I said, trying to sound casual.

Tara smiled and offered me coffee, telling me, 'I like mine black with six sugars.'

She said this as though she drank coffee all the time and like she was sixteen and all I could say was, 'Same! Me too.'

Her dad hollered from the lounge that he couldn't find his car keys and Tara shouted, 'They're under the newspapers, by the cushion . . .' then shook her head and rolled her eyes and walked towards the doorway to the lounge.

'I'll keep an eye on the kettle in case it boils,' I offered.

'You don't have to watch it, it's electric.'

I looked at her blankly and she explained, 'Electric! It switches itself off automatically.'

She seemed so grown up. She wandered out to help her father find his keys and I could hear them in the other room.

'There.'

'Where?'

'Oh, for crying out loud, Dad . . . here!'

'Oh yeah . . . thanks. What would I do without you, princess!'

Mr Collins said he'd left some money on the side for her lunch. They talked about dinner, Tara said she wanted spaghetti and then he laughed and went out the door saying something like, 'Again? You'll turn into spaghetti one day, no wonder your legs are so long! Spaghetti legs!'

They kissed and said *I love you*, and then he got into his car, beeped the car horn and was gone. Tara's brother was still asleep in his bedroom.

'Take your jacket off then. Come on, let's take our coffees in the lounge.'

I sat in the lounge and I looked at the photos and felt conscious of the silence. Tara reappeared, changed into a stripy T-shirt and purple jeans. She sat with her feet tucked underneath her and held her mug in a cupped way, as though she was warming her hands. I mimicked her. There was a slight awkwardness as I remembered that the last time I was in this house her mum was alive. There was a photo of her on the sideboard. The room was messier than before too, with some clothes on the floor and newspapers, but it was really homely and comfortable. Then Tara asked me if I wanted a bit of jam on toast. We watched telly, a black-and-white Harold Lloyd where he's hanging precariously off the hands of a clock. We talked about school and the netball team we were both in. Well, me as a reserve, Tara actually really on the team. Sitting in her lounge, I remembered how when she first returned to school she'd quietly thanked me for the card I made her and how I playfully punched her arm and told her it was a real American dollar bill. Now, though, we did not mention the death thing, my death thing or hers. Suddenly, it dawned on me we didn't have to. Instead we deliberated over how to spend the day; it had started to rain again and the school holidays yawned ahead. I suggested we do some colouring and she looked at me and screwed her face up.

'Colouring? You are joking?'

'Yeah. I just thought . . .'

'Colouring?'

Tara started laughing, and then coughing, and I laughed too, nervously. I felt like an idiot for saying colouring. My mum had told me if I went to see Tara that she might want to be gentle, she might want someone to sit with her quietly, to do some colouring or a collage. Clearly, Tara thought colouring books were for babies. She made us more black coffee, spooning in heaped teaspoons of instant granules and white sugar. Then she washed up the breakfast things, sighing and telling me how she needed her coffee to get her up in the morning. It did taste nice the way she made coffee with six sugars. It felt as though the house was her own, and we were both much older, and I suddenly blurted, 'We should play that we are really old and both sixteen and this is our house . . .'

'Yeah, I know. Let's say we're seventeen even, and we live together and share a house, yeah, ace . . . and let's pretend we have to get ready to go to a disco.' Tara flapped her wet hands excitedly, suds went everywhere and she pulled off her rubber gloves,

'Oh, I know, I know! Listen to this then!'

Tara turned the TV off and beckoned me down the hallway and into her bedroom. She had a tape of Adam and the Ants' 'Stand And Deliver'. On came the rolling drum beats and we danced. We rewound it and played it again and again, high as kites on coffee and sugar. We put on eye shadow and lip gloss, we tied our hair up in colourful elastic bands, and bounced madly on her bed and sang along at the top of our voices. We were doing the hand gestures and the dance that particular song required – a stomping pose with the crossing of the arms in front of the face.

After that first caffeine-fuelled day of dancing and lip gloss, that particular holiday I went around to Tara's almost every day. We sang and danced to Sheena Easton, Eurythmics, *Grease*, Kate Bush and our favourite, Adam and the Ants. We drank lots of sweet coffee and played that we had jobs as secretaries. We sat opposite each other typing on imaginary typewriters. We somehow converted half of her bedroom into an office and the other half into the disco where we'd pretend to go after work to meet our two boyfriends and dance. We chewed gum with our mouths open noisily and pretended to talk on the phone to each other, taking it in turns to be each other's boss or boyfriend.

'Yours are really growing now.' Tara said to me one day.

'No, they're not, not like yours,' I replied dolefully.

'Yours are! Look, so are mine, look at mine . . .'

Tara closed her curtains and lifted her T-shirt to show me her nipples. They were swollen to different sizes, like two sweet plums pointing out in different directions, pink and mauve-coloured. I thought hers were amazing and I told her, 'Mine hurt sometimes. Do you really think they're growing?'

'Mine hurt sometimes too but that means they're growing. Look at them, yours have grown loads lately. Look at them now, show me them and I'll show you what I mean . . .'

I lifted up my T-shirt to show her and we both stared at my bumpy nipples in the mirror.

'My mum calls them bee stings,' I complained, and then realised I said 'mum', but Tara grinned.

'My gran's got whoppers and she thinks mine are going to be big as hers one day!'

We stood side by side with our tops up under our chins to compare in the mirror.

'See mine were like that, like yours at first, but yours are coming along nicely now . . .'

Tara sounded like she knew what she was talking about. The golden news that mine were growing normally too gave me a rising bubble of excitement inside. Tara taught me how to smoke sherbert. We'd buy Refreshers — oblong yellow fruit chew sweets with sherbert in the middle – and she'd break them open and roll the sherbet in the sweet wrapper to make cigarettes. Then, when they were rolled up, she'd gently blow the sherbert out the other end so it looked like real smoke. Tara also showed me how to take two rolled-up socks and twist them into your vest to make a bra. She taught me that if you tuck the extra vest material up the middle, pull it through and down to make a knot, your vest becomes a kind of sexy bra top with the socks sitting in place like real boobs. After the disco dancing, we would lie on the bed and take it in turns to be the boy and the girl and pretend to kiss, with our mouths closed and our heads smooching mechanically from side to side. We took our socks out of our tops and put them down the front of our trousers so we'd know which of us was being the boy and which was the girl: Sandy or Steve, Candy or Chris. We'd get it wrong and make Chris and Steve kiss.

'Oh, Chris, I mean Steve . . .'

'No, I'm Sandy now . . .'

'No, hang on, my socks aren't in right then.'

I have such vivid and happy memories of lovely Tara and of that particular school holiday. We'd both lost a parent, but she seemed to be getting on with living and I followed her shining example. I remember her once showing me photos of her mother and sharing memories with me, but only once, while we waited for the kettle to boil and switch itself off.

We were almost ten years old, but we escaped into caffeine and sugary bubblegum play days, each day inspecting our growing pains. It was all glittery silver disco and lip gloss, it was all pretending we were not where we were, and for that school holiday we were really old and grown up and all of seventeen.

Game, Set and Match

It was June, and although my tenth birthday was coming up that month, June really only meant one thing in our household: Wimbledon. In our street everyone got Wimbledon fever, and that particular year everyone was tennis crazy. John McEnroe was making televised tennis dramatic with his outbursts, his infamous tantrums, coining the catchphrase *'You cannot be serious!'* which we in turn mimicked and cried out while lobbing tennis balls across the road at each other. After school and under long, rose-perfumed, midsummer evenings we hurled grassy-green balls against walls and sent them crashing against garage doors. Tennis balls got everywhere, on rooftops and in guttering. We bounced them so high they hurtled over the telephone wires.

Sometimes I went with my mother and stepfather to the tennis club. While my parents competed in tournaments, I'd push my sister in her pram and talk with Aunt Doreen. Having a tennis coach as a stepfather ignited an ambition to play tennis to please him. I tried, but I was never good enough. I was heavy-handed and lacked any of the natural skill or patience required. My stepfather even looked a bit like John McEnroe; he had similar curly hair and wore a headband. I saw sharing his enthusiasm for the game as a way to maybe creep into his affections, and for that season I even harboured aspirations to be a ball girl at Wimbledon one day. It was the only time I really ever talked about him to my friends. I cringe to admit this, but at school I might boast, *My stepfather is a tennis coach. He actually goes to Wimbledon every year for the special dinner and for strawberries and champagne and everything.*

On the morning of my tenth birthday I opened a present from my mother of new running shoes. They were two shades of pink and I loved them. I was excited that morning at breakfast, skipping about in the kitchen in my new trainers and pyjamas. I told my stepfather, 'It's my birthday today!'

'Is it? How old are you now then?'

I thought he was joking so waited for him to smile. When he didn't, I replied, 'I'm ten, and that means I am now in double figures.'

Still I waited for him to smile, to say he knew how old I was really and *happy birthday.* I held up my leg to show him my new trainers. He nodded but, clear and sharp as glass, I remember feeling ignored. Mum had made a fuss, telling me it was an important and monumental birthday because I was nearly a teenager. Patrick flicked back at the newspaper, crunching on his toast.

*　*　*

At his tennis club there was an older girl who befriended me. Lucy was at least seventeen or eighteen. She wore her blonde hair in a sporty bouncy ponytail and had smooth brown legs. She was being coached by my stepfather and would often ask me to walk with her. We'd take our rackets and balls and walk, bouncing them off the grit on the nearby athletic track. Walking around the circles of white chalk lines, she'd grill me about my stepfather. Lucy asked me about my mother and how long they had been married. She talked a lot, in fact Lucy talked too much – she told me that my stepfather was a brilliant coach, an inspiration, that he was so smart and handsome and on and on she would blather . . . I played the dumb kid and took all the Coke floats and bubblegum screwdrivers Lucy wanted to buy me. It irritated me how much she idolised Patrick.

A few weeks later, I remember overhearing Mum on the phone complaining that Patrick was always out at the tennis club and coming in late. Then I heard Patrick and my mother rowing about some girl who had a crush on him. Later my mother quizzed me about these weekly walks; she asked what Lucy talked to me about. I told my mother everything, I told mum the truth, that Lucy thought Patrick was the bee's knees.

The Nightmare

The Montys were Patrick's parents – my step-grandparents. They were Irish Catholics and lived in Surrey. Ma Monty was a scatty, curly redhead who wore her hair in a bouffant bird's nest balanced on her head. Pa Monty was a stern bruiser of a naval man. Pa Monty was an ex-boxer too and he liked to clench his fist and shake it at us. He'd stand above us like a boxer and growl, 'I'll give you a zonker.'

He was tough-talking, hard and weathered. They were both a bit scary and mean from a child's-eye view, but they meant well. Ma Monty was partially deaf but never wore her hearing aid and so misheard everything. She and my mother were almost as bad as each other. I can picture them now in the kitchen cooking together, boiling vegetables or making gravy out of the grease of roasted meats, both with their glasses steamed up over the stove, hovering over a huge broiled ham.

Mum would start, 'I'm just going to see if the potatoes are done.'

'What?'

'The potatoes.'

'What tomatoes?'

'Doesn't matter . . .'

'Hang on, Lorna, let me see to the potatoes first.'

'That's what I said.'

'What?'

'What?'

Then they'd collide at the stove, both holding a fork to test the spuds. Meanwhile, in the lounge, Pa Monty gave us swimming lessons. He taught us how to swim front crawl through the air. Lying on my belly across the dining chair, I learned how to straighten up, keep my body in line and scoop the water away with my hands and how to turn my head to breathe. On the walls of their home were framed black-and-white pictures, now faded to yellow, of my stepfather as a schoolboy in an old-fashioned blazer and cap. Next to them stood pictures of a younger, more dapper Ma and Pa. In one picture, a ship dominated the background, while Pa Monty stood upright and smart in his naval uniform and Ma Monty turned to the side and posed holding his arm. Even in black and white, she looked vivid. A blazing redhead in scarlet lipstick and fur coat and heels, her stockings with black lines running up the backs of her long legs. Now in his dotage, Pa still stood to attention. The skin of his face was lined with purplish threads from sea, salt winds and weather. Ma Monty still wore pillar-box red lipstick and a fur coat and she jangled with gold and pearls just to go to the corner shop every day.

* * *

That June then, after my tenth birthday, it was Wimbledon. We were to stay in with Ma and Pa Monty while Patrick and Mum went out for the night to the Wimbledon dinner. My stepfather was in a tux and bow tie. My mother looked stunning in her new cocktail dress.

It was royal peacock-blue chiffon and it floated around her. I thought it was the kind of dress Princess Diana might wear.

It was a small house, so Gus and my stepbrother would share the box room and I was sharing a room with my parents and Jo-Ann. I was lying on the makeshift bed on the floor and that is when I heard something I wish I hadn't, words too brutal for a child aged only ten. I stayed quiet and as still as possible, facing the wall, eavesdropping and letting them think I was asleep. Mum was seeing to my baby sister, and she and Ma Monty were talking in loud hushed whispers.

I heard, 'What, Lorna?'

'Hung himself . . . ?'

I could hear the hiss of whispers, their jaws clicking, the wetness of mouthed words, and caught only parts of sentences.

'. . . the staircase . . .'

I had the covers over my face as I listened to snatches of what was being said.

'It snapped.'

'Snapped?'

'What?'

'Cracked . . .'

'Radiator at the bottom of the stairs . . .'

'What?'

'It broke . . . split clean . . .'

'Ooh no!'

'. . . bottom of the stairs, imagine? . . .'

'That's terrible, Lorna . . .'

Jo was being given her milk and I heard her gurgling, soothed by the breast. The deaf women whispered loudly for a few moments more like this, then I heard my mother say *shush* and there was a very long pause and then they left the bedroom. I lay in bed and thought about that for a new sentence: *my father hung himself.*

Whenever I had asked my mother how my father died she had avoided telling me any exact details; she just used the word *suicide.* Now I could imagine a noose, the knot and the thread unravelling, the sound as the rope snapped, the crack of the broken bannister and Dad falling, falling and falling. I saw him landing with a thud, his head split open on the sharp edge of the radiator and the brain and blood oozing down the sharp edges of the world below, the carpet, the walls, all thick black blood and the insides of raw sausages. I tormented myself with horrible details, brain tissue and bone, muscle and matter. I pictured a staircase, a balcony and a hallway in a house I had never seen. My father jolting and his feet kicking then swinging lifeless.

He's hanging and I am scared to look up past his feet to his face. I just watch his swinging feet and then I hear a snap . . . he is falling . . . thud . . . radiator . . . crack . . . dark blood.

Now I had a whole film to play. I tortured myself picturing my father wobbling on the top of some stairs as though he was jumping from a burning ship that is careering into an iceberg and either way, fire or ice, it's clearly the end. He couldn't stay and burn, he wouldn't survive if he tried to swim. He deliberately jumps to certain death.

I imagined the texture of gnarled, thick brown rope against the skin and then I imagined him trying to use his tie or a belt. I had difficulty imagining him knowing something as practical as how to tie a noose, but boys often know things like that. Maybe he didn't tie it well enough and that's why it snapped . . . *of course . . . that's why it snapped.* I imagined him waiting for an opportune moment. Self-murder would take purpose and planning. Pre-mediatation. I put myself in his shoes and wondered how he spent his last few hours.

Did he go out walking that dark December afternoon?

Let's say he did. It would have been nearly Christmas; the streets would have been garish with a shrill chorus of carol singers, that grating, incessant 'Jingle Bells' pouring from all the shops. I imagined him going to buy cigarettes and then finding himself walking by the water and stopping to buy rope at a chandlers by the docks. I tried to imagine the misery and violence he must have felt towards himself. Perhaps, though, he felt eerily calm knowing he'd made a choice, perhaps it was soothing to know that it would all soon be over. During those last hours he must have been desperate, waiting for the end of waiting; waiting for the raging pain to go away, waiting for a reason not to live, waiting for a reason not to die.

I imagine Dad on the top of the stairs; he swigs neat brandy straight out of the bottle. I imagine him weeping and finding there are yet more tears under there. I imagine every bitter swig taking some of the waiting away, dowsing the fear and the misery in hard liquor. I imagine him convincing himself everyone would be better off without him, that it was for all our good and that none of us would even care. Then I see him suddenly calm, silent and still. With conviction and surety, he sniffs hard and wipes his wet face and grinds his cigarette out. He stands, makes a knot, fastens it rough and tight around his throat. That was it. He made a decision and let go . . . fade to black.

69 Pink Pass

It was a crisp and bright Tuesday on 11 December 2007. The sky was cloudless, truly blue, as we drove through Bristol. The winter sun cast long, cartoon-like shadows. We had seen a sky dog, a beautiful flash of rainbow in the distance, and we drove towards it, taking it to be a good omen. December the eleventh was the anniversary of my father's death and also my friend Sam's birthday. As Sam drove, his helium-filled birthday balloon bumped lazily against the rear window. I had always imagined I would do this journey on my own. I was grateful for his company.

We travelled in silence, gliding through the traffic. I felt I was following a path, being led by fate and destiny. I took nothing for granted: my eyes were open, my senses were alert. I found myself admiring the beauty in pedestrian things: sunlight on the river, faces in the rocks by the suspension bridge. We nosed our way through the city towards Shirehampton, counting magpies, finding significance in one for sorrow and two for joy. Uncanny road names gave us odd clues that we were close. The hairs stood up on my neck as we passed Hung Road, and then a Springfield Avenue.

My brother Gus stood alone at the iron gates smoking a roll-up. He looked lost and cold, tight around his features. He was relieved we'd arrived, he said, he'd been there since nine that morning. We'd arranged to meet at the graveyard gates at midday but he'd got there keen and early. He'd found it, he said and nodded: this was it. It wasn't a wild goose chase; this really was the final resting place of our father. I felt a quick, sharp wave of envy that Gus had been there first, without me, that he'd had time alone with the grave. Gus showed us to the local shops and I went into a flower shop and bought pink freesias and a small pink rose bush. The roses, I decided, were from Mum. My father's plot address is 69 Pink Pass. Even in death his grave number is loaded with innuendo. When I telephoned and told my mother, she said, *That's your dad for you, he was always the one with both the wife and the bit on the side. He just couldn't make up his mind what he wanted.*

When we entered the cemetery gates, magpies flew in pairs above us. This is it then, this is where he is, I remember thinking, I am going to see my father once and for all. I had telephoned ahead and the cemetery caretaker was there to show us to the plot. Although Gus knew the way, we followed him, walking in single file. I walked last, I walked slowly, I wasn't sure how I would feel to see it. I was afraid I would feel nothing. I was afraid I would feel everything. For all my life I had imagined this moment in film noir images. In my mind I always imagined I would be doing this alone under a thundery black sky, collapsing melodramatically to my knees, dragging at clumps of wet grass, sodden earth under my nails, trying to climb in or dig him up, drunk and inconsolable with rage, with fury and grief. But there was no stormy weather, no melodrama. The wintry light was primrose yellowish, the cemetery serene, peaceful and calm. On a modest, arched headstone of grey shiny granite I found the words:

PAUL GODDEN
POET & MUSICIAN
1941–1981

So, there you are. I thought it was nice that they included Poet
and Musician. I am sure he'd have liked that. For a moment I felt
as though I was seeing my past and my future, my own grave. I
stared at the name on the stone and did the maths – he was only
forty years old. *How long do I have left?* I looked at my brother, who
looked down at the grave. We stared in silence at the headstone
and the grass for a very long time. It was tidy, the gravestone was
tasteful. I imagined his funeral, more than twenty-five years ago,
and I wondered who had been there. I started to feel faintly embarrassed and awkward, as though I was gatecrashing. I had made all
these plans of how I would like to react and they all suddenly
seemed far-fetched. My father was long gone; he wasn't here at all,
not really. I wasn't sure what to say, so instead I crouched down
and kept quiet and thought about the person my mother loved to
describe, the bones and the heart of the man six feet under the
ground, under the grass roots. In my head I said, *There you are, there
you are, I found you finally, nice to meet you again . . .*

I knelt on the wet cold grass and touched the letters. Although
they were engraved into the granite, some of the white paint had
faded. No religious waffle or even a *greatly missed father and son*, just
his name, his poetry and his music. There were no other flowers
there, no evidence of recent visits. I was jumpy and half-hopeful
that we'd be caught here, that someone might catch us trespassing
in the past, others he'd loved, others he'd left behind. Gus said he
thought he had seen a young lady earlier who may have been
someone, but she went to a different grave. We both dared to hope
that by finding the dead we might find the living. And then suddenly

I felt ridiculous. I felt self-piteous, pathetic, and I hated myself for making such a fuss. *Is that all there is then? Is this all there is then, Dad?* I felt cheated.

Directly above our heads the sky was a chilled December blue. Two planes crossed paths, white lines making an X to mark the spot, or maybe it was a kiss. I sat with my legs crossed on the cold muddy grass, running my thumb over the letters on the headstone. I brushed it clean, the ledge where the flowers go. I heard Gus saying that the stone was protected by the hedge beside it. He said Dad's was the only grave without morning frost. I placed the pink freesia and the roses beside my brother's pink carnations. I took a swig of brandy and then poured some on the earth at the head end. *There you go, cheers, Dad.* Sam asked if we'd like it if he planted the roses; he said they'd last longer. I stood back and watched as Sam knelt down and dug into the earth with a stick, getting mud on his hands. As he jabbed the stick into the earth, I pushed away horrible thoughts of being underground and seeing the stick from the underside, the view of the tip of the stick from inside my father's coffin. In horrified flashes I pictured my father's skeleton. Sam poured water on the freshly planted rose bush and I told him indignantly he had just watered down Dad's brandy. I felt an awful aching in my chest and throat. I squirmed inside, hurting. I asked Sam to put the roses in straight, they were slightly askew and too far to the right side. This was me trying to get things perfect, lost in a compulsion that it mattered, that we had to get things in the right order. Sam dug up the roses and shifted them along to the left a bit.

'Better?' Sam asked gently and touched my sleeve.

I nodded. 'Yes, that's better.' I was still thinking about the watered-down brandy. I took another little sip and poured some more straight onto the roses and the earth.

Sam wandered off to leave us alone and I felt Gus put his arm across my shoulder.

'I cried when I came on my own this morning, but there were workmen and I . . .'

Gus didn't finish his sentence. I heard him crying. Just like when we were children, his weeping moved me. It sounded like off-key laughter. I wanted it to be laughter. I was hoping he'd laugh instead. I kept my jaw clenched tight until it started aching. Hearing him crying, my eyes grew hot, but I pushed it all down. I whimpered gruffly, a short and soundless sob.

Then Gus said thank you. He said in a broken voice, 'Thank you for finding him, Salena.' Then he said, 'Oh dear,' and sniffed, holding me close around the shoulders. It was Gus and me again, Gus and me and our real dad. This was what was meant that day when we went fishing all those years ago. This was the unsaid, this was the conversation, and this was what we wanted to find together.

I closed my eyes tight as a school bell rang on the other side of the fence. The silent cemetery was littered with the sounds of children's laughter and a cacophony of kids shouting and singing. I liked that my father could hear children at play. Gus wandered off towards the car, and when I was alone at my father's grave, I took out a piece of writing from this book. I read the last paragraph under my breath to the headstone and saw it for what it was: I saw that once upon a time there was one day, it was a once-in-a-lifetime moment, and now I was here. That was all we ever had, my father and I – I was a thirty-five-year-old woman, standing in a cemetery staring at the letters on a headstone, trying to make sense of my need to see this, rationalising my sense of the importance of counting magpies, sky dogs, flight-path kisses and street names. I started to weep but pushed it down again and coughed. I told myself *cowboys don't cry.* I don't know, I have no idea why I was trying to be a tough cowboy about it.

I wondered if that was all there was to a life and a death. Perhaps the most we can hope for is that twenty-five years after we die, someone may remember us, that someone will come looking for us and put pink roses on our grave. All in the name of what could have been, all for the promise of those *what if*s and *but*s. Is that the most we can hope for? I felt emptied and said goodbye and walked away. I left the writing in a sealed plastic wallet by the flowers and walked toward the exit, hands in pockets and shoulders hunched, shivering. I couldn't help looking back to see my father's granite headstone, so small next to the grander graves, and so very small in the grand scale of things. I faltered and found it impossible to actually leave and for a few minutes I was that lost little nine-year-old girl, looking for her father in a crowd, looking at his grave among all the others.

I remembered all the anniversaries and all the Decembers before. Days when I had wandered into random churchyards to cry at the feet of strangers' headstones and lit candles in unfamiliar churches. There were times at school when I'd sit in my classes silent and withdrawn for that day. The times when I had walked miserably along the city streets of London alone, searching for ways to numb this feeling I got on this date every year on this day. I was pale as the rain and thin as December, and always so sad and so skint in the weeks before the holidays. How I walked around Soho, with Christmas music jarring me, surrounded by normal, happy, plump holiday people with rosy cheeks and bellies warmed with mulled wine and mince pies. There were times I sat and drank by fires, burning writings to my father so he could read them in the smoke. And times as a teenager I'd cry and throw pebbles into the sea at Hastings, searching for him and a way to let go and a way to heal.

I bowed my head and wept into my scarf and coat collar, kicking a stone at a puddle through fat hot tears. I found I couldn't leave the graveyard. I kept looking back and then walking towards him. I couldn't let go, I couldn't just leave. *I don't want to go now I have found you, Dad.* In the back of my head I heard the reply: *You are on your own now, kiddo.* And with that I cried, *Am I on my own now, is this really goodbye? Will I still be watched over? Will I be able to sleep with the lights off? Will I still wake up sometimes and feel something, someone, at the end of my bed?*

Perhaps you were never there. Maybe I really am blessed and lucky and it wasn't my father's intervention that ever helped or guided me. Perhaps I was always on my own. Perhaps there are no such things as ghosts and guardian angels – *you are on your own now, kiddo* – maybe we were all always alone.

I heard children laughing and playing in the sunshine in the school next door, alerting me to life and the poetry and beauty in living things. I heard the squawk of a crow, and as my tears dried I watched it take flight overhead. I looked up and felt a rush of relief, a certainty that everything was going to be better. I said several times out loud, *it's all going to be all right now.* I felt like I had closed a door and opened another inside myself. It was as though this wouldn't hurt quite as much again. This was the beginning of healing, the start of this story and not the end. I finally had the evidence I needed. Maybe now I would no longer look for my dad in strangers' faces or seek him across a crowded world. I had been given the chance to say hello and goodbye properly and I walked away under the canopy of tall trees this time without looking back.

✳ ✳ ✳

We drove away in convoy towards London. Behind us and in the west, the winter sun set in a vivid and breathtaking fire of scarlet and fuchsia. The birthday balloon bumped against the car window. At the back of my mind I remembered a poem I had been writing, 'Today I Found My Father', and as we drove, I remembered the ending lines:

And the nine-year-old inside me,
the lost little girl is found,
she is released like balloons into the sky.

I played with the mud on my fingers and under my nails. I looked over at Sam's hands, filthy on the car steering wheel, and at the muddied knees of our jeans, and felt somehow comforted, that we were both covered with earth from my father's grave. There was something real, something tangible about it. I smoked a cigarette and listened to the radio but whenever I closed my eyes I saw my father's granite headstone. With the lull of the engine and the car heating I started to feel sleepy, memorising every moment and detail, the exact fading letters, the rose and pink petals against the flecked grey headstone. I put that image firmly in my mind, just as though it was a photograph of his face that I wouldn't allow to fade. Just like the eternal picture I have imprinted of the time I looked into my father's eyes, how he crouched to my height and looked into my face, and I swear I saw love, and that was all we ever had, Dad.

SPRING

The knee-high banana-yellow boots

Mickey

When we visited the Montys in Woking I had a friend called Mickey. I must briefly mention her here because I never forgot her. I wanted to be like her. When I think of her now, I imagine her at Glastonbury or Burning Man Festival with a whole crew and circus – she was a wild and free spirit with a magnetic charisma. Mickey had long black curly hair that fell in beautiful ringlets, untidily, out of her ponytail. It was a great friendship because we'd just pick up where we left off each holiday and it was always as if no time had passed, it was as if time were rubber.

Mickey whistled and walked with a confident gait, slouching with her hands in her pockets. She was skinny and shabby and always had holes in her plimsolls. I liked that about her. I was scruffy and had holes in my world too. She spoke like a Cockney, dropping her Hs and saying *I ain't going . . .* rather than *I en't going . . .* the Midlands slang I used.

Mickey couldn't walk past anything without investigating it. If she saw a low branch, she had to swing off it. If there was a post, she had to try to leapfrog it. She skidded on any surface that promised you'd get a good slide out of it, especially in supermarkets. She always had some bruises or a cut covered with a dirty plaster. She rooted around in bins, skips and gutters, stuffing things in her pockets, winking at me and telling me that these items would mean something or come in useful later. Abandoned shopping trolleys were a favourite. We had many precarious, white-knuckle rides in shopping trolleys we'd found. I remember on one occasion Gus and I pushing her up a steep hill and then letting go. The trolley zoomed away and we ran down after it and found her in a crumpled pile in some bushes at the bottom of the hill. She just brushed herself off and laughed crazily. We asked if she was hurt, but she found it hilarious and wanted us to do it again, and, well that was Mickey.

I remember we'd go to visit Truck-Man. He was an old tattooed hippy with long white hair and a grey beard and he lived in the car park behind the shops. His truck was not always parked there, but when it was, he'd let Mickey and me nose about inside. It was bigger than you'd think inside. It had a real toilet, a sink and a bed, loads of cassettes, books and his guitar. He sat on the bunk and rolled cigarettes while we poked about, and he let us sit up in the cab and talk on his CB radio. *Roger Roger . . . over and out.* He said he could hear the police signal on it and we tried to listen in. He showed us how he could make tea in a stained chipped mug and demonstrated how the electric kettle worked. We thought it was cool to be allowed to look inside his truck, with the incense burning and the Indian tie-dye wall hangings of elephants and monkeys. I remember the tapes he played too and in particular that song about the Marrakesh Express. We watched him playing guitar with his long yellow dirty nails with a roll-up drooping from his coppery-grey tar-stained beard.

Heading to the swings, Mickey said she'd like a truck like that one day.

'Imagine if you had one of them, you'd be free to go anywhere. House on wheels, you could just pitch up and take a snooze, then have a cup of tea and drive off as free as a bird!'

As she said this, she made a little run and extended her arms like wings as if to fly.

'You could travel the world with no cares, just you and your truck, your own kettle and make tea and stuff, you could even go to France.'

'You could go further than France even!'

'Yeah, yeah, Sal! You could go further than France even!'

'America.'

'Yeah, America, imagine that . . .'

'How could you drive to America, though?'

'Dunno . . . under the Atlantic? I know, I know! Mine would be a submarine truck.'

'Ha! Then mine, mine would be a flying truck.'

'If mine goes underwater and yours is a flying truck, I reckon I'd like yours more if it's going to fly.'

'I'll tell you what, let's both get one of each, yeah . . . Or, I know . . . we could get trucks that can fly and go underwater at the same time.'

We stole matches from Pa Monty's garden shed and went down into the woods behind the swings. We had sour fizzy cola bottles, salt and shake crisps and cans of dandelion and burdock in her rucksack. Then Mickey taught me to smoke. She sniffed knowingly and, with her dirty bitten nails and bony fingers, showed me how to straighten out a fag butt she'd found in the gutter. She lit it and took the first drag, making it look easy, then passed it to me. I tried puffing on it, but it was disgusting and it made me cough. Mickey took it back, holding the ashy butt expertly between her thumb and finger, and gave it a good pull, then she collapsed in fits of coughing, her eyes watering as I banged her on the back.

We were always busy with mischief and on missions, making fires with cardboard, crouching down and blowing into our cupped hands over smoking twigs and melting plastic. We stank of smoke and tree bark and our clothes would get stained moss-green and filthy. Leaning logs against trees we karate-kicked them to break them up for firewood and we smashed up dank wooden crates. We spent hours in the woods by the river, amongst the broken prams, shopping trolleys and junk. Best of all, we climbed inside a burnt-out, rusted old car, with ivy on the bonnet and growing inside, but the steering wheel and gear stick still intact.

We never talked about any of the outside world or the crazy adults – why would we? It was about escaping, running away, smoking and making fires. Instead we felt tough if we managed to smoke fag butts without coughing. We imagined driving to wild places in that mildewed, rotten and rusted-up car, which to us would be capable of being both a submarine and a plane. We had a secret camp and a burnt-out car in the undergrowth, we didn't need nothing and we didn't need nobody. We acted like we could sleep out there any time we liked – but we never did.

Six Times Six

My stepfather had a special stick, a switch reserved for hitting us. I have no idea where he got it, but it appeared in our bedroom one day and was thereafter used mostly to hit our outstretched hands. I can distinctly remember Gus and I putting it precariously behind the heavy books on the top bookshelf, hoping the encyclopaedias would fall on Patrick's head the next time he reached for it. Needless to say the books never came crashing down and the use of the switch continued. My mother wasn't usually witness to this. Looking back, I suppose if she heard a commotion coming from our room, she assumed it was Patrick sorting out another sibling squabble, and that was often the case.

Our stepfather terrorised us. I was frightened of him. If he found some mud on the precious white carpet, he would come into our bedroom, inspect the soles of our shoes to identify the culprit, then demand we polish all the shoes as punishment. We didn't own many shoes, but we had to polish them perfectly to his almost military liking. On other occasions he'd come into our room, stand in front of my brother and me, and demand answers to maths problems.

'Six times six?'

We looked at him blankly, neither of us daring to speak or move. I knew if I said the answer, then I would have to watch Gus getting hit, and if Gus answered correctly, then I would get it. Gus would always remain stoic and silent as Patrick would repeat: 'Six times six?'

'Thirty-six!'

'I was asking your brother! Are you stupid?'

After my father's death I often found myself in terrible rages and sometimes I was unable to contain angry tears. It took years to try to learn how to manage or comprehend these emotions. It took even more years to recognise this was unresolved trauma and grief. One night, my brother and mother were both out, I was alone in my bedroom and looking for a worksheet I had to finish for school homework. I couldn't find it and I began ripping the bedroom apart as I looked for it, working myself up into floods of furious tears. It felt as though there was a pressure valve in my head, and once I opened it a little bit, much more would follow than anticipated. I screwed up and tore apart papers that were the wrong ones. I even bit them and jumped on them and slapped inanimate objects as though they were hiding my particular piece of paper on purpose. I hit the side of my own head with my fists and sobbed. Eventually, I collapsed onto my knees, hitting myself in the temple with my fist. My teeth were clenched so tightly that my jaw hurt. I was curled over, growling and bawling into the carpet.

I looked up when I heard the bedroom door fly open. My stepfather stood there and saw me in this hysterical mess, amongst the ripped paper all over the floor and the books all strewn. Seeing him there made me howl even harder. He shouted and told me off, telling me to stop making a racket, to shut up and stop grizzling. He was furious and said that I had woken my baby sister. Terrified by the man, I cried even louder, my head hot and throbbing. He must have seen I had worked myself into a state, but he lost any patience he may have had. He picked me up by the scruff of the neck so I was standing, my legs buckling under me. He shook me and asked me again if I was going to be quiet, and then he lifted and threw me down, somehow clouting me mid-air. I landed face first on the bedroom floor. He yelled at me to bloody keep it down, to clear all my crap away and behave. Then, as suddenly as he had appeared, he left. I picked myself up from the floor and felt my mouth. My bottom lip was bleeding a little. I looked in the mirror and the sight of blood stopped me dead. I was stunned. It was stinging. I looked again at my lip in the mirror and sucked it. I blew my nose and saw blood on the tissue. I examined it, then threw it in the bin. I felt very calm as I tidied up the torn pieces of paper I had thrown around the room. I put everything neatly back in its proper place. I was numb – the physical shock and fear somehow counterbalancing or quelling the fury. Once the bedroom was immaculately tidy, I made my bed and then lay on top of it and stared blankly at the ceiling, waiting for tomorrow to start.

I never spoke of that night or other times like these; I didn't tell Mum. I felt like I had made a racket and had a tantrum and I deserved it. I knew I had to learn to control this rage, the fury and the grief I was feeling. Looking back, I now know I was a child in mourning. I suppose this attention from my stepfather was better than being ignored. His temper was his feedback. To be honest, I am not sure how I would have reacted if my stepfather had ever put an arm around me or hugged me; any affection or kind word from him would have been alien.

Around this time a double bedsheet was hung across the centre of our bedroom. We dismantled the bunk beds to make two separate single beds. The sheet was to give the illusion of two bedrooms in one. We were running out of ideas and outgrowing the rooms of the bungalow — and of this story.

The Red Suitcase

Under the bottom bunk, Gus's bed, was my mother's red suitcase. It was battered and covered with peeling old stickers of faraway countries. On rainy days, I'd remember it, drag it out and go through its secrets. There was an old photo album with *Cyprus* written on the cover in gold lettering. Inside were photographs of my mother as a skinny teenager, her cocked head looking too big for her body and her face not yet grown to fit her big smile. She was dressed like Nanny, the two of them in identical outfits, wearing lace gloves, standing side by side, squinting in the sun.

My favourite photos were a sequence of pictures of a wild-looking fancy-dress party. I didn't recognise anyone but my mother. In one picture she stuck her tongue out at the lens. In another, a man with a comic moustache picked her up, twirled her around and nearly dropped her. The party people were all laughing, dancing the twist, elbows stuck out like chickens. My mum was dressed like a pirate, wearing a beard and an eye patch. I wished I could turn the volume up on these images and hear all the laughter and the music. And later in the album there were the few photographs of us as babies with Dad.

A flat yellow envelope held all my mother's stunning modelling shots and contact sheets. She was so beautiful; in some she was lying on sand dunes and in others she was dressed in her go-go dancer's clothes – a waistcoat, top hat and black, short wig – and looked like Liza Minnelli. And I remember there was the burgundy and pink paisley silk cravat that had once been my father's. The material was crumbly and worn; I sniffed at its musty perfume of roses and cinnamon.

That red suitcase was like a Russian doll, with hidden pockets and bags within bags. I'd discover theatre programmes and old bus tickets, silver glitter stick-on stars and gold eye shadows, handker-chiefs folded around lost single earrings, bags of beads and hippy jewellery and four-leaf clovers wrapped in tissue. There was a bag of wigs, a pair of knee-high banana-yellow platform-heeled boots and a tiny black PVC minidress. This was the evidence of my mother's life before I was born. Her triumphs as a young athlete in the All England championships; her Olympic dream and her Royal Ballet dream; her Gold medals and *Swan Lake* dreams; her teenage years in Hong Kong and Cyprus, and also her wild go-go dancing days. My mum used to hint that she had partied and performed with a cool 1960s crowd, mentioning the likes of Engelbert Humperdinck, Tom Jones, Stevie Wonder and Georgie Fame. Mum was the tall skinny dark one and her best mate Leslie the tall blonde, and the way my mum tells it, the world was oyster-like for the pair of them. During the day, she had a civil service job before she met my dad. She told me they made her sign the Official Secrets Act. I used to imagine my mum was a spy, that one day I'd find her fake passports and a gun in that suitcase, and that she used the modelling and go-go dancing as a cover but accidentally went native when she fell for my dad.

The truth was it always felt as though my mother could drag her suitcase out from under our beds and slip back into herself if she wanted to. I thought of these things as her superhero costume. That she could stick the glittery stars back on her face, put on the yellow platform boots and use a bus ticket from before to get back to then and who she really was.

* * *

My mother was often on the phone for hours talking *grown-up stuff* and chain-smoking. I'd play peek-a-boo with my sister, holding her on my knee while eavesdropping on these long conversations, often with Aunt Doreen. Mother suspected that Patrick was having an affair with a woman from his work. I heard her saying his car was spotted, parked up on one of the country lanes with the windows steamed up. It was sleazy and it was almost the last straw.

Then one day I came home from school to find my mother dressed beautifully in her red suitcase clothes. It was four in the afternoon and she was in full make-up and lashes. She was stunning, immaculate in a long flowing gypsy skirt, patterned with huge purple, lilac and orange flowers. She wore a belt of bells and a bobbed black Cleopatra wig. We went out together, strolling down Braybrooke Road, the High Street and through the village. Everybody looked, cars slowed down and the people inside turned and stared. I pushed Jo-Ann in the pram as my mother walked by my side with a confident stride and her head held high. My mother looked sensational and she kept repeating to me, 'This is how I looked when he fell in love with me . . . I think you-know-who needs reminding.'

Every time she said it, she seemed stronger, more convinced.

'You know what I think? I think a certain someone has forgotten exactly whom he married . . .'

We walked past Mark MacGowan's place and his mum was out

255

front in pink rubber gloves, watering the flowers with a hose in her hand.

'Wow! Lorna!'

They talked above my head for a very, very long time.

Mrs MacGowan grinned and patted my mum's arm, saying things like, 'You show him, Lorna, that's right . . .'

When Patrick came home and saw her he chuckled and said, 'Ha ha! What's the big occasion then? What's with the get-up? Did I miss something? Are we going to a fancy-dress party or something?'

Before they started to argue, I was told to go outside and play with my sister in the front garden. Much later, I saw my mother had been crying and was back in her dowdy jeans and jumper. Hugging her, I felt as though we were in some unspoken alliance. Perhaps we were silently unified by the finality of Dad's death, but something had shifted: the worm had turned and my mother wasn't taking any more nonsense. She had borne my stepfather a child, but this still didn't strengthen their bond; they were not closer for their new daughter – if anything quite the opposite. I sensed there were some great changes in the air.

Big Lessons

There were tears on the last day at Loatlands, our little village primary school. I cried and hugged my classmates while saying goodbye to Anna Parris and Sheila Sparks – we roared our eyes out as though we'd never see each other again, and some of them I really didn't. It is funny how even now I remember so many names from the school register: Theresa Fitzpatrick, Hannah Parry, Kate O'Keefe, Shelley Luxon, Joanne Green, Claire Maslen, Claire Munday, Janet Reay, Tammy James, Nicola Hughes, Jason East, Darren White, Christopher Perkins and Anthony O'Donnell.

We were not all going to the same secondary schools; we were spreading out and beyond the comfort of the village. No more walking up and down the hill, chubby-faced, sleepy-eyed, scabby-kneed with our hands full of blackberries or a cardigan full of conkers. No more sitting on the gate and feeding crab apples and grass to the old horse. No more lolling about making daisy chains or charging with war cries into the long grass of the backfields. No more soft, easy teacher reading us milky afternoon stories. Now we had to wear stiff white shirt collars, ties and blazers and we'd have real homework. We had new tin pencil cases with protractors and compasses to learn how to use. We had to take the school bus up the hill to the big school where the older kids smoked fags and gobbed on you from the top deck. We were told the big kids stole your lunch money and flushed your head down the toilet when you were a new first year.

I remember the night before my first day, how my new school uniform hung on its hanger looking like a headless ghost of a schoolgirl in the dark. September skies were crisp and blue and russet leaves gathered in the gutters. We were so nervous and scared, like frozen-stiff penguins, in the queue at the bus stop in our new uniforms and sensible shoes. We stared up in awe at the older kids smoking and swearing, pushing and shoving past us to get to the front.

Montsaye Secondary School was a castle compared to our tiny village school. I joined the swimming club and skipped lunch just so I could swim every lunch break. My blazer was huge on me, my tie worn with pride. I was very keen. We rushed to find friendships to replace those we missed from primary school. These alliances ended in tears. Eleven-year-old girls fell out and made up every week. We were fickle, giggling over special sign languages and sending notes to each other using secret words and code names. I took after-school classes in athletics, drama and music. I joined the school band and tried to learn the euphonium and then the cornet. I played jazz instruments and ran in cross-country competitions – with my lips pressed against the cold brass and my feet never fitting into my mother's old spikes, I felt I was literally following in my parents' footsteps.

Every morning my mother made me take cod liver oil. It was bitter, foul stuff. One wintry morning I refused to take it. My mother angrily asked me why and I said, 'Because it makes me sick! All the way to school! Every morning!'

'Really? Why didn't you say? Maybe I'll see if I can get the tablets instead.'

She told me if I had spoken up I would not have had to take it. I took note of this.

Runaway

I will never forget the morning my brother went to school with a black eye. That morning, the rooms had the kind of silence you find in a house where illness has been, as though something got lost and sick; there was a scrubbed wet bit of living-room carpet, a scent of bleach.

I absorbed myself in the routine of morning class. There was the usual talk about last night's television. Somebody picked on somebody else's new pudding-bowl haircut. And all the while I replayed the events of the night before, and in my head I imagined scenes where I ran in and saved the day. I hated the passive role I played as onlooker and witness. I felt guilty for being the girl and being younger. Perhaps if I had been older, if I had been a boy, then it would be me sitting with a black eye in class today.

I listened. I couldn't do anything else. I listened at the door to the living room and so I saw nothing. Gus had been summoned to the lounge by stern voices, and then I heard shouting. I crept out of our bedroom and crouched down small in the hallway, between the doors leading to the two bedrooms, the bathroom and the lounge. I knelt on the white carpet, rolling balls of fluff between my fingers. If someone came, I planned to dart back to the bedroom where I had a book lying open on my bed.

I heard Patrick read my brother the riot act, the list of his crimes. This was not such an unusual domestic scene: an angry stepfather figure reprimanding a stormy teenage boy about his CSE mock exams or lying about a party or smelling of cigarettes. Then the teenage boy digs himself in deeper by denying everything as the adult becomes more irate and impatient. We have ringside seats and we mouth the answers. We know it's a trick question. The answer is to just apologise. Own up to everything, act humble and contrite, say sorry a thousand times and maybe if you are lucky, you will just get grounded and it will all blow over.

This time, though, my brother was defiant. But he got tongue-tied, his answers became confused, and his story came out different each time. From the wings, I heard him slip into slang and I tried to nudge him the answers telepathically. To use the letter H before words like *haven't* and say *cannot*, not *ken't*. With each misuse of the Queen's English, Patrick grew meaner and more vitriolic.

Gus seemed to always be in trouble with my stepfather. This wasn't an isolated incident, but this was the worst in my memory. What was his crime this particular time? Was it that he came in late after curfew? Was it simply that he was a normal teenager dreaming of living with his friends' freedoms? Or that he was growing into a young man and becoming some kind of threat? I don't remember, and, as usual, the crimes and misdemeanours were never as memorable as the punishments.

I was frozen there, by the door, crouching down. I stared at the door hinge with the bits of white paint on it and the place where the carpet and wall meet the skirting board, my eyes misting over. All I could do was be there, listening, just feeling everything. I wished that Mum would speak so I could tell if she was there in

261

the room. I wished that my stepfather would back down and be gentler. I wished that Gus would say sorry, accept blame and let it pass over like a black cloud. I wished that my brother and I were smarter and faster and more like the kind of kids Patrick liked, more like his real kids. Mostly, though, I wished I was as small as the piece of fluff between my thumb and first finger, so I could cram myself in between the wall and skirting and disappear beneath the carpet.

Then, with the first blow and the bang that followed I jumped out of my skin. I heard a heavy weight thrown against the very door my ear was pressed against, and I leapt to the other side of the hallway. I guessed that perhaps that had been my brother's back hitting the other side of the door between us. It sounded like someone fell, there was a scuffle, something got knocked over. There was a crash accompanied by the sound of a struggle. Maybe my brother threw a punch and was fighting back, maybe he got one in. With all that boxing Gus did, it was bound to come to blows one day. My heart thudded. My mouth filled with the dry metallic taste of fear and I could not move, frozen by awful, conflicting feelings, until finally I heard Mum scream.

'That's ENOUGH. STOP!'

I ran into the bedroom to pretend to read the book lying on my bed. Gus was sent to our bedroom while Mum and Patrick continued shouting. My baby sister started crying from the other room. After it was all over, Gus climbed onto his bed.

I whispered, 'Are you all right Gus?'

I remember the sense of dread. The sound of Mum and Patrick having the most terrible fight once Gus had been sent to the bedroom and how we passed fear and blame like a hot coal between us. I remember lying in bed in the dark, hearing Mum and Patrick fight, and then that horrible silence. I listened to Gus's breath calm, his restlessness cease, and I sensed him falling asleep. While he was sleeping his eye grew purple and swollen. My mother has told me that she slapped my stepfather and told him he had gone too far and yet again all hell broke loose. I'll never forget the next morning, standing at the bus stop to school, and how ashamed I felt when I saw that my stepfather had given my Gus a black eye.

* * *

My brother got into some scrapes as a youth and the police came to the door a handful of times. Once they came because Gus and some friends climbed into somebody's house. While the other boys were upstairs in the bedrooms rooting around for things to steal, for money or jewellery, my brother sat in the strangers' kitchen and ate chocolate biscuits and drank milk. This was my brother, the kind of lad who just wanted to be able to watch telly, eat biscuits and be left alone. All Gus ever wanted was peace and quiet, an easy life, without melodrama and confrontation. However, the fact remained that some jewellery and things were stolen that night and hidden. The police were called, and a week or so after the event, they came knocking on our door looking for my brother. Gus was made the scapegoat – Mum always said in his defence that he was easily led and kept getting into the wrong company.

To this day, Gus belly laughs about it. He swears he just sat in the strange dark kitchen and ate chocolate biscuits. I believe him. I know my brother: a packet of chocolate Wagon Wheels is worth all the gold in the world to him. What use was jewellery to my brother? Sharing a bedroom with his irritating little sister in a tiny bungalow, he was left no privacy for secrets and no safe hiding places. Once the police had come and gone, Patrick laid into him for it. Gus had to do youth community service on Saturdays while

I believe the other boys got away scot-free, which I never thought was fair.

Mostly, though, the police came regularly to our house because Gus started to run away from home. He ran away a good few times, and on each occasion Mum called the police and gave them another recent school photograph. I remember their efficient manners, their little black notebooks, the way they noted every tiny detail; everything Mum said they scribbled down. Mum chain-smoked fags, worried sick, her eyes red and watery. The truth is, deep down, I was so impressed each time my brother ran away again. It was courageous how he managed to hitch rides heading south with lorry drivers. By the time the police caught up with him, he had covered hundreds of miles, across the whole country, all the way from Northamptonshire to Hastings, to Springfield Road and Grandpa George.

Until now I never told a soul, but I saw Gus go. One night I saw him get dressed and silently open the bedroom window. I asked him to take me with him. In fact, I begged him, but he told me I was too young, I wouldn't be able to keep up, and that it wasn't safe for girls. He told me I had to stay to cover for him and look after Mum and Jo. He held his finger up to his lips for me to be quiet. I loved him then, so very much, in the darkness. And so I obeyed him when he asked me to close the window after him and go back to bed and pretend I didn't hear or see anything. I thought he was brilliant and brave. I let him go. Afterwards, I lay in bed listening to the night and imagining his journey. He would have trouble getting through the rusty back garden gate without it creaking. Then he would have to pass down the side of the house, remembering not to tread on the wobbly grate, which I also didn't hear. The crucial point would be when he would have had to pass the living-room window, on the very other side of which sat Mum and Patrick watching late-night television. I pictured it all: my brother legging it up The Ridings and turning the corner onto the high road.

There would have been miles of black open lanes, nothing but night and solitude. There would be rustling in the woods, night creatures: wolves, badgers, foxes in the shadowy ditches and hedge-rows. Acres of fields with sleeping animals and the jingling of scarecrow bells and tin cans. There would be so much black ahead and surrounding him, just the occasional flash of oncoming traffic, a sprinkling of car lights. I wondered whether he would hide when a car came or if he'd stick his thumb out. I worried if the driver might be the Moors Murderer or the Yorkshire Ripper. Restless in my bed, I imagined my brother jogging steadily to keep warm, with his hood up and his fists clenched in determination, his breath visible, his heart racing in his chest. I didn't imagine him being at all scared.

I pictured Gus running down dark, open country roads until the streetlights of Desborough were just a glint in the distance behind him. He ran and then he spat up a ball of phlegm with a snort from the back of his nose, the way he always did, flicking it off his teeth and tongue and flobbing it onto the wet tarmac. He wiped his nose on his sleeve, looked behind him and saw how far he had gone and how far he had to go. He thought of the road ahead, maybe driven by the thought of his destination – Hastings and his freedom. He'd look behind him to see the bungalow, the street and the whole bleak town become inconsequential and finally disappear. Until we were a blot of lights on the landscape that grew smaller than an expiring star.

One Knife, One Fork,
One Cup, One Plate

Gus had to come home to finish his exams and the tension in the bungalow continued. Until one Sunday morning, when my brother and I were woken by the sound of an argument and a slammed door. My stepfather had driven off, leaving my mother sitting on her bed in tears nursing a bloody nose and a cut on the bridge of her nose that would later leave a small scar. She said she had knocked it on the wardrobe door. I got her some tissues and we switched the kettle on. Then I took my reluctant brother by the hand into the dining room where Mum was drinking a cup of tea. After an awkward pause I blurted, 'Mum, we don't like Patrick.'

'What do you mean?'

'Like cod liver oil, Mum, he makes us sick.'

'What do you mean?'

'He makes us sick, we don't want to stay here, Gus say something—' I nudged my brother and then continued, 'He makes me sick! All the way to school! Every morning!'

'Why didn't you come and talk to me before now?'

We had tea together around the dining table; the three of us had a very long talk. We remembered the good days in Danesholme, recalled our lives together in the pink house when Mum and our real dad were still together, when Gus and I were babies. My mother said Patrick had been a big mistake and repeated what she always said: 'The day he got that ring on my finger, everything changed, he changed.'

Shortly after that, Mum told Patrick there was a teachers' strike and that we had no school the next day. I don't know if she waved him off that morning, but I like to think she did. She had told us the night before to stay in bed until he was gone. This was it then, this was the last day. This was my last morning waking up in that bedroom, in that bungalow, in that street and in Desborough. We didn't say goodbye to anyone, to my new school classmates or our neighbours. As soon as Patrick had gone to work, Mum got us up and out of bed and we started packing. Mum was a frenzy. She zipped about the rooms repeating to herself, 'Leave everything! I'll leave this marriage with everything I had when I walked into it. I will not take anything that is his, let him have it all. He can keep that for a start, urgh, and he can keep that . . . leave everything that's his! I'll take my own clothes but leave him the rest, he can have everything, he can have it all, the sofa, the bed. I want nothing to do with any of it, he can have it all!'

It was like a warped Christmas, it was that exciting. There was the rustle of paper everywhere, the filling of black bin liners and the sound of wrapping, boxes being filled, taped up and packed. I had to run to the shops for more boxes. I thought to myself, *This is the last time I will run to the sweetshop around the corner.* I sprinted all the way. My breath steamed into the wintry air and my heart pounded in my chest. When I asked for the boxes I thought, *Goodbye, scary sweetshop lady, goodbye, scary shopkeeper with your stumpy digits, you'll not give me nightmares about my thumb-sucking ever again . . .*

This made me laugh and I ran back home clutching cardboard boxes in one fast gallop. Mum asked me to pack up the kitchen.

There was an almighty crash from the back of the house, where Gus was dismantling the bunk beds with a screwdriver – end of an era, end of a war. Mum was busy caring for the plants and boxing up her cuttings. I started on the kitchen stuff and I remember thinking, *I'll never forget this day, not ever, not for as long as I live.*

I opened the cutlery drawer and looked into the plastic compartments, wondering out loud what to take and what to leave. I grabbed the knives and counted: one, two, three, four and leave one for Patrick . One fork, one knife, one spoon, one teaspoon. The crockery was next. I counted one, two, three, four cereal bowls – we are four, and one bowl for Patrick. I left him one bowl, one plate, one cup, one saucer, one pot. I counted and Mum heard me and we laughed together wickedly and nervously.

'One knife, one fork, one cup, one plate – now that's all he'll ever need, won't he, Mum?'

We loaded up the truck and left, we drove away from that bungalow and never turned back. Leaving my ex-stepfather with a lonely one of everything – *now that's all he'll ever need, won't he?*

Patriarch

For a couple of wintry months we went to stay at my grandad's house in Danesholme, Corby. Nanny was away working as a nurse in New York and only Grandad and Uncle Gerry were living there. We were back at another beginning. I walked around the estate and towards our first home, where we lived when Mum had left my dad. The immense Danesholme of my imagination now looked small and compact as a rabbit warren. The streets were inhabited by ghosts and memories. I heard the eerie music of the ice cream van and the sound of little children counting, skipping and hiding in doorways just as I had before. My dreams so often took place in a surreal version of Danesholme, that the sensations of the memories of those dreams and actual events of my infant life were merged and jumbled.

Digging around in memories and the past often leads to another, unexpected piece of your story. Once you start recalling the past, you keep remembering, and it can arrest you, alarm you, as though you are momentarily trapped in the then. In that moment, it is as though you are under ice, scratching at the underneath of the surface of what it is you feel or hear. Memories don't always come when they are summoned but creep up and flash back to you when you least expect them. And so it was, as I walked around Danesholme, I found I slipped into a trance, lost in a chain of nostalgic thought, and it wasn't until the present moment interrupted me, the smell of food or feeling cold, that I realised I had stopped walking. I was standing still and staring dead into space, lost in the sensation of layers of memories. I suppose that is why the mind forgets, so we can function in the present. I expect that is why we should be glad we don't remember absolutely everything.

I found myself stopped outside our first house, gazing into space. I blinked a few times, shook my head and carried on walking with no real destination. Ahead of me I could see the tunnel that led to the woods where the bears lived, where Mary and I followed Gus when he found the chicks that died in the airing cupboard and the hillside where Gus and I once caught grasshoppers in a jam jar.

'What are you doing here?' Mary said when she abruptly answered the door. She had grown taller than me. She wore a Catholic school uniform, a striped tie and bottle-green skirt. I grinned, taking that as a *hello*. From inside the house I could smell a familiar warmth. Her mum appeared behind her, wiping her hands on a tea towel.

'Well, well, don't leave her standing there . . .' Her mother ushered me in. 'Well, come on in! How's ya mam, love?'

Mary showed me upstairs to her bedroom. A clutter of clothes and pop posters adorned the walls. I thought, *Here I am in Danesholme then, we are here again*, and I thought it felt safe, as safe as nostalgia would allow.

✳   ✳   ✳

Grandad mellowed a little as he got older. As his hair grew white he seemed to shrink, or maybe I grew, but he still scared me and made me feel nervous. In his prime he was a hard booze, knock-it-back kind of man, a tough guy. His voice remained deep and smoky, and when he said *honey* it was literally honeyed, syrupy and smooth. He would quote entire passages from Shakespeare or Wordsworth and he never hid his disappointment when I couldn't name the author or the piece. Even if I did recognise parts, I would freeze, terrified, in case I got it wrong. He delivered explanations of Greek gods and mythology, how the planets work, the historical and Latin meanings of words, but as soon as he went into it and reached for a pen and paper it became a lecture, heavy data, condensed dates and numbers. Just as I was with my stepfather, I always feared forgetting to listen properly and failing his tests and lessons. It's hard to listen when you are thinking the word 'listen' over and over again.

Grandad is a big old lion, the patriarch, rumbling and restless. Maybe I am a lion too. Our dirty guttural laughs are similar, we are frightfully alike when we are loud and boisterous. I sometimes feel I inherited more of Grandad's bravado than the patience and quiet dignity of Nanny. My mother is his daughter; I will always be my mother's daughter and I believed everything she told me. I know she tried to protect me when she instilled a wariness of men, in particular my grandfather.

*　*　*

For two or three months of the winter of 1984, we stayed there at Grandad's. The three of us, my mother, baby Jo and I, shared a bedroom. My mother and grandad got along and muddled through and managed somehow. Those weeks were anxious, highly

271

strung, and my mother was adamant she would not go back to Patrick and Desborough. She spent long hours on the phone to my stepfather in tears as he tried to gaslight her into coming back to him. *What a mess I've made with you kids, I'm so sorry . . .* she cried often.

We were planning to go to Hastings for the Easter holidays, and we were dreaming about moving there – Gus was already staying there and happy living with Grandpa George. Mum and I grew closer than ever during this transitional time in the small confines of that shared bedroom. When Mum got dressed in front of me I saw her body, the stretch marks of her pregnancies and mother-hood. I saw the scars on her back.

'Mum, when did you move to England?'

'You know!'

'Tell me again!'

'I was seven years old when I arrived in Dover in 1951. It was winter, and the first and only thing I remember is the cold! Oh, it was so cold, and all I had on was a cotton dress, white socks and red shoes. How I hated to wear shoes . . .'

As she speaks she lilts in the slightest sing-song of Jamaican accents, her eyes twinkle, then she pretends to go back to her book. I've heard it all before, of course I have, but I still say, 'More, tell me more. Then what happened?'

'You know what happened. I remember how I loved to chase my chicken . . .'

'Chicken, what chicken?'

'Oh yes, back home, I had my own chicken, and we killed it and ate it on the boat to Dover on my birthday . . .'

'I don't believe you!'

'It's true. I remember my mother making a birthday party for me on the boat to England and cooking my chicken . . .'

Of all my mother's stories, I never believed the story about the chicken. I have heard it one million times: it was her seventh birthday on the boat from Jamaica and they had a party. It still always makes me laugh, picturing my grandmother, Nanny, slaughtering a chicken and plucking it on the deck of a boat, which took six weeks to sail from Jamaica to Dover. Was there no health and safety in those days? I ask her to tell me more.

'What do you want to know?'

'OK, what was Jamaica like? What was it like there?'

'OK, let me think. I remember swimming and splashing in the cool river and I remember walking through the coffee groves. In the evenings my Marma told us stories as she fed us fruit, fresh mangoes . . . she smoked a clay pipe and wore a red bandana . . . When she died, my afternoon naps were taken on her grave of white marble under the mango tree and—'

'You slept on her grave?'

'Oh yes, either there or in my feather bed where the hot rain beat on the tin roof and lulled you to a sweet slumber . . . now you go to sleep! You have school in the morning!'

'But tell me more! What was it like to come here? It was cold and what else, what about the first time you met Grandad?'

'Well, he was stationed here and waiting for us. He met us off the boat and – I remember King George had died – I asked, why is the flag at half-mast? He snapped at me, *Quiet, child, can't you see I am talking to your mother?* That is the first thing my father ever said to me.'

'Were you afraid of him?'

'Afraid . . . yes. I can remember overhearing my father saying to my mother, she isn't a baby, you mother her too much, you're too soft with her, this world is hard, when you gonna realise you a black woman in a white man's country now? You not on Colonel's Ridge now, you know!'

Mum pulls that face and mimics my grandfather's deep baritone and frown and then looks more serious as she continues.

'I remember him telling me, you're no good at anything, you will never be any good at anything. And I remember him once waking me from bed to beat me because I had forgotten to brush my teeth. And then—'

'The teacher?'

'Then yes, well . . . Then one day my teacher noticed blood on the back of my shirt and how I flinched if anyone tried to put an arm around me or touch my back. For the first time I was encouraged to talk and my dad had to see the headmaster and she called him in and he laid off me for a while.'

'But what did Nanny do?'

'When?' Mum looked at me over her glasses.

'Well . . . what happened after?'

'Nanny would bathe my cuts and bruises and then send me off to school the next day.'

'But why?'

My mother took off her glasses and pinched the bridge of her nose, then looked directly at me as I pushed for answers.

'Didn't she ever do anything?'

'Oh, there would be tears, but she said we would work it out.'

'But . . . why?'

'Why what? Darling, don't upset yourself, I don't know why. I suppose she just thought that it was best to just soldier on. You know things were so very different back in those days. You forget your grandparents are Victorian, they are from another era . . . we just carried on, much like we do now. We stay calm and we carry on.'

'Then what happened?'

'Then I left home and I started dancing and . . . well, that's when I met your dad. And it's all in the past now, isn't it. Now you go to sleep, you have school in the morning. Actually, I know someone who needs new winter boots. What do you say we go into town on Saturday?'

'Yes! Can I have pixie boots, please?'

'They'll ruin your feet . . .'

'I could save them for best. Please!'

'Well, we'll see. Now get some sleep. Night night, love you.'

'Goodnight, Mum, I love you.'

'Love you too, sweetheart.'

That night as I fell asleep I dreamt about grey leather ankle boots with a kitten heel. I wished hard, I prayed for pixie boots with pointed toes and buckles. I thought they would look great with leg warmers . . . but I wasn't a little girl anymore, and the distraction and shine of new boots wouldn't ever quieten the things we never talked about. All the pretence and the scars and all the secrets and the lies were nicely swept under the lumpy carpet. Keep the past in the past and let sleeping dogs lie, lie, lie. In my family there wasn't an elephant in the corner of the room but a whole herd. My mother confided in me, she told me all her secrets and the lessons she has learned – probably to protect me – but this left me with so many questions burning in my head: questions to which sitting here today, as a grown woman, I still have no answers. And all of these questions begin with the same simple single word: *why?*

Voodoo

Every Sunday, I'd take Jo-Ann to Desborough to visit Patrick. Mum would say she was paranoid Patrick would kidnap Jo if he had her alone. Gus was in Hastings, and he said that if he ever saw Patrick again, he would knock him out, so I had to go. My ex-stepfather was odd, alarmingly nice to me, and much more relaxed and jokey than he had ever been before. I didn't mind going back to Desborough because I got to see my old school friends like Anna Parris and Sheila Sparks.

However, during these wintry months living back in Danesholme we were on a threadbare raft in a sea of transition: our clothes and belongings were all in black bin liners and boxes, and we had no space or room. I started going to an ugly new local school, Kingswood, while Mum figured out what to do next. I stood out at this school and the kids could smell the shiny keenness on me. There was no uniform, but for some reason I still wore my old one. Combined with my National Health glasses and my huge afro, this just made me more geeky and weird-looking. This school was rough. There was no swimming pool, and the possibility of continuing swim training or lessons in the euphonium or cornet were greeted with smirks and whispers. I remember in music class we had to sit through *Peter And The Wolf* and the teacher had us guess and discuss each instrument portraying the narration of each character. I owned a copy on vinyl and knew it very well, so I sulked and sat in that class feeling like I was in some thick kids' school.

Worst of all was during PE. I was always paired off with the only other girl of colour in our year, an Indian girl called Ruby who was introverted and nerdy. She was lovely to chat with, but I knew she couldn't catch a ball to save her life. She hated sports and resented being lumped with me too, I suppose; I loved athletics and was keen to run. When teams were picked for hockey, it was always us two brown girls, Salena and Ruby, left until last on the icy pitch. Forced to pair up, we eyed each other, standing side by side, shivering in gym knickers and knee-high socks in the snow. The two of us tackled the wintry wind up and down the freezing pitch, volleying the ball to each other for practice. I used to wish she could for once return a serve or run a bit faster so I could at least keep warm.

* * *

I eventually made friends with a bony girl with huge eyes called Michaela. She was also into athletics and we started meeting up after school to run cross-country together. We'd jog across the woodland and back fields of Danesholme, past traveller sites, junk-yards and burnt-out cars, towards the cereal factories and the industrial estates. I also made friends with a tough Scottish girl called Mandy, who had acne on her chin. Mandy liked to put on make-up and listen to Cyndi Lauper on her Walkman. I remember Mandy wore a white fake-paint-splattered denim jacket. The three of us would walk about Danesholme with our hands in our pockets and spend Saturday afternoons in the cinema watching amazing teen films like *Flashdance* and *Footloose*.

Kingswood was a red-brick box of a school, covered with scrubbed-out racist graffiti. I was often called names like *Blackie* and worse by girls who hung about outside the school smoking fags, their hair sprayed in flicks, black kohl and stripes of neon blue and pink eye shadow across their eyelids. Many of the people in Danesholme had come down from Scotland to the Midlands in search of work in the 1970s. As a result, almost everyone spoke with a thick guttural Glaswegian accent. The Scottish accent was nice when we were reading poetry in class, but terrifying when I heard it shouting *you're going to die, you black bitch* as I ran through woods.

I ran, pursued by about fifteen kids, five or six of them on BMX bikes. I saw them all waiting for me at the school gates. I went out through the lower gate and ran blindly through the traffic across the main road – a car horn beeped, alerting them. I ducked under barbed wire and made a run for it into the woods. They were shouting *get her, get her, Blackie, Blackie.* As I was running, branches scratched my arms and legs, but I tore through and kept going.

There was someone with me, a kind and gentle girl called Claire. She was my partner in home economics and she was running next to me. She said something like *uh-oh, look, they're all at the gates.* I thought she was stirring me up but that was when I looked and saw the gang, all waiting, waiting for me, waiting to fight me.

'Come on,' Claire said, 'if we go this way, they won't see us.'

Claire and I ran through the woods. My heart was in my throat, I was catapulted by adrenaline and fear, I had never run so fast in all my life. I was way ahead, but they were passing Claire, leaving her alone, and the BMX bikes were cutting in front of me. I swerved, jumped over a broken old tree trunk as the bike tyres cut into the earth and dead leaves. I was a fox and the BMX bikes were dogs with my scent on their tyres. I could hear them behind me, a braying crowd who ran behind the bikes on foot, shouting names and jeering.

I was outnumbered and out of breath. My legs were pistons, running without me. I could not feel them, and if I had stopped running they would have given way like watery jelly beneath me. My eyes were focused on finding any clear path, but the bikes kept appearing in front of me. I switched direction, ducking and diving. I ran and ran, until I ran out of options. The way was cluttered with bracken, with brambles, and the trees were in the way, thorns and thistles that twanged and snapped. Two bikes pulled in at once, then another raced in behind, and I was finally surrounded by trees and bikes, and circled by a crowd in the centre of the woods, miles from anywhere, miles from anyone, miles from home, and this had all gone too far.

'You've been getting too big for your boots!' said Mandy – it sounded like *youse bin gittin too big fer yerr booootz*.

Earlier that day, my friend Mandy had decided she wasn't my friend anymore. At lunch break she and some other girls with hair-sprayed flicks had said to me, 'Youse betta watch yer step, youse got a wee surprise after school . . .'

'A surprise? I love surprises!' I had laughed it off.

Then she spat at me, 'Don't youse be getting so cocky, youse got a fyeet t'night.'

'A fight? Woo! I'm scared.'

'Youse betta be!'

Now I was scared and I was cornered in the woods. They stood around hurling racial abuse and calling me hateful names and discussing who was going to fight me. Then they said that they could smell shit, that I was covered in shit, that's what made me black. They told me I didn't come out of my mother's vagina, I came out of her arse.

'Have you seen her black mum? Her mum's got shit all over her . . .'

'Listen, I don't know why we have to fight . . .'

'Youse bin getting too big for yer boots, ya need t'be brought down a wee peg or two, you black bitch' Mandy snarled at me, pulling off her coat and rolling up her sleeves.

'But I thought we were friends.'

'Well, you thought wrong, you black coon. And what's that shit you have around your neck anyway, some African voodoo black magic shit, is it?'

Everyone laughed and jeered. I looked down and saw I was wearing one of my mother's 1960s necklaces. It was a peace symbol in black, orange and yellow, a flat beaded circle on a string of orange beads. The gang sniggered. They said I should be wearing it in my bottom lip, like when I was *with my tribe in the jungle and shit*.

Claire was bright red in the face. She often blushed, but it was especially beetroot colourful. She started saying, 'Why don't you all just leave her alone . . .'

They jeered at Claire and teased her, asking her which side she was on. She shouldn't spend too much time with me or she'd get shit all over herself. She'd better watch it or she'd get a fight too. Mandy squared up to me, a boxer getting ready for a bout. She looked like she knew what she was doing. I knew that if I so much as flinched, she would throw the first punch. I didn't want to be hit, I didn't want to fight and then she surprised me.

'Fight me then!'

I didn't know what to do. I avoided her eyes and fiddled nervously with my necklace.

'Come on then, bitch . . . you scared or something? Come on, fight me, Blackie . . . Blackie . . .'

The crowd started calling me names and chanting.

'Fight! Fight! Fight! Blackie! Blackie! Blackie!'

Improvising, desperate to do anything to avoid coming to blows, I held the necklace up like a crucifix, my hands shaking. I found my voice was steady, though, and then my mouth suddenly started speaking.

'Curse you . . .'

'What?'

'I curse you . . . May your crops fail . . .'

'What? Yeah, right . . .'

There was a pause, a silence, and then I took a deep breath and continued: 'I curse you. Your crops will fail and your water, may your water be poisoned, may your children all be born deformed, may your fields be ridden with flies and your food rotten. I curse you all. May you all suffer disease and hunger and may you . . .'

I had no idea what was coming out of my mouth. I allowed my watery, tear-filled eyes to gently go out of focus as though I was in a trance and talked in tongues, repeating things about disease, deformed babies and failed crops, holding the necklace up like a crucifix.

Mandy was the first to shout. 'Are you doing black magic voodoo shit on me?'

Kids started backing off, getting on their bikes and then riding off, swerving in the leaves and screaming, 'Shit! She knows voodoo shit! Run! Shit! Wait for me!'

The stragglers ran off into the woods as I was still casting my spell: '. . . may this curse follow you for all eternity. No matter where you go, this curse will follow you. Your crops will fail as long as you are under the same sky. You will be eternally cursed!'

When everyone had run off I burst into tears that dried as soon as they came. Claire was still there, standing still, scarlet-faced and trembling. My tears turned to relief as she touched my arm and asked if I was all right, and I thanked her for sticking up for me. The woods were quiet and growing dark; it was getting late. I bent down to pick my satchel up off the earthy leaves and brush the muck off it. I saw my hands were still shaking, and then the crying suddenly was laughing.

'Crops?' I said. 'What crops?'

I looked up at Claire and a rush of brilliant laughter overtook us. I was kneeling on the leaves, holding my bag, hardly capable of picking myself up for laughing. Both of us were in total hysterics. We hooked arms and starting walking slowly homewards, through the thick of trees towards the flickering of urban orange streetlights, doubling over in fits of laughter every time one of us said, 'Run! She knows voodoo shit!'

And We Don't Wear No Shoes

It was May, the warm spring of 1984, when we finally arrived to live on Springfield Road.

I now had my own room on the second floor, but I also had a single bed in my mother's room. Jo slept in the king-size bed with Mum. I slept in the spare bed in Mum's room most nights in the beginning; I liked being close to her and I thought the house was haunted – at night the old floorboards creaked and the sash windows rattled. Grandpa George had lived there all alone since Edith's death in 1972. There were four floors of disarray and dust. It took some work, but Mum got it shipshape and homely, and the kitchen in the basement cleaned and almost hygienic to cook in.

I started a new school called The Grove that was very close to home; the lower school was situated right at the bottom of Springfield Road. It was a narrow, crooked and decrepit old schoolhouse, which they have demolished now and rebuilt. There was a national teachers' strike that year, so we finished classes at lunchtime every day. My afternoons were deliciously idle and often spent on the promenade and beaches. Sometimes we'd sneak into the closed-down Lido on the Marina, or go to Alexandra Park to climb trees and play on the swings. Grandpa George gave me an old grey tape recorder, and every so often I'd go up into my father's old room in the attic where nobody went, and in contented solitude I made my own radio shows and recorded poems and songs.

My brother and I liked to go down to the seafront to an amusement arcade called Out of this World. For the price of a day pass, you had unlimited plays on all the electronic games, Pacman and Space Invaders. There was a darkened room that was an all-day music video disco. I remember watching Chaka Khan's 'I Feel for You' and realising that my big curly hair was *cool*, thanks to her. Racism was now *uncool* in the playground, thanks to breakdance and hip hop, soul and rap music. Suddenly it seemed being in any way black or of colour gave you a certain street cred. Hip hop and beatbox and rhymes crept into the popular consciousness. Breakdancers wore nylon tracksuits and wet-look hair gel and strutted about Hastings town with chunks of linoleum or cardboard under their arms. They were always preparing for a burn; to impress the girls they'd spin on their heads and caterpillar across the polished floors. With legs twisting they'd spin in a windmill. You'd see their hands and necks jolting and juddering with robotic moves. There was a constant rivalry between the body-poppers, the robotics and the breakdancers. I also remember a cool older girl whose dancer name was Boogie Bush and she could breakdance as well as the boys. She also had big curly hair, and I looked up to her and cheered for her to win.

We loved to mimic the film *Breakdance*. I remember with great amusement Gus scribbling a letter G, turning the title of 'Ain't No Stoppin' Us' to 'Ain't No Stoppin' Gus' on the cover of his seven-inch single. I also remember my brother playing the latest Prince album, which I'd steal to learn the lyrics off by heart. I'd study Prince intently when Gus was out, feeling I was privy to a whole new exciting world, and I started to try to write political poems and songs with sexier lyrics and go up into the attic to sing and record them on my tape recorder.

Sometimes, my brother and I would stay home and watch the big television down in the basement together. It was wonderful. A channel called MTV had just been launched, pumping out the hits of Michael Jackson, Wham!, Madonna and Tina Turner twenty-four hours a day. I now prayed for Mum to let me have crop tops and lace fingerless gloves. The basement was still almost as Edith had left it – cobwebs hung heavily from the ceiling and mice scurried in the corners – and to my delight the pantry light still worked, illuminating the same tins of beans and corned beef dating back to the 1970s.

The very first friend I made in Hastings was a freckled girl called Florence, who showed me how to soak secondhand jeans in the bath so they'd fit better. I also made friends with a red-haired girl called Caroline, and we went to Christchurch every Sunday. We liked church and especially Father Jonathan, the cheerful young vicar there; he had a pot belly and glasses. We all got confirmed because of him. He was enthusiastic and funny and he started a church youth club called TCs – the Christ Church Crew – the Three Cs. Every Monday evening, we'd meet and play pool and ball games. Father Jonathan's energy and generosity seemed to have no limits; he organised Shrove Tuesday pancakes, trips to the cinema, swimming and camping holidays. I went to church every week, not just for Grandpa George, but because of my friends, the cute choirboys Scott, Justin and Andrew. How I'd applaud and cheer, watching them burn and compete, attempting windmills on a piece of linoleum in the churchyard which we all thought was the ultimate in cool – spelled *kool*.

In that first year while we were living in Springfield Road, my mother discovered that my sister Jo-Ann had a rare condition called Williams Syndrome, as well as asthma and eczema. This meant it took my sister a long time to learn to talk and speak in proper sentences, and she remained elfish and fragile. She was my living doll and I doted on her. That first year in Hastings we nearly lost Jo-Ann when she had a chronic asthma attack. Her breathing was so laboured that we had an old kettle on constantly until we could find a doctor, turning mother's bedroom into a steam room to help her breathe.

Hastings is a long drive from Desborough, but that's no excuse – Patrick visited Jo-Ann only once. I had to go with them, as Mum was still paranoid he'd kidnap her. (What on earth she thought I would do if he did try to abduct her, I still have no idea.) We sat on the beach near the town and had ice cream. It was a grey, boring day. Patrick was staying at the Queen's Hotel on the seafront and he disappeared in there, leaving me with Jo in the pram waiting for him for a while. Then he came back out and we sat and stared out at dull sea some more before he dropped us back home and left. Apart from divorce proceedings and lawyer's letters, we never heard from him ever again. Not that Gus and I expected anything, there wasn't even a birthday or Christmas card or anything for his real daughter.

Now I lived in Hastings I became one of the naked summer children and *we don't wear no shoes*. Writing this, I am listening to that song by Jane's Addiction, 'Summertime Rolls', and remembering us.

We were barefoot all summer. We lived on the beach and scooped rivers and irrigated moats around pebbled turrets of wet mud-castles. We jumped from rock to rock with nets, paddling in shallow crab pools. Teenage girls in jelly shoes slathered coconut and olive oil on each other's shoulders, cooking themselves in the midday sun, trying hard to get the attention of young wannabe surfers with no real waves to catch who lay on their bellies on their surfboards, basking on a flat green sea. From the beach you could always see the distant lush green of the West and East Hills, rising like two plump mounds. Walking towards Fairlight, you'd find beautiful places to think or fly a kite. We'd go meandering along the wild, yellow gorse-lined paths of the Firehills in a daydream. Hastings Castle was a broken tooth above the chalky, jagged jaws of the cliff face, which in later years became the place for the sweetest flush of first love: teenage secrets, stolen cigarettes, French kisses and bottles of cider.

When the tide was out, standing on the rocks and looking back towards land, as far as the eye could see the beaches stretched in shades of mineral, copper and granite, swirls of slate and smooth amber-coloured stones, pieces designed especially for skimming and skipping stones across the water's surface. If you found yourself a lucky pebble with a hole in the middle, they said, you would always return to Hastings. I always thought that was a good thing.

That new beginning of May 1984, Hastings was in bloom, awash with cherry blossoms, and the summer was ahead like a promise that we would surely keep. For the rest of my life I told people that this was where I came from. I never bothered to mention the life before – Springfield Road was always my home, this was where my life began, and this is where another story begins.

✳   ✳   ✳

'Where are you going now?'
  'For a walk.'
  'Where?'

287

'Just a walk.'

'Can I come too?'

'No, not this time. I'm going to leave you in Hastings in 1984.'

'What do I do next?'

'Lots . . .'

'Like what?'

'You wear wet-look hair gel and blue mascara, you obsess about Prince, you'll get into books like *The Color Purple* and you'll keep writing poetry. But, listen, try to go gently and enjoy the journey more, smell the roses on the way. I know you think you know it all, but try to listen to Mum sometimes.'

'I know.'

'No, I know. Listen, when you get to fifteen take it easy with the cider and the cigarettes . . . in fact, don't smoke, it's so stupid.'

'I don't smoke.'

'Yes, you do.'

'And what about Dad?'

'I think he'll be at peace now.'

'But are you still afraid you'll die like Dad did?'

'Are you afraid?'

'Yes.'

'Then I am too.'

'Always wait and see if you feel better in the morning?'

'Yes, that's right – wait and see another sun rise.'

'Sleep is the great healer.'

'That's right, love. Oh, and one last thing: please try not to be so hard on yourself so the people who love you don't have to work so hard.'

'What?'

'I know, easier said than done. Goodbye, then, Salena.'

'Goodbye . . . Salena.'

I walk up the beach towards the pier and leave my twelve-year-old self paddling in rolled-up jeans, flat-chested in a striped T-shirt, short-sighted and squinting in the sun. I leave myself there in 1984, where I am content and safe with my family on the beach in St Leonard's, opposite the statue of Queen Victoria. The soft green sea sparkling in May's lemony sunlight, bright and warm out of the wind. Seagulls cry overhead and sit like ducks on the calm, still water. I turn back and see the tall bony silhouette of my brother Gus, staring out at the horizon and skimming stones. Jo-Ann sits in a sunhat on a sandy ledge, playing with a bucket and spade. Mum is head-to-toe in turquoise; she turns, shielding her face from the sun. I see her smile and I walk away. I know we are going to have a wonderful summer, we are going to get some ice cream in a bit, and we don't wear no shoes, there is sand between our toes, and at last we live on the holiday.

Facebook 2008

Hi Salena,

This is probably the strangest message you'll get this year but my name is Claire Godden (used to be Godden anyway) and I just wondered if you were trying to find me on the genealogy website thingy???? If you are I'd really like to hear from you and if you're not I'm sorry to have sent you this weird message.

Take care Claire x

Hello Claire,

How are you? In a word – yes! I have been looking for you, Claire Godden daughter of Paul Godden. Did you leave a message on a genealogy website like back in 2001? I found the query and my name and replied last year and left a note there. Wow! hang on . . . OK . . . I just checked and opened the site and now see your new note! I am gobsmacked and so pleased you found me here. Not sure what to write now . . . stunning.

Guess what, after seeing your posting, I wrote to every Claire Godden on Facebook and MySpace, to lots of dead ends . . . I got lots of very nice replies, one very nice letter from a 14-year-old Claire Godden whose grandfather does Godden family trees. It's been quite a road to Damascus. I am very excited to find you here. You are right, though, this is the strangest message I got this year. What shall we do now? If I was standing in front of you in the pub I guess I would look at my shoes and then ask you if you want a fag or fancied a pint . . . or something like that.

I just looked at your page, are you based in Bristol? I am in London. Write back when you can.

Take care too,
Salena
     x

* * *

London
December, 2008

Dear Dad,
The most wonderful thing happened this summer; we found Claire. We met in August, one Saturday lunchtime, at Reading train station, a halfway spot between Bristol and London. The moment I saw her in the station I felt I knew her and we threw our arms around each other and held on tight and for a long time. I might have imagined it, or longed for it, but I felt something warm and familiar in that embrace. My eyes were welling up and I had to catch my breath to stop myself from crying or making a fool of myself or she would think I was soppy.

We had so much catching up to do, so we went to a quiet place on the river. We sat at a table outside a restaurant and it was a perfectly sunny day, blue sky, still green water. We ordered white wine and shared starters and chatted and when she spoke, I watched her, I couldn't help it, I knew anything she did that I did, we had both inherited from you Dad. I was readily observing any similarities in our mannerisms and personalities and enjoying them. She makes up words like I do and loves books and writing; she's got glittery eyes and a mischievous nature; she likes a drink and belly laughs at rude jokes . . . it's in our genes, then, and I thought she's one of us all right, Dad.

We were there drinking wine all day and I wanted to know everything, stupid things like her favourite colour and what were the names of her childhood pets and of course the other side of the truth, like what did her mother say about you. Where were you on those last days? I think I understand more now.

I made Claire a scrapbook, with poetry you'd written and pictures of you when you were younger on Springfield Road, and she showed me pictures of you in the late 1970s. You changed didn't you, Dad, I mean your sideburns grew and you looked older. It was strange to see photos of you appearing a little more portly in your thirties. I never imagined I'd see you like that, older I mean, we've only ever seen pictures of you from way back then, in black and white.

Claire and I laughed about you, Dad – we compared our mothers and figured your type out in no time – you were a legs man, that's for sure, down in the pit looking up at our mums' high-kicking legs.

Finally, on a weekend in October all of us were united for the first time. Paul, your grandson and your namesake, was climbing all over his new uncle Gus. It was a very noisy and chatty weekend, there was plenty of laughter and a glass or two of champagne was raised to you, our dad, you know you should have been there.

I look forward to showing Claire around what is left of old Soho, the poets, artists and jazz musicians that still drink here; I'll take her to Gordon's Bar down Villiers Street, maybe Ronnie Scott's and there's still a few drinking dens you'll no doubt have frequented, the Colony and Gerry's. And I'll take her up Primrose Hill or Hampstead Heath too, to listen to the wind in the branches of the William Blake tree and to look across the frosty rooftops of a wintry London from up on Parliament Hill.

Dad, it's your anniversary again, but this year I don't feel the way I have before. I think that is why I'm writing this letter, because it's not that I don't still remember you, Dad, because I do, but this year I won't seek your ghost and soak in your memory. This year I won't burn poems so the smoke can reach you, or walk the streets of London alone at night in some private melancholic vigil. This year it's different. I know where you are and that you must surely be resting now, and for the first time, this year, it's all to do with living with the living.

Suddenly, I know that in a way I have always had you in the stories from my mother, in the quiet strength of my brother and now in the laughter of my sister and the hugs from my nephews and nieces; I am not alone and that state of waiting is done. The search is over. We all always think of you whenever we hear Gilbert O'Sullivan.

So you can sleep now and rest in peace Dad,
With love.

From your eldest daughter,

Salena Xx

Eulogy

So, I tried to write this under a mango tree remembering you,
your love of mangoes,
how Marma used to slice up the fruit
and tell you stories at bedtime.
I tried to write this in the Blue Mountains
on the road to Melbourne and Victoria,
knowing I'd soon be on the road to take you home
to these Blue Mountains I've only dreamt of in your stories.
Then I wrote this in Darling Harbour in Sydney
and I thought of you there too, watching the boats
and the Maritime Museum, recalling your history,
and I remembered your passage to Dover,
to England, with my mother.
And whilst walking through tranquil Chinese gardens
there were ornate waterfalls and fountains
reminding me of photographs of you
in Hong Kong and Singapore.
Then wandering the markets of China Town
the aroma of rice and ginger —
well, I thought of you there too,

how you'd wag your finger
and tell me to eat my greens.
Walking along a beach at dawn
a coconut washed up on the white sand.
Again I thought of you and how you warned me that
coconut was bad for the cholesterol.
I was convinced that very coconut had sailed
from Jamaica, from you to me,
to tell me it was time to go home.
I realise now that I will
always be writing this;
no matter where I go,
you walk beside me.
I can hear you nagging me
to quit cigarettes
to look when I cross the road
to take care not to trust strangers
to work hard and to take my time.
I can picture you now,
your eyes like tiger's eyes
and so gold.
I can sense you in the room,
a gentle and quiet dignity,
your infectious chuckle.
The last time I saw you, Nanny,
I asked you to wait
until I could give you a grandson.
You laughed your laugh then
when I told you I plan to begin this work
when I am fifty
and then you asked me

to write something to read today,
but words are not enough
and it is in the silences
I still try to write this.
There are no words, my Nanny
with tiger's eyes,
just the calm in the pauses
as we all share our memories of you today,
memories that will live on.

A tribute written for Nanny, my grandmother, read at the service of thanksgiving at the Mount Carmel Church, Colonel's Ridge, Clarendon, Jamaica, 24 January 2011.

My grandmother, Nanny

Kingston, Jamaica

January 2011

It was 4 a.m. when I was awoken by the raging storm. I pulled the curtain aside to witness this almighty cacophony of thunder and fork lightning, followed by a downpour, the like of which I have never seen before. I got up in the darkness and went outside onto the veranda. It was first light, a strange dawn with dark green clouds.

I'd picked up my telephone and cigarettes. How strange, I thought, not to have picked up my notebook and pen, as was usual, but my phone – and it was then I knew it was time to make that call to England and get confirmation of what I already knew to be true: my grandmother, Nanny, had passed away only four hours earlier.

I was so far away from home: that December and for Christmas and New Year we were on tour in Australia with the Book Club Boutique. My bass player Max Doray and I were staying and playing with our Australian friends and fellow bandmates Melania Jack and Patty Bom. We were travelling along the east coast; from the rainforests in Nimbin, sacred Bundjalung country, to Byron Bay, Sydney, and finally down to Victoria and Melbourne. We were throwing parties, doing spoken-word and music events, playing beach shacks, cocktail bars and alternative theatres with local artists, and meeting up with poets, authors and musicians in each town to jam alongside us. Admittedly, sometimes the locals were quite baffled by the arrival of us four looking all weird and wonderful in the town hall or bar but we took it all in our stride. We made some great friends, met lots of lovely people, writers, poets and artists along the way.

Queensland was suffering the worst floods in history; eighty per cent of Queensland was affected, and the tides were rising with flood warnings escalating. There were images on the internet of a shark that was sighted cruising down the waterlogged Brisbane high street. The rain: I have never seen such rain. It was like we were white-water rafting down the highway in the car. I easily imagined humans as ants and that giants, gods, were having a water fight, throwing huge bodies of water at each other above our heads. It was a constant bashing, it sounded like horses galloping across the roof. Many roads were closed; the rivers were swollen and bursting their banks. We were in Lismore in limbo; we watched the weather and the news unfold via the internet.

Following the news that my grandmother had finally passed away, that night we had to do a performance in a bar in downtown Lismore. It was all right, not my best show, but we made it through. I was distracted and I was hurting. But when we came home from the gig, there was a tawny frog-mouth on the veranda; a beautiful rare bird, like a fat silver owl, a reptilian kookaburra. She – we knew she must be a she – she stayed there as if she was watching over us as we drank Jamaican rum, raising a glass to my grandmother. We played music, improvised songs and poems. I recall we were with The Hussy Hicks, and the brilliant

Julz Parker played slide on a guitar made out of a wooden cigar box as Leesa Gentz sang the blues beautifully. When I went up to the kitchen to get more ice, I watched the bird for a while. Staring at its round gold eye gave me a chill, goosebumps. I whispered, *Nanny?* And the bird ignored me. Then I said, *Marma?* The bird's head spun around 360 degrees and then it winked and stared right at me, both gold eyes unblinking. *Marma is here,* I thought, *Marma is a bird.* Marma, I whispered and put my hand out. She flew, sailed high up into the banana tree above us. I believe she was there, watching over us, up in the branches of the banana tree throughout the whole of that night.

Phone calls to England were very strange, distant and tearful. We made plans to all meet in Jamaica on 24 January, where I was determined to fulfil my grandmother's wish that I write and read her a eulogy. And there we would meet all our many relatives and take my grandmother home, back up the mountain to Colonel's Ridge. Organising flights and transfers was frustrating, becoming very expensive and the time-zone differences were irritating too. Was it even possible to get from Australia to Jamaica in time?

Far away on another continent, I heard my mother's voice breaking on Skype and felt her heart was breaking. My sister Jo-Ann was in tears and my brother was quiet and shaken. I was homesick and felt guilty, I felt I should head home to England, but Gus wouldn't let me cancel anything and my mother insisted I complete my trip and meet them in Kingston.

Continuing the tour was quite epic. Brisbane airport was closed down. We drove and dodged wild weather south from Lismore, to Newcastle, to Sydney and Melbourne. I recall squalls where visibility was zero and brown chocolate rivers oozed from burst banks. I remember the full moon in Sydney sent us doolally. Four girls in a hot cramped car under the full moon? It was heady and emotional.

I went off on my own in Sydney, I took a hotel room in China Town alone. I did a solo show, reading poems in Bondi Beach for a friend, a musician called Jont from London, who had established a weekly residency there. I soaked in the moonlight, took in the full moonshine, which often gets me into the worst kind of trouble. I was happy to be kidnapped; I dived in secret waters; I sat in a magic garden and drank bubbly wine and watched a beautiful sunrise. By the time we drove those last two long days to reach the Melbourne show, we were all officially tour fried. We all needed a good bath and our own beds.

The Melbourne venue, Bertha Brown, was a converted warehouse in the financial district. The crowd, though small, was warm and friendly. I look forward to returning to Melbourne one day – my twelve hours there could not do it justice. Throughout the gig my heart was heavy, knowing my suitcases were in the wings. I was in the departure lounge. I had travelled and unravelled, laughed and cried and worked hard and played so hard alongside this gang of brilliant women for two months and now it was all done. I hate goodbyes – but now it was time to go home to say goodbye to my grandmother.

I left Australia at 4 a.m. and flew from Melbourne to Auckland to LA to Miami and as if by magic I arrived in Kingston at 9 p.m. on the same day, the evening before the memorial. I had never been to Jamaica before. We had not been to Jamaica before, my brother, Gus and I. And it had been dozens of years since my brother, my mother and I, had any time together. I had been rewriting this memoir for more than five years and now suddenly I'd see for myself these places we'd only ever heard about through stories from our grand-parents. Here I was, walking onto the bamboo tray, the parishes of Jamaica once signified by pictures of coconuts and birds of paradise.

✳   ✳   ✳

At Kingston immigration desk, the passport control man looked at my visa for a very long time and then he asked me if it was my first time in Jamaica.

'Yes, it is!' I said with a huge idiot grin on my face. I was practically skipping on the spot to have arrived, thinking, clever me, I came all the way around the world from Australia. I was so relieved I had not missed any connections. I had written *writer* next to occupation, and the passport control man asked me, 'Do you know the stories of Anancy?'

'Yes! Of course I do.'

He frowned and stared at my passport and my face in turn, slowly, his features bearing grave concern. 'And what do you write about?'

I then wished I had written as my occupation 'teacher' so that I wouldn't get asked these tricky questions. When people know you write they say things like *everyone has a book in them* and smile knowingly as if you've never heard that before. Or they say, *You're a poet and you know it.* I felt that if I answered incorrectly he would interrogate me further so I said, as casually as I could, 'I write about anything, life, dreams, you know . . .'

'Do you think it is best that you write from your own perspective or somebody else's?'

'I think both are equally as good, I think there is no best or better. There is no wrong or right answer to that one. Do you write?'

'Hmmm . . . a little . . .'

He looked thoughtfully at my passport and took a long time, reading all my paperwork and then choosing a page to stamp. He pointed his pen at me and said, 'While you are in Jamaica, you should write a story about an English person's first time in Jamaica. Write about a writer who writes the stories of Anancy but with the English perspective.'

He looked at me directly, eye to eye, but I shook my head *No!*
'No?'

'No, I know what — I'll write all about you, the man at the passport desk in Kingston airport who clearly loves writing and good stories.'

He grinned at me, beamed brilliant white teeth and bonny cheeks. He nodded, then as he handed me my passport he said, 'Welcome to Jamaica!'

Welcome indeed. Stepping out into the tropical heat, the night air embraced me and that first hug from my big brother let me know I had made it home and dry.

We were up and dressed early for the ceremony. It was already hot at 7 a.m. as we drove through downtown Kingston heading up and out to Clarendon. Kingston is a lively city, with street vendors, hustlers and bustlers. I have never been in the Caribbean before, but this place initially reminded me of East Timor. The distant blue hue of forest and mountains, fish on poles being sold on the side of the road, tin shacks selling fruits, cigarettes, tinned drinks and bottled water. At every street corner a heartache, at every stop sign a beggar. I was told it was best to keep your windows rolled up or you'd be harassed at every junction. I saw gulleys and alleys, humble shanty towns where people lived in makeshift homes, corrugated iron rooftops, just like the ones I once saw in Dilli, East Timor. And I saw great grandeur too, an abundance of beautiful white and marbled embassies, old colonial buildings, museums, churches and universities.

Driving through Kingston, delirious with jet lag, I could easily make believe I was in the film *The Harder They Come* or a Bob Marley video. I saw tiny rum shacks; a topless, toothless, bearded old Rasta with dreadlocks grown matted down past his bum; coconut trees, palm trees and birds of paradise; signs for tasty patties and jerk chicken; the two boys riding a 1970s-style motorbike with a box of plantain to sell, balanced precariously on the handlebars . . . all that Jamaica, in real time, zooming past my car window.

The road up to Colonel's Ridge grew steeper, winding and potholed. As we continued, it grew narrower, and we passed shallow muddy rivers, fields of sugar cane and bamboo. Rainforest. Up and up and up we drove until we came to a shop, a sign for a barber's, some chickens and a donkey, and we had arrived somewhere, somewhere special — we were at Colonel's Ridge. The view of the mountain range was spectacular from way up there.

Mount Carmel Church was high up on the top of a mountainside. It was light and airy and the walls were painted pale primrose yellow. Inside were rows of pews and my mother pointed to our old family bench. On the back wall there were marbled plaques with the names of both sets of my great-grandparents, Robinson and Robothan, named as elders of the church which they helped build. My other great-grandmother's name was Lena May Robothan. My mother tells me she had no idea, but what a strange coincidence that we are so similar — Lena May, and I was christened Salena Faye. And also strange to me, below the carved dedications, dates and names were these bold words: Well Done.

The church bell rang twice and everybody came inside and sat down. We were in a congregation of cousins I had never met, some from Jamaica and others from America, and people from the village and their families. We looked at the altar, the flowers and my grandmother in a box. It was suddenly overwhelming, and as the first hymn 'All Things Bright And Beautiful' began, it suddenly hit me that somehow we had all made it, gathered here, to this isolated village on a mountaintop — we were finally together. I looked at my mother and we cried.

I was the first up to read my poem, my offering, which had been written on the road in Australia, scribbled in a scuffed-up notebook. I hoped that it was close to good enough for such a crowd of strangers-yet-familiars. As I stepped up, I heard a quiet voice telling me to be myself. *Don't try for trying's sake, just do what you can do and be honest, just be yourself.* All I remember about the actual reading is that I managed not to bawl and kept a steady voice. This was followed by another hymn and then my mother's cousin, son of my nanny's brother Sam, Patrick Robinson, read his piece.

He began by saying: 'My father had two kinds of sisters. There were those who had the more typical Robinson woman, dominant and imperious character that brooked no foolishness from anyone, man or woman. The other set were softer and more forgiving. I loved both equally. My own father, were he a woman, would have fallen into the first category. The nieces here today and elsewhere have inherited those traits. But in the interest of my own security I will not categorise them . . .'

As he said this there was a lovely pause, full of giggles, nudging and knowing grins, for it was a certainty that we Robinson women all knew which category we might fall into, or at least we thought we did.

Patrick Robinson was no stranger to us. We had met him on numerous occasions visiting my grandmother and love and admire him greatly. He continued, 'Aunt Muriel fell squarely into the second set. She was eternally sweet and gentle but possessed of a great inner strength that was to serve her well throughout her life, and in particular throughout her illness. Aunt Muriel was born and raised in Colonel's Ridge. She was the fifth child in a family of ten, born to Rudolph Robinson (Papa) and his wife Theresa (Muma) née Robotham. She was the last surviving child and the one that lived the longest. Papa was an elder and lay preacher of this church when it was the Mount Carmel Presbyterian Church. Aunt Muriel would have seen her parents work hard, and although not well off, always giving of others. Many are the stories of Muma cooking and feeding the village . . .'

Now, I pictured the stories Nanny told me about her mother feeding all the children after school. I looked out around the elderly congregation and wondered who went to school with my grandmother and her siblings.

'She told me how it fell to her to care for her grandmother until her death and she carried out this duty willingly and lovingly . . .'

Marma. In my head I whispered her name, *Marma*.

'. . . It was in Hong Kong that Aunt Muriel started to become interested in nursing as a career. On returning to the UK, they spent some time working, before going to the USA where Aunt Muriel worked as a nurse in a prison. Naturally the prisoners loved her, calling her their angel, and respected her so much they wouldn't swear in front of her . . .'

When Patrick finished we bowed our heads in prayer and there was a stillness and peace. I squeezed my mum's hand as the Mount Carmel choir sang old Jamaican hymns I hadn't heard before. I recall liking a particularly bluesy, soulful hymn with lyrics about the pearly gates and your place in heaven.

Then the whole church sat down to listen as Reverend David Tucker stepped up. He was a giant, with a bald head, ebony skin and bright eyes. His voice was deep, booming and resonating as he belted out the sermon. The lesson was brutal, based on 'you reap what you sow'. It was passionate and soon stopped any weeping. The Reverend clenched and pounded his fists, he told the congregation to look into their hearts and he bellowed: 'Do you live for just today or for today and tomorrow? When you get to heaven to meet your maker will God say "well done"? Will the Lord look upon you and say "well done"? Muriel has passed. Muriel has gone. But when Muriel enters the pearly gates will the Lord say "well done"?'

And throughout this blazing speech there was a murmur of *praise be, hallelujah!* and *amen!* and thereafter I felt differently about the meaning of those two words: well done.

After the service, we walked down the dusty track to the family plot. It was ten minutes from the church in the midday heat and as we walked we seemed to attract more attention. More villagers joined us, people wanting to pay their respects, and everyone came to their gates to watch us go by. A gaggle of schoolchildren of all ages followed, giggling and whispering. It was no longer so sombre, with different cousins introducing themselves to us. Some folk remembered my mother as a baby, and my mother met cousins she might have played with as a very little girl too.

The family plot was beside the abandoned house that my grandmother lived in alongside her ten siblings, Papa and Muma — my spelling, Marma. We stood amongst the tombs of our great grandparents and my great-aunts and uncles, beside a house that could not have possibly housed them all. It was derelict, and I could see through a jagged window into the kitchen where my great-grandmother would have cooked. There was a broken old stove there. I saw the porch where Nanny may have been sat in a tin bucket filled with roots and herbs, blinded by malaria. Now the black-and-white drawings my grandmother had described to me as a girl were full colour, those tales of Nanny as a child were suddenly in 3D, moving around me, a living, walking and talking picture. Vivid blue and violet, the world was humming in a hundred shades of life and lush green. The neglected house was swarming with hornets; I was told it was dangerous and so I couldn't risk actually going inside. I really wanted to, but I could see enough to know

308

we all come from very humble beginnings, from hard work and love. And looking at the congregation from the outside, I was proud to be part of this family.

My brother laid Nanny to rest; he put her box in the hole already prepared. As soon as he did so, they sealed the grave with cement and began laying the headstone, rushing to beat the hot sun baking the cement too dry. The Reverend said some words of prayer, the choir and old ladies began to sing, and everybody joined in, old Jamaican hymns from long ago, trembling voices, the rumble of blues under the yellow midday sun. I was crying quietly, looking down through my lashes, the cement slapped cold and grey, wet and final. Then one huge orange butterfly, the colour of a tiger lily, settled on the grave. It stayed for a very long time, tiger lily, Nanny.

We stood at the graveside in the shade, talking politely and waiting for the headstone to be in place. I suppose I must have stood out because of the way I was dressed, I was wearing a black Westwood dress and heels, and children started gathering around me. Eventually a pretty little girl with braids, by far the boldest in the school, came up to me and asked, 'Excuse me . . . why you no got no church clothes?'

'Do you not think these are church clothes then?' I laughed as she looked up at me and shook her serious young head. I tried to explain that this was the only black dress I owned and that I had just come from Australia.

Soon her friends came over and we asked each other our names and they stared at me until my new bold friend said, 'Can I have your phone number?'

I managed to convince her it would be very expensive to phone London, and with that she ran off and returned with her school notebook and a pen and said,

'Can I have your name, I want to see your name, please write it . . .'

Before long I was surrounded by schoolchildren with notebooks, writing my name over and over again. They all watched and said I had nice handwriting and then someone asked, 'Can you write "I love you" and then your name?'

And so I found myself writing *I love you, Salena Godden xxx* in all the notebooks of all the village children while they bombarded me with questions.

'Where do you come from?'

'England. London. You know, it's the place where everyone is in a hurry and it rains all the time and the Queen lives there in a palace and she has a little dog . . .'

'Who's the Queen?'

I laughed. Hallelujah for Jamaican Independence!

Eventually, the headmistress appeared and shook hands with us too. My brother laughed at me and took photos because once every notebook was signed, the children all mobbed and hugged me. I haven't been cuddled by twenty-five small pairs of arms at the same time before. I wondered what my elders would think if they saw this display, and I hoped I wasn't being disrespectful. The children asked me to sing to them. I couldn't be persuaded and instead I managed to have them sing for me. They nudged and whispered, and then began an up-tempo, energetic version of *riding through the snow, on a one-horse open sleigh, over the hills we go, laughing all the way, jingle bells, jingle bells . . .*

I started laughing and joined in, and we sang. I couldn't help but wonder if perhaps these were the great-grandchildren of my grandmother's school friends, distant cousins and friends. Perhaps if we went in a time machine, I would find I am somehow connected to them. For sure I felt anchored to the geography and energy there. And I promised myself I would go – I will go – back up there to that school one day, back to Mount Carmel Church and back to Colonel's Ridge. It really was magic and as beautiful as Nanny had always said it was.

*　*　*

Some days have passed, and I am alone now and writing this in Kingston. I am high on the top of a hill, high enough to watch the city waking up; it is very early morning, and a blue hazy smog lies above the peppery city below. Kingston hums with life; it feels fast and dangerous to me. When I wouldn't sit and be calm my grandmother told me I had pepper on my tail. I think Kingston has pepper on its tail. I am absorbing everything. This is a proud country, rich with culture, academia, sports, music, literature, food, breathtaking landscapes, history and art. It will take my whole lifetime to learn all of this, to know my history, the differences between my fictional Jamaica and the real Jamaica, but I'm an eager student. I couldn't begin to capture it all here, but my cousins have not let me rest, from historical buildings to places of great beauty; Dunn's Rivers Falls, the Jazz and Blues Festival, the Bob Marley Museum and the National Gallery. And how they have stuffed us with food: breadfruit, callaloo, salt fish, dumplings, patties, jerk chicken, festival, red snapper and bam bam.

My grandmother tried to teach me two fundamental things: to save money for a rainy day and that it was important to study and work hard. I never saved a bean, but I did choose a path I enjoy and so I like to work hard at it. I remember the food my grandmother loved to eat and tried to pass on to me. I'd phone Nanny whenever I cooked ackee – just to hear her voice I would ask her how, even though I knew the answers. I'd put the receiver in the

311

crook of my neck and listen to her voice as I did these meals for one, alone in my little London flat. *Just fry up the onion with a little oil then add the tomatoes, just a little seasoning, some salt and you cook it up, on a low heat . . .*

During my grandmother's illness the food theme continued. I knew she was ill when she stopped eating. She lost her appetite, and I knew she was losing the fight against cancer. I made soup and took it to her, frozen in batches. I laboured over my recipes, as though I was making spells in a cauldron, convincing myself they would make her feel strong and well, mastering the combinations of spinach and nutmeg, broccoli and stilton, yellow lentil dhal, sourcing the best organic herbs and spices I could find. Being sure to use Jamaican root ginger and freshly ground nutmeg. The last time I saw my grandmother, she was frail, papery thin, and the most I could get her to eat was a plain boiled egg with a little salt. I tried so hard to conjure something of Marma, some healing power in those soups.

We are descendants of the Maroons of Jamaica. And now I am in Jamaica I learn that in some company this is something to be proud of and in other company perhaps not. I have been told the Maroons were the rebels who began the fight for independence to abolish slavery. And also that some people think the Maroons were turncoats who sold out their own brothers and black slaves to the white man. In some books I have read how Maroons were brave soldiers, using early guerrilla warfare tactics to beat the British. But at other tables they are something to fear with Obeah-practising magicians and ancient witchcrafts.

Some of my cousins are certain we are direct descendants of Colonel Robinson, a white man, a Scotsman, who captured Maroons with the use of huge hunting dogs. He was rewarded with land

and properties as payment for his work, and the area was called Colonel's Ridge thereafter. Another cousin goes as far as offering further explanations – that his real name was Robertson but they spelled it wrong at the Post Office and it was never corrected. Another cousin added that he misspelled it on purpose, so he could stay in Jamaica and hide from going back to his life back home, neglecting his first wife and abandoning his children in Scotland. Colonel Robertson used this new misspelling of Robinson to begin a new life in the blue mountains, where he took a wife and started a family. To this day I still do not know the whole truth of it, however, I have seen the grave of Colonel Robertson; his mausoleum is at Greyfriars Kirkyard in Edinburgh.

We cannot turn back the clocks, but I do find myself wondering how things might have been if my brother and I had come to Jamaica for our school holidays as children. How very different this story would be, this memoir would be. For a start, if my childhood had been filled with memories of Jamaica in the 1970s, the title of this book might have been *Colonel's Ridge* - but money was tight and I know it would have been expensive to come to Jamaica for the summer holidays back then. Globally, we didn't view the world the same way; international travel now is not what it was back in the twentieth century. The world is smaller and shrinking more and more.

I can, however, imagine what it would be like if I had been in Jamaica as a child. It is for sure I would have early memories of white sands and warm turquoise oceans instead of rocky beaches and shivering in the sage-green Hastings sea. I would know that ackee actually grows on trees like red apples, but here I am, like a child, looking up with wonder and anticipation waiting for them to ripen.

I would also know now that when you drive towards the stadium in Kingston, there is a long wall of paintings, all in a row, of the heroes of Jamaica, and you'll see a portrait of Leila Robinson, my grandmother's sister (incidentally, the netball court is also named after her). I would know that I come from a family who continue to achieve great things in sport, politics, law and medicine. If I had spent time in Jamaica as a child, I imagine I'd have picked up slang and patois easily; it is probably no coincidence there is a trace of dancehall rhythm and rhyme, bold language and ska beats influencing the music and poetry I've made.

If I had come here as a little girl, I might have had more of a grasp of the geography and history of here. In UK schools they didn't teach us about the Maroons. In fact, the entire history of slavery was brushed over; teachers focused on war, with only the briefest mention of the Windrush. It was only yesterday, when I was driving out on the road to Hellshore through Spanish Town, where I saw the forts and cannons, the remnants of colonialism, that I could picture the struggle for independence and abolition. And when I visited the Jamaican 2010 National Biennial, the art of Barrington Watson, Alexander Cooper, Lou Davis and many others depicted a more accurate and real beauty within this island.

Most of all, if we had come to Jamaica as children, we would have known our ancestors, as well as our many cousins, our dead and our living, and we would know them as well as the ghost of our father on Springfield Road. As one Jamaican saying goes: 'plantain ripe, can't green again' – we cannot go back in time. I know now that Colonel's Ridge is a big part of the salt of my earth and Kingston the pepper. And looking out across this Caribbean landscape, with the palm trees, the distant blue mountains and the glittering port in the distance, I am no longer just gazing upon a bamboo tray on the wall. There is Jamaican soil beneath my feet and turquoise blue skies above and ahead, and I find myself imagining what it would be like to live here, on this holiday.

Afterword

London, 2024

My dears,

Thank you for coming with me on this journey.

As I revisit this memoir, I am back at the beach, crouching down to touch the sand. I feel a familiar vibration, see the knotty-haired girl I once was, laughing and cartwheeling along the sandy shore. I recall my young self sitting here, at this exact spot, by Hastings Pier, staring out at the the horizon, as waves wash the years away.

If I could, I would climb into these pages and hug the loving child and the hungry poet who wrote this down so faithfully and tenderly. I want to protect them both and thank the young poet for listening to that child so that I can now hold both visions of them in these pages. The truth is that if it were not for the tenacity and perseverance of the young poet, I would not be here now.

I used writing as a way to hear myself, to navigate feelings. I narrated my life, used my imagination as a tool to make sense of the world and to make myself feel safe. Books were and always will be a place to hide and a place to grow, a place of comfort and a place to learn to fly. Writing as medicine, writing as escapism, writing as survival and a way to put food on the table, writing as a superpower. As adults one day we can become our own hero; we can come back to save ourselves.

I wish I could show the poet who wrote this memoir that despite how much pain she was hiding, I was inside there, blooming, growing, holding on, and I was not going to give up on myself. I'm fifty years old now: my first day at school feels like such a long time ago, as does the day I learned to ride a bike or the first time I borrowed a book from the local library. It also feels like a long time since I sat down at that wonky fold-out table in that yellow kitchen in my tiny London flat, where the rent was always overdue, where comfort was scarce and where I struggled to complete this memoir for the first time.

Preparing to publish this 2024 edition, I read the diaries of this era, in which I recall writing this memoir on borrowed writing equipment and dodgy word processors. I remember lost chapters, glitching Word docs and floppy discs, and the now-obsolete turquoise-blue box-shaped Apple G3 computer that a friend gave me. I must say a huge thank you to old friends: you know who you are, you know that this book wouldn't be here, I wouldn't be here, if it wasn't for you. Thank you for every generosity: every meal or cab fare, every sofa I stayed on, every all-night soul-searching rum session, every lecture and every laugh along the way.

In these diaries I write of hunger, of longing, of wanting to feel safe, of wanting to be healthier and happier. I write about wanting to have food in my own fridge, of yearning for my own warm and quiet space to write in. I fought so hard for so little, for some peace, for the freedom to make the work I wanted to make, to write the books I wanted to write. I wanted to love and be loved, and knew deep down I needed first to love myself, which, of course, is never as easy or simple as it sounds. It takes a lifetime to live well. It took years to learn to love myself and take care of my big heart.

I remember when I began writing the first draft of *Springfield Road* I found myself in Paddington Station with an impulse to run away. Fight or flight. At random I got on the first train heading west, towards Devon and Cornwall, St Ives and Penzance. As the train bumbled towards the coast, I woke up to the slow realisation that no matter where I ran to, I would be there when I got there. It took six hours to Penzance. Staring out of the window at the lush West Country, I realised I had already started the work. And once I started to write and remember my childhood, memories flooded my head, a clutter of moments – some of which I wished I had forgotten.

In my thirties I asked myself: *What would writing this book teach me?* And I answered that *rather than being careful what you wish for, you should be sure to dream harder.* I did wish hard and dream big. But you cannot go poking at death without making the maggots wriggle. Writing this book felt like I was picking up rocks and looking at the worms and truths underneath. Now, in 2024 and in my fifties, I would answer a little differently. I now know that focusing on this book and fighting for it saved my life. It changed my path, as tumultuous as it was; this work was my job in the 2000s, it took a decade to make, but it was a life raft. It was also the first time I had to face myself, the first time I kicked a door through and jammed my foot in and elbowed my way into a room I was not comfortable in.

As I write this letter, I am home, writing at my own desk and in my own room surrounded by brilliant books, many written by people I am lucky to call my friends, my heroes and my poetry family. I have a mug of tea and a view of the sky. Isn't this the wish, isn't this all I asked for? I have so many beautiful books in this room that I would like to share with the young rebel poet who wrote this memoir. I have a myriad of books by Black poets and authors, queer writers, working-class and feminist writers, outsiders whose stories tell of lives lived fearlessly. How she will love these people she finds in the future, this library, this room, this tea, and the roses and tomatoes I grow every summer.

Since signing with Canongate and publishing *Mrs Death Misses Death*, I've been doing the difficult work to heal some of this pain. I recognise that I have an archive of historical trauma which manifests itself in my words, actions, choices and decisions. I have no idea why or where or how the young woman in this book managed to find courage to write this memoir. Knowing what I know now, it is remarkable to me. And reading the diaries of this era, I am moved by the vulnerability and tenderness of my younger selves, the soft parts of me that I barely nurtured or protected. The young person who wrote this book was in so much danger; there was so much self-sabotage and untangled grief. However, I was determined to complete this book and see it in print – rewriting it, and rewriting it again, in spite of so many obstacles, self-doubt and such unhelpful advice, then eventually crowdfunding it and hustling it into life. I had to get out of my own way.

I must not apologise for my optimism, this idealism, the natural joy and passion I was born with, not anymore. If you're a young writer, I just hope you'll read this and stop apologising for burning brightly too. I want to see you all shine!

Reading these diaries of the young poet, I recall lugging a suitcase of first editions of *Springfield Road* on trains and buses to events and festivals all over the world to share this work. I walked the rainy streets of London and visited bookshops and asked booksellers to stock it, to take just two or three copies, offering my services to do readings in shops. Most of the time the baffled staff would chat to me kindly but explain that isn't how it worked: they didn't book the gigs or choose the stock or do the bookshop windows. But I didn't know any of that back then.

Everything changed with my fortieth birthday and the year I outlived my dad. I felt as though his shadow lifted. Or a curse was broken. Or a light switched on. I got my first two books published at the age of forty – my first full collection of poems *Fishing in the Aftermath* and the first edition of *Springfield Road*. Now, I know they say that age is nothing but a number, but this was a huge transitional time for me.

Now I am older, I feel differently about some things in this book: for one example I feel sad that so many of the children at my schools had been taught to be so racist, bitter and bigoted, and frequently used racial slurs such as the N-word and the P-word at such a young age, and that this bullying went unchecked, not just in my schools but in playgrounds up and down the UK. These racial slurs were used widely in popular culture and television in my childhood. So in this 2024 version I have made the decision to remove most uses of the N-word and P-word. However, I have kept one example as reported speech where it felt necessary, to give an example of violence and truth and the power of words.

In the first draft of this book, some names were changed to protect people. I have honoured that decision and kept it so. Many of the people in this book have died or disappeared now. Some of the people in this book still haunt my nightmares. Looking back, I feel protective about my young self with these adult male figures, namely my father, stepfather and my maternal grandfather.

However, I also see a young person with a glorious sense of wonder about the world, a wonder I maintain now. May we all keep a hold of that wonder, that curiosity, our ability to seek the wonder in things. On this note of wonder, I recently met up with my childhood classmate Anna Parris and asked if she would like her real name in this new edition. Anna just asked if I could make her taller, so for the record: Anna was the tallest tall person at my primary school.

How strange is the passing of time and what we recall and what we forget. It seems when we are younger we are closer to the sting of childhood and closer to memories of growing pains and loss. I promised myself I wouldn't change this memoir too much; as I said at the beginning of this letter, I stand by the imaginative child and how I once remembered how it felt to be her. I stand in solidarity with the fierce and passionate young poet who was compelled to write this book and who just couldn't catch a break. I imagine in twenty years' time, when I am seventy with wild and white curly hair, that I will feel differently about all of this again. The fact I can even imagine my white-haired magic soul at seventy shows you where I am and how I feel about living now. For the record I highly recommend living: I highly recommend getting old. It seems to me the older I get, the more I become who I was meant to be all along, and it is mad that this is the person I was always running from.

The sad truth is this: I wrote parts of this memoir with very little belief that I would live. I can see the pauses and breaths, the tears between the lines. I know elements of the early drafts of this memoir were a goodbye letter. Who to? Perhaps to my siblings or my cousins in Jamaica, or my nephews and nieces; perhaps it was a rallying cry to other Black or queer or working-class writers and poets struggling with identity and scarcity, unable to catch a break, seeking peace and longing for love. However, the sad part of this book is also the bold fire inside it. I see her, this young determined poet writing at 4 a.m. with little hope of light or dawn. This early morning writing habit is a routine I kept. I have grown to become a dawn-chorus writer because of this one book.

I can remember believing I would die on the book's completion, but this macabre feeling didn't scare me; rather, it became a motivation to see the work completed. While absorbed in the violent imaginings of my father's last hours, I pictured my own demise. I am so grateful I didn't die, but some myths around suicide smashed instead. I started to learn that my fears are not prophecies. I am so relieved that rather than a swan song, this was to be the beginning of a change of heart and a new path. I made medicine from poison. I weaved gold out of fear. I know now this was the intention, and I hope my story resonates with your memories of you as a child when you were perhaps also filled with wonder and light, or when you were shrinking and running away from yourself too. This writing is rooted in so much resilience; there is so much courage embedded here. This is a story of survival, of holding on to your integrity and dreams. A reminder from me to you that we must not count how many times we got knocked down, but how many times we get back up, again and again.

I was often asked, why memoir? Why was this book written as memoir? I have to stop and wonder too. Perhaps if I was writing this book in this decade, I might try to hide myself and write it as fiction. I might disguise myself, change geographies, fictionalise myself and my family. I might take it out of the raw and vibrant first person of *I* and *me* to a much easier and more anonymous *she*, *her*, *they*. We are so fearless when we are young. I wrote it real and poured it raw and downed it neat. Memoir is a powerful tincture: one gulp and you can capture an era like a ship in a bottle.

* * *

I love reading and writing memoir. They are letters to time, a glimpse into who we all once were and how we all got here. If I could, I would climb inside this book and hold the remarkable young woman who wrote this memoir: I know how hungry she was and how hard she struggled while navigating the difficult business of living. The author of this work is a young woman writing at the turn of the century, a time that was so entrenched in dodgy toxic masculinity, sexism, elitism and racism. How bizarre it is to me now, to see how that young poet would believe a person behind a desk, in an expensive suit and nice shoes, rather than her own gut instincts. A majority of memoirs being published in that era were 'misery memoirs', which I was adamant this would not be. I remember taking Toni Morrison's sage advice and looking for my story in bookshops and libraries and then going home and writing the book I wanted to see.

When this book was originally being written I did not see myself or my story represented much in the world. It seemed to me that the 1970s and 1980s were primarily depicted through a white male gaze, much like the punks and skinheads we see in Shane Meadows' *This Is England*. But there has been a massive shift. For one shining example, the brilliant *Small Axe* anthology of films by Steve McQueen, with powerful writing from Courttia Newland, depicting the same era through a Black and Caribbean lens that I can recognise and see myself in. I really loved those *Small Axe* films, they were a huge inspiration to get this book back into print. They highlighted epic Black talent both in the writing room and on screen. So here is hope, and perhaps a new era of powerful Black-centred talent and film and books. Maybe now, finally, in 2024 it isn't so very difficult to imagine this brave brown girl with her scabby knees and rainbow socks and roller-skates finding her voice in this world and using it.

Here we are in the 2020s, and my powerhouse agent is Crystal Mahey-Morgan — I am represented by the film, TV and literary agency she co-founded with Jason Morgan, OWN IT! — a company that puts a diverse diaspora into the centre of the story. When you work with friends and people who share mutual love and respect, the work feels more like playing and like flying, instead of treading water at sea alone. Just as my mum always says: *Go where the love is.*

Ever supporting and encouraging all I do, when I began work on the first draft of this memoir my mother gave me her diaries. In the early 1970s, after my mother left my father, in her newfound solitude she sat down and wrote out her entire life in her own words. I remember sitting up in my teenage attic bedroom in the house on Springfield Road and spending some furious tearful weeks labouring to type them all out, word for word and blow for blow, only to destroy the files, finding them too painful to share. So just a glimpse of my mother's story in her own words remains in this book. My mother's life story, her survival, my Jamaican roots and history could be a whole book all of its own. My mother is my champion; she has always told me that my writing *is* a proper job. She has continually supported my choices, cheered at my success and consoled me in my failures, my many near misses and close calls. My mother has encouraged me to try, try and try again, and I thank her here and every day. She helped to nurture this passion and a mantra of never quitting. This, then, is our bond, this is my understanding of her hurts and trauma. This is the spirit of our elders and ancestors. Thank you, Mum.

As for my dad — back in 2006 I started seeking my father and his final resting place. I applied to Bristol registry for his death certificate. When the letter arrived, I burst into tears, holding his death certificate and seeing my father's name written by the word *death* for the first time. His cause of death: vasovagal inhibition due to hanging. His occupation was given as a 'sub-contract progress chaser'. I suppose I had hoped and expected it to read: 'charming libertine jazz dude'. I received the address for the cemetery where Dad was buried and I will always be very grateful to the person who took the time to give me this information – I cannot tell you much more than this, that a stranger took the time to write to me. So I now knew he had been buried and not cremated, and at last Gus and I could go and say a final goodbye. The journey to Bristol to see his grave was a huge healing moment for us. With this chapter in mind – and particularly after publishing *Mrs Death Misses Death* – I firmly believe that children should be given more space to share their loss, that children should be permitted to be involved in the process of death and dying, the ritual of funerals and of saying goodbye. I think it is so important that children should be included in the big grief conversations and the navigation of mourning.

While I was editing the final chapters of the first edition of this book, a friend of mine took his life aged forty years old, just like my father. Tarka Cordell was stunning, a gifted and charming musician. Since then I have lost many other friends.

We are all so fragile. We are fighting the good fight, but we are way too harsh in the way we measure our success and failure, the way we compare our lives and reward and penalise ourselves. Perhaps loathing and punishing ourselves enough to convince ourselves that we will not be sorely missed by every person's life that we touched. I met Tarka when I was in my twenties doing poetry gigs with poets Tim Wells and Cheryl B in New York. Tarka made me *feel* like I was a real poet. If there is a place where we meet in the afterlife, then I like to imagine that they will all be there, partying and jamming together, all the good people and all the big wild hearts.

During the 1970s the seasons of my childhood seemed so much more distinct. There was the throng of cut grass in spring, the hot yellow of summer and the droughts, the pumpkin and conkers of autumn, and heavy snow and electricity cuts at wintertime. Due to the escalating climate crisis and global warming the weather is forever changed. This book is a time machine to a before-world: where shopkeepers smoked fags while serving slabs of warm cheese, where fish and chips were served in newspaper, we had paper one-pound notes, and recorded the Top 10 off the radio onto cassette tapes. Once upon a time, the UK only had four television channels to choose from. As children, we played outside in the streets, interacting without any health and safety, without crash helmets or internet or mobile phones. If you wanted to find your gang, you'd knock at the door of the house with all the bicycles outside on the front lawn. I hope I have captured something of that era for those too young to remember and for those old enough to know.

Writing memoir is making maps and connections between past and present, linking dreams and connections with the long-lost people of before. It's a loose thread that most of us fear pulling in case we unravel the whole sweater. But I pulled it and it unravelled and I sat there untangling the knots I had made. Revisiting this book, I learn that remembering never meets you face to face: it sneaks up on you like a sharp corner when you least expect it; you take the turn and find yourself down an alleyway of memories you never knew were there. The things we want to remember are so different to the things we had forgotten. Now, for the first time in my life, I sleep with the lights off. I also pay more attention to dreams and all that I wish for. If a fear conceals a wish, perhaps this original fear of death was a wish for rebirth and reinvention.

Now, I must send this letter. As I wrote all of this, the sun came out and a copper morning light fills this room. I want to plant bulbs for spring – metaphorically, figuratively and literally. It is time to be in the present and plant tomorrow's flowers. We water the seeds we sow and nourish our dreams and gardens. I have always pictured this book as a full bucket of dreams. I was always prepared to carry this bucket myself. And you must do that too, with your own stories and pasts and ghosts, your own wishes and dreams. You owe it to yourself. I believed that if I ever let anyone else carry that bucket they might spill it. I knew I would always carry it and not spill a drop.

Springfield Road is in the far away and the long ago now, so we'll remember it as it was. A place to find the lucky marble, a place like a pebble with the hole in the middle, and a place we called home.

Salena Godden
London, 2024

'Where are you going now?'
'For a walk.'
'Where?'
'Just a walk.'
'Can we come too?'
'Yes.'
'And me?'
'Yes! I won't leave you in Hastings in 1984.
I'm sorry I did that.'
'What about me? Can I come?'
'Yes! I'm not going to leave you in the past either.'
'Where are we going?'
'I'm going to take you to the now.'
'What is that like?'
'It is like being whole.'
'What happens to us?'
'Not sure, but we'll write about it.'
'What do we become?'
'Our own hero.'

Acknowledgements

Thank you to our ever generous community of readers and writers and poets who inspire me every day. Thank you to all book lovers and book bloggers. Thank you to bookshops, booksellers and libraries. This book may not be here if it wasn't for so many amazing conversations, inspiration and the encouragement of so many of you. Thank you to Maggie Gee, Colin Grant, Benjamin Zephaniah, Nikesh Shukla, Lemn Sissay, Dean Atta, Joelle Taylor, Nikita Gill, Jean Binta Breeze. Thank you, Matt Abbott and Nymphs & Thugs. Thank you to Unbounders, John Mitchinson and Rachael Kerr. Thank you to the Society of Authors, the Royal Literary Fund, the Royal Society of Literature and West Dean. Thank you to all beautiful venues, live events and festival organisers. Thank you to all podcasters and radio makers. Thank you to Kevin Conroy-Scott for suggesting I write this memoir all those years ago. A special thank you to Catherine Davies for all of your support. With BIG love and forever thanks to my beautiful mum and to Richard and to my siblings and family and friends who have supported me and cared for me and nourished and loved me. Love you. Thank you, team OWN IT!, and Canongate.

With love and thanks to

Agent	Crystal Mahey-Morgan
Editor	Aa'Ishah Hawton
Copy-editor	Martha Sprackland
Commissioning Editor	Leah Woodburn
Managing Editor	Leila Cruickshank
Proofreader	Alison Rae
Typesetter	Palimpsest Book Production
Head of Publicity	Lucy Zhou
Deputy Marketing Director	Caitriona Horne
Cover Design	Valeri Rangelov
Rights and Contracts Director	Jessica Neale
Senior Rights Manager	Charlie Tooke
Rights Executive	Phyllis Armstrong
Head of Production	Kate Oliver
Sales Director	Joanna Lord
Head of International Sales	Stephanie Scott
Senior International Sales Executive	Rebecca Scott
Head of UK Sales	Sasha Cox
Publisher	Jamie Byng

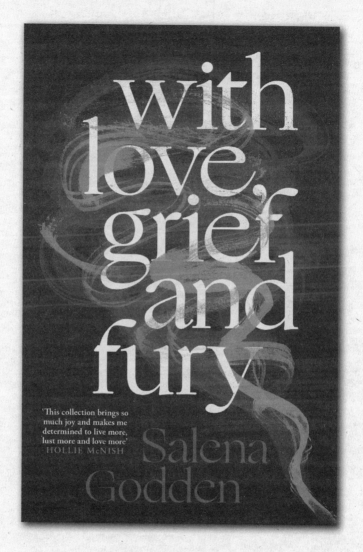

with love, grief and fury

'This collection brings so much joy and makes me determined to live more, lust more and love more'
HOLLIE McNISH

Salena Godden

'Uncompromising'
Joelle Taylor

CANON█GATE

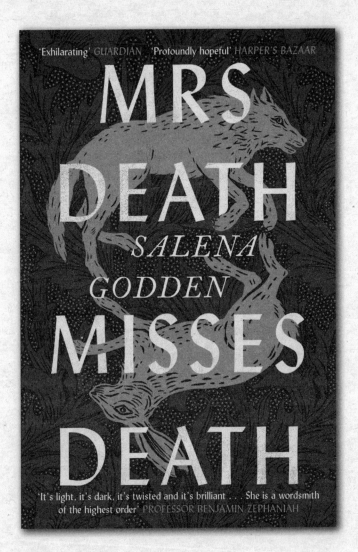

'Exhilarating' GUARDIAN   'Profoundly hopeful' HARPER'S BAZAAR

MRS
DEATH

SALENA
GODDEN

MISSES
DEATH

'It's light, it's dark, it's twisted and it's brilliant . . . She is a wordsmith
of the highest order' PROFESSOR BENJAMIN ZEPHANIAH

'Devastating'
Irish Times

CANON‖GATE